Native Florida Plants for Shady [

UNIVERSITY PRESS OF FLORIDA

Florida A&M University, Tallahassee
Florida Atlantic University, Boca Raton
Florida Gulf Coast University, Ft. Myers
Florida International University, Miami
Florida State University, Tallahassee
New College of Florida, Sarasota
University of Central Florida, Orlando
University of Florida, Gainesville
University of North Florida, Jacksonville
University of South Florida, Tampa
University of West Florida, Pensacola

Native Florida Plants for Shady Landscapes

University Press of Florida
Gainesville
Tallahassee
Tampa
Boca Raton
Pensacola
Orlando
Miami
Jacksonville
Ft. Myers
Sarasota

Craig N. Huegel

VIVA FLORIDA 500
1513-2013

A Florida Quincentennial Book

Title pages, left to right: Columbine (*Aquilegia canadensis*) and wild blue phlox (*Phlox divaricata*) mix with native azaleas beneath the canopy of a north Florida woodland landscape (photo by Eleanor Dietrich, by permission); a male common yellowthroat finds habitat in the understory of a shady landscape designed with native plants (photo by Christina Evans, by permission).

Copyright 2015 by Craig N. Huegel
All rights reserved
Photographs by Craig N. Huegel unless otherwise indicated

Printed in the United States of America on acid-free paper

This book may be available in an electronic edition.

20 19 18 17 16 15   6 5 4 3 2 1

Library of Congress Control Number: 2014949013
ISBN 978-0-8130-6059-0

The University Press of Florida is the scholarly publishing agency for the State University System of Florida, comprising Florida A&M University, Florida Atlantic University, Florida Gulf Coast University, Florida International University, Florida State University, New College of Florida, University of Central Florida, University of Florida, University of North Florida, University of South Florida, and University of West Florida.

University Press of Florida
15 Northwest 15th Street
Gainesville, FL 32611-2079
http://www.upf.com

To every Florida gardener faced with the very real desire to create shade with an environmental purpose. For all of you willing to dig a little deeper beneath the traditional approach to landscaping and to add purpose to aesthetics, I add these words and photos to the discussion.

Contents

Preface and Acknowledgments

Florida is a fascinating place. Within our uniquely shaped border is everything needed to create magic within our own property boundaries. There is nowhere like Florida, and the heritage that is ours as Floridians is something we should cherish. We should not be so quick to cast it off to make this special place like everywhere else or like something it never was.

As residents of the Sunshine State, we understand the value of shade. We experience more hours of sunshine annually than anywhere else in North America except the arid West, and they at least have months of cooler temperatures where having shade is less important. With summers that seemingly last for more than half the year and with high temperatures that remain locked at 85° Fahrenheit (F) or above, we seek shade as a survival mechanism. Unlike other regions of our nation, shade is built into our landscapes as a matter of principle. We either have it, or we desire it.

Shade has real value in keeping us cool. During the heat of summer, shade lowers the air temperature by as much as 4.5°F. That's because shade reduces the component of sunshine that causes us to feel heat, infrared radiation. The infrared portion of the light spectrum is "heat radiation." This is very different from the portion that causes sunburn. That part of the spectrum is in the ultraviolet range, the opposite end of the light spectrum, which is why we can get sunburned on overcast days even when we feel cold.

Shade has an even greater impact on the soil surface than it does on air temperature. Direct sunlight, reaching the ground, can heat the soil on warm days to temperatures greater than 15°F above air temperature. I learned this the hard way early after my arrival in Florida when I left my sandals off as I hiked across a wide open beach in the middle of summer.

By the time I reached the water, I had burned the soles of my feet to the point of blisters. Thankfully, most Florida beach sand is white and not the darker color I had walked across, but most of the sandy soil we have in our landscapes is dark. During a typical Florida summer, this soil gets extremely hot. Plants adapted to our growing conditions must cope with overheating as well as our relatively low-nutrient soils and periods of water stress. Providing shade at the soil surface improves the ability of most plants to thrive. That is one reason why mulches are so universally used here. It's not just about reducing water loss or about making the landscape appear more attractive. Mulch protects a plant's fine surface roots from literally getting cooked.

Shade at the soil surface affects plants quite differently from shade on its foliage. Plants need sunlight for photosynthesis, the complex process by which they convert solar energy into body tissue. Plants cannot grow when it is dark and they grow very little if they do not receive enough sunlight over enough days. Most plants are sun lovers. They reach their full potential only when they receive ample amounts of sunlight. In reduced light, most plants become weak and lanky, they fail to flower, and they produce few, if any, seed to carry on the next generation. That is the dilemma we face as gardeners seeking to create shady places in the landscape. As Floridians wishing to enjoy the outdoors, we are drawn to establishing shade, but as landscape artists we find our potential palette limited to a small subset of plants adapted to low light conditions. Gardening in the shade is a balance between how much shade we want and the species of plants that can tolerate those conditions. Shade limits our plant choices, but it creates the respite we seek and the conditions we need to feel comfortable outdoors during most months.

To complicate the situation further, our plant choices become further limited if we also seek to accomplish ecological goals with our finished landscape. What plants remain are only those that *truly* thrive under low light conditions. They must produce flowers and fruit, they must be lush and healthy, and they must persist over time without a lot of excessive care and attention. Our plan will consider providing habitat for birds, butterflies, and other wildlife and it will not require us to add a lot of inputs such as irrigation, fertilizers, and pesticides. That is not an easy task, but it is certainly something we can accomplish with a little thought. Adding ecological considerations to our overall plan will involve using plants native to Florida that thrive in naturally shaded plant communities.

This book is about several things. For one, it is about creating and using shade more effectively in our Florida landscapes. Nearly all of us have shade, so it is not so much about making more of it but about making it work better on our behalf. As I explore the developed landscapes of my neighborhood and those elsewhere in Florida, I am struck by how poorly most of us do with the shade we have inherited. For far too many, shade becomes a sort of landscape curse. We look at our yard and equate it with lawn, we equate that with grass, and we then throw our hands up in despair when our shade makes growing a traditional turf-grass lawn impossible. Recognize one important fact about turf grass—it abhors shade. Shady landscapes will have to rely on something other than turf grass if we are to have anything other than bare soil or the weed of the season. In this book, I seek to provide answers on what the alternatives are and to show you how to use them effectively. Just because the shady portion of your landscape will not include turf grass does not mean that it won't be beautiful, functional, and valuable to you. If you don't have shade already, using this book will help you design a shady retreat that also meets those goals.

This book is also intended to guide you in making your shady landscape areas more ecologically valuable. It is a book specifically devoted to Florida, and the plants included in these chapters are native to our state. Native plants, when used correctly, are beautiful, but this is not a book solely devoted to making your shady areas an aesthetic masterpiece. It will not include plants from around the world that do not occur naturally here in Florida. Though I admire the beauty of Japanese maples and exotic hostas, they do not belong in the landscapes I write about. Florida is a treasure trove of beautiful plants all its own, without the need to venture outside our borders, and by "staying home" we ensure that the landscapes we design will require fewer inputs in terms of valuable natural resources (e.g., water and fertilizer), use fewer lethal chemicals (e.g., pesticides), and will ultimately make these areas significant habitat for the rest of the living world (e.g., birds, butterflies, etc.). I am not a native plant purist and there are non-native plants that do not cause ecological harm, but overall, native plants fulfill these roles far better than plants from other countries.

I believe we are entering a time when landscapes will become more than pretty faces and that we will embrace the ecological purposes that our landscapes could achieve. We do not live on this earth only to consume. We have the ability to give something back as well, and we can do that by allowing the rest of nature to live alongside us. This is true whether we are landscaping in shady locations or sunny ones.

In many respects, this book is an outgrowth of a movement first started by William Robinson with the publication of his book, *The Wild Garden*, in 1870. *The Wild Garden* was revolutionary because it urged landscape planners to look more toward nature for design ideas than the highly ordered and artificial gardens and expansive manicured lawns that were almost universally mimicked at the time. Although I am not a landscape architect, my sense of what is right and wrong with traditional landscape designs had its embryonic outgrowth from the ideas of Robinson.

I also owe much to the works of other landscape designers and authors who have taken Robinson and expanded it to modern-day concepts and values. My personal library includes a great many excellent books that have shaped my thoughts. I am most indebted to Rick Darke and Ken Druse for their pioneering works on incorporating nature into landscapes. Others have written specifically about landscaping in shade. Of these, the works of Larry Hodgson, Beth Chatto, Ken Wiley, and George Schenk have been the most influential to me. I have read each of their works with enthusiasm and have taken away a great many ideas from them that have shaped this book.

My knowledge of Florida native plants was founded on my association with the Florida Native Plant Society and my more-recent involvement with the Florida Association of Native Nurseries. Both organizations are filled with knowledgeable and enthusiastic members, eager to share what they know. I am most indebted to Mike Kenton, Brightman Logan, Bill and Nancy Bissett, Peggy and Don Lantz, Walter K. Taylor, Gil Nelson, Roger Hammer, Richard Wunderlin, Bruce Hansen, David Drylie, Richard Workman, Steve Riefler, Bruce Turley, and Dan Miller.

I have also been extremely fortunate over the years to be able to supplement my average photographic skills with the work of others. For this book, I have enlisted the support of good friends: Pam Anderson, Bill

Bilodeau, Eleanor Dietrich, Christina Evans, Roger Hammer, and Gil Nelson. I have credited each photograph that is not mine with their names. The beauty of this book is a testament to their artistic abilities.

This book, like the others before it, has been possible only through the faith and assistance of the staff of the University Press of Florida, Meredith Babb, Nevil Parker, and especially my copyeditor, Gillian Hillis. Their attention to details, their knowledge of English grammar, and their attention to beauty have taken my prose and photographs and made it the work of art that it is.

I have a sense of purpose crafted by a supportive family. I owe the roots of that to my father and mother, Jack and Louise Huegel, who nurtured my interests from childhood until their passing. I dearly wish they could have been with me on all the roads I have traveled. My sons, Tyler, Nathan, and Evan have been there from their births and have always indulged my curiosity with nature. I value their companionship. Last, my best sounding board, companion, and friend has been my wife, Alexa Wilcox-Huegel. This and my other works would not have been possible without her support.

The endpoint for all of this is the book before you. I trust that I have got it right and that it serves you in some way as you seek to provide meaningful shade into your landscape. Those of us who dig holes and put plants in those spaces are by nature the world's greatest optimists. I believe we are making a difference and that the earth is better off because of what we are doing. I hope that we are shaping the next chapter of landscape design and that this book will help us create beautiful and ecologically functional landscapes in the shade.

Light and Shade

Sunlight is the energy source on which all life depends. Nature runs on energy, and that energy comes from the sun. Plants use sunlight for photosynthesis. They cannot survive if placed under 24 hours of darkness. Sunlight, a very narrow portion of the overall solar spectrum, starts the chemical process by which plants convert solar energy to body mass. Each species has a minimum requirement of light energy and even the most shade-tolerant species need some sunlight to meet their basic life requirements. Just as we consume food to meet our basic metabolic needs, plants consume sunlight,

Sunlight is the ultimate plant food and fuels all of the chemical reactions that allow plants to grow and reproduce.

and their daily intake of sunlight "calories" is measured by the solar energy they absorb over a 24-hour period. To grow, all life consumes more calories than it burns. Plants ingest sunlight for this purpose.

Every chemical reaction plants use to grow and respire takes energy, and every mineral they use is necessary because of the role it plays in photosynthesis. In short, everything you need to know about a plant is based on its sunshine requirements. Over the millions of years since plants left the oceans and found ways to grow on land, some adapted to thrive in lower light levels than others. None (except a few that do not photosynthesize) have evolved to live without light. As we plan a shady landscape, we must meet the sunlight needs of the plants we want to use. We cannot force plants to meet our expectations. We must meet theirs.

In the world of plants, there are heavy feeders and those that "eat like birds"; everything from those that can withstand the blistering solar energy of tropical deserts to those that find enough solar energy in the understory of dense tropical rainforests. The plants that need high levels of light can survive for periods of time on a low-sunlight diet, but forcing this on them for any appreciable length of time will cause them to weaken and die. Plants grown under suboptimal conditions will burn off their stored energy, just as we would burn off excess fat in order to survive, but this will eventually take its toll. Over time, plants ill adapted to low light will exhibit signs of stress; they will fail to flower and set fruit, their stems will get thin, and they will be more prone to insect and disease damage. They may survive like this for years but will do so in an emaciated condition. We want plants that can thrive in the shady places we plant them.

No book about landscaping in the shade can truly begin without first defining the terms. Shade is a more complex concept than what appears on the surface. There are different degrees and types of shade, everything from total darkness to the slightest dampening of full sunlight. Each presents unique challenges and opportunities. To be truly successful in our endeavor to put plants in shade, we need to know which type we are dealing with.

Shade can come from merely filtering out some of the harshness of full sunlight, much the way we use shade cloth in a pool enclosure. Sunlight is filtered as it passes through the leaves of a forest; each leaf takes some of the sunlight and lets the excess travel on. The more layers of leaves and the smaller the gaps between them, the more energy is absorbed. Filtering diffuses the energy of the light as it works its way from the canopy of a forest to

Shady landscapes provide a respite from the heat of a typical Florida day.

the forest floor, and it removes portions of the light spectrum differentially. The portions most filtered, of course, are those most important to photosynthesis. Plants that reside beneath a dense canopy not only have to adapt to low light intensity, they also need to use more efficiently the portions of the spectrum remaining to them.

Different canopies filter light differently. Pines (*Pinus* spp.), for example, are much different than broadleaf canopy tress like oaks and magnolias. In most forests, pines intercept less sunlight than oaks (*Quercus* spp.) and magnolias (*Magnolia* spp.), and most pinelands have more plant diversity beneath them. Filtered sun increases the variety of plants that can grow beneath the forest canopy as long as it is filtered and not intercepted. Canopy trees with needle-like leaves are sunlight filterers.

Broadleaf canopy trees, however, are sunlight interceptors. The vast majority of leaves on such trees are held parallel to the ground. This aspect maximizes the ability of leaves to intercept light for photosynthesis and it

A canopy of broadleaf trees, such as oaks and maples, creates very different shade conditions than one created by evergreens.

makes good evolutionary sense from the canopy tree's perspective. Broadleaf trees intercept light and absorb much of the useful portions of the spectrum for themselves. They leave little for others beneath them; there is no such thing as altruism in the plant world. As landscape designers wanting to use broadleaf trees, our flexibility lies only in selecting the breadth of canopy we desire or the spacing between the trees we plant.

Not all broadleaf trees are created equal when it comes to canopy structure. Each species tends to develop a shape based on its inherent genetics. Live oaks (*Quercus virginiana*) and southern magnolias (*Magnolia grandiflora*), for example, have evolved to form extremely wide crowns. They dominate the areas where they occur and they tend to prevent other trees from getting established close to them. In this way, they are the ultimate competitors. Other canopy trees are not as greedy about space and sunlight. Turkey oak (*Quercus laevis*) and sweetbay magnolia (*Magnolia virginiana*) are narrow-crowned trees that capture sunlight from a much smaller area around their main trunk. Both types of canopies shade the area beneath them, but narrow-crowned trees leave a lot more sunny space to work with.

Short canopy trees shade the area beneath them to a lesser extent than taller ones. It is a simple exercise in geometry. Given an equal breadth of canopy, the taller a tree grows, the wider the shadow it will throw. This is an important consideration during the design phase of your planting plan. The amount of shade you will create in your landscape will change significantly as your trees mature, and understory plants that might have been appropriate initially may become poor choices in those intervening years. Plan your landscape for the mature canopy, not the initial one.

Most horticulturalists consider "full sun" to be 12 hours of direct sunlight per day, at least during the summer months when day length is at its maximum and the sun is at its highest point in the sky. Anything less than this is, by definition, "partial sun." A great many plants that grow best in sunny locations can tolerate less than 12 hours of direct sunlight, especially if some of those hours are spent under partial sunlight and not complete shade. Therefore, 6 hours of direct sunlight, followed or preceded by 6 hours of reduced sunlight might still meet the overall sunlight budget required by a plant that needs "full sun." In reality, it is the total amount of sunlight energy received by the plant per day that is the bottom line. As long as the required light budget is met, the plant will thrive. This can be accomplished by any combination of direct and partial light that adds up to the necessary total.

As a rule of thumb, the plants covered here require no more than 4 hours of direct sunlight, or some combination of sun and partial sun that adds up to that amount. In fact, some shade-tolerant plants disdain any amount of direct sunlight on their foliage. These are adapted to longer hours of indirect light. Direct sun scorches their foliage or causes other types of distress.

The time of day direct sunlight is received also plays a significant part in this. Midday sun bathes a plant's foliage with far more solar radiation than does morning or afternoon sun. An hour of midday sun can equal the same amount of solar energy received in 4 hours of early morning or late afternoon sunshine. Clouds, atmospheric water vapor, the ozone layer, and a host of other factors reduce the amount of solar energy reaching the earth's surface. When the sun is lower on the horizon, these influences play a greater role in reducing the energy of the sunlight reaching the plant's foliage.

For the same reason, sunlight changes throughout the seasons. Here in Florida, where we are still some distance north of the equator, the tilt of the earth as it orbits the sun causes summer sunshine to be much stronger than winter sunshine. The sun is lower on the horizon as it arcs across the sky in winter. Consequently, the amount of solar energy that reaches a plant's leaves and triggers photosynthesis is much reduced. Shade-tolerant plants handle direct sunlight better in the late fall to early spring than they do in the middle of summer; they react to morning and late afternoon sun much differently than they do for direct sunshine during the middle of the day.

While full sunlight is a concept that seems pretty straightforward, the concept of partial sunlight is relative because it includes everything else. How *partial* does it have to be not to be considered "sunny?" When does *mostly* sunny become shady enough not to be considered "sunny" at all? These are important questions as we seek to create shade in our landscapes and select a palette of shade-tolerant plants.

Shade is defined by all types of relative terms in the literature. *Partial shade* might be the best term when a plant receives full sun for part of the day and is shaded for the rest. This situation is the one most plants find at the outer canopy of a large shade tree. In such a situation, they might receive direct sunlight during the early morning or late afternoon but are protected during midday, when the rays are at their strongest. This situation also occurs when there are gaps in the canopy. Gaps can be variable in size; they allow unfiltered sun to reach the plants below for a limited period of time. A great many plants do extremely well in partial shade, but the challenge is in giving them the right mix of sun and shade. Canopy trees continue to grow over time and the extent of their canopies grows with them. Often, plants beneath still-growing shade trees become too shaded over time unless the canopy is kept pruned.

Understory plants also grow, and it is natural for many of them to bend toward the sunlight. When they do, they can become contorted or misshapen. No amount of pruning will stop a plant from growing toward the light if it wants to. Most shade-tolerant species avoid too much light by not responding this way, but those that do well in sunny as well as partly sunny locations will almost always grow toward the sun. When planted near the canopy's edge, they will soon grow sideways and attempt to get around it and into the light.

It is important to consider the physical orientation of the plantings in relation to the canopy tree. Sunlight shifts in the landscape throughout the seasons. What is shady in the summer may be sunny in the winter, and vice versa. I operate a small native wildflower nursery in my side yard, directly south of my house. During much of the spring through fall, this area receives ample light for my nursery needs. The sun is relatively high in the sky and my next-door neighbor's home is not a factor in shading it. Winter, however, is another story. For about three months, much of this area receives little to no direct sunlight. This doesn't really impact my dormant plants, but it does affect the growth of my evergreen species and the seedlings emerging in my flats. I cannot alter the shade of a neighboring home or other such structure; I can only plan around it. If you are planting beneath a preexisting canopy, make sure you understand how shade changes throughout the year. Most shade-tolerant plants welcome sun in the winter and early spring. They just don't cope well with the opposite arrangement.

Areas shaded by walls or other objects can be difficult to landscape, but because light is a wave, it can be reflected. Such light does not seem as bright as direct sunlight, but it can contain nearly the same amount of light energy, and it's the energy that plants use to grow. Light-colored walls reflect far more sunlight than those painted a darker shade.

Plants that might not receive a lot of direct sunlight because of a wall can receive ample amounts of it if a nearby wall reflects the sunlight in their direction. You can sufficiently change the amount of light your plants receive by reflecting light toward them or by preventing it from doing so. This can have significant effects. North-facing walls, painted white, will allow for a much greater diversity of plants than those painted dark brown or green. Landscape ornaments that reflect light can also provide the same service, but in a more directed way. What all this means is that the concept of shade

Walls painted white reflect far more sunlight back to the landscape than those painted a darker color. This additional light energy can make a significant difference to the health of your plants.

is truly relative. Different plants adapt themselves differently to degrees of light. Some require lots of light energy to thrive while others abhor all but the lowest amounts. Somewhere in the middle of this spectrum are all the other plants, those adapted to less than full sun. This group includes plants that perform well under partial sun, filtered sun, dappled shade, and nearly full shade. They simply have a lower sunlight energy budget. These "shade plants" are the minority, but the list available to us is still significant. Our goal is to match the right plants to the amount of shade we desire.

2

The Challenges and Advantages of Shade Gardening

There are challenges and advantages to landscaping shady areas. Of course, the foremost challenge is selecting an appropriate plant palette, and we will examine that in a lot more detail in a later chapter, but assuming we make the right choices, shade-loving plants often act differently than those that favor sunnier places.

By necessity, shade-loving plants have a lower metabolic rate than sun-loving plants. Because they feed on a lower energy diet, they tend to grow at a slower rate. That is one way they cope in reduced light. They have less extra energy available to them to add bulk, once their basic metabolic needs are met. With less energy to work with, they simply put less of it into growth. I have seen this firsthand in my own landscape. Several years ago, I planted two fringe trees (*Chionanthus virginicus*) of equal size in my developing woodland at the back of our house. One is in relatively deep shade while the other gets several hours of direct sun each afternoon. The first has added only a few inches to its original height while the other has more than doubled in size and stands two feet taller than its mate. Fringe tree naturally occurs in the understory of deciduous woodlands. It is a shade tolerant subcanopy tree, but though it can tolerate reduced light levels, its growth rate is influenced by the total amount of sunlight it receives. Plants in shade will grow more slowly than you may expect. This slower growth rate should be considered in your landscape design. You may wish to select plants a bit larger to start with than you might normally, and you may want to plant some of them closer together than you normally do in sunny locations. This is especially true for those plants that will form the understory of your landscape if you do not want to wait years for the full effect.

Sapling trees grown beneath the canopy of a mature woodland often produce significantly larger leaves than those grown in the sun. This enables them to capture the most sunlight possible.

Under low light conditions, plants increase their ability to intercept light. They frequently do this by increasing the surface area of their individual leaves, especially those at the top. Saplings that come up under the canopy of their parents often produce oversized leaves. These leaves tend to be very thin and pliable, but they can be more than twice the size of those grown in more sun. As a balancing act, they may produce fewer leaves below, where there is less available sunlight. To survive in the shade, plants need to conserve energy wherever possible.

Another way plants compensate for lower light is by putting more energy into gaining height than in gaining girth. Such a response makes ecological sense. There is always more light higher in the canopy than near the ground. Using light energy to produce stouter trunks or wider crowns is not as efficient as using it to gain height to a level where the sunlight will be more abundant. This is especially noticeable in our own landscape where we have planted Simpson stopper (*Myrcianthes fragrans*) in both our shady woodland and along the front of our home, where it receives full sun. In the full sun, they have remained short and full, but in the shadier woodland they have grown much taller. Visitors to our home could easily mistake them for two different species. In Florida, Simpson stopper occurs in both scenarios naturally. It takes shade to make it act like a small tree. It takes sun to make it work as a shrubby hedge.

Most plants bloom less and set fewer fruit and seeds as shade increases. This too is based on the plant's overall energy budget. Plants that naturally occur in the shade are well adapted to completing their life cycle in such conditions. All plants need to reproduce to survive over time, but plants adapted to shade generally do not have the same amount of energy to devote to reproduction as plants in sunnier locations. They do not produce as large a number of flowers and fruits as their counterparts, their flowers and fruits may be smaller, and they may not produce them as often. Shade-adapted plants often have understated blooms. They can make up for this tendency by having colorful and interesting foliage. We use ferns, for example, for this purpose.

The exceptions are those shade-loving plants that live in deciduous shade, species like our native azaleas (*Rhododendron* spp.), violets (*Viola* spp.), and the like. Such species require protection from the harsh sun of summer,

Deciduous woodlands allow sunlight to reach the forest floor during the winter and early spring. This sunlight is the engine that allows ephemeral wildflowers, shrubs, and subcanopy trees to bloom in profusion before the canopy closes over once again.

but the months of direct sunlight they receive in winter and early spring is the engine that allows them to flower, fruit, and set viable seed for another generation. Shade-tolerant plants in deciduous shade need sunlight. They just need it at times of the year when the intensity is reduced. These are, with few exceptions, the species that we most admire for their color. They are the spring-blooming plants we most often incorporate into our landscapes and they are often the ones we most often misuse.

Planting these types of spring-blooming species at the edge of an evergreen canopy tree, such as a live oak or southern magnolia, is not equivalent to placing them beneath the canopy of deciduous trees. In a deciduous woodland, the understory receives many hours of direct sunlight for the time of year when it is needed and receives very little when it is not. Both the high light levels and the eventual protection are important for achieving their optimal growth. Plants at the edge of an evergreen canopy get trickles of light daily. Sometimes this is adequate, but too often there is not sufficient light in the spring for them to bloom normally and too much light in the summer to adequately protect them. If you must use these types of shade-loving plants beneath an evergreen canopy, do your best to plant them at the edge that allows for sufficient winter/early spring sunlight and lower light levels during summer.

Plants in shade take longer to become established. Though we see the above-ground part of a plant and can easily monitor top growth, we do not see the roots. All parts of a plant, however, grow because of photosynthesis, and reduced sunlight slows this process. The root system, so vital to the health and development of a plant, grows slower in shady areas, and almost no growth occurs in deciduous plants during the winter once the leaves have been shed. The same is not true if the plant is evergreen.

Because roots develop slower in shade, getting plants established properly in your shady areas will take more time and effort. New plants may need more water from time to time if the soil is not staying moist. You may also want to use a root-stimulating fertilizer (one low in nitrogen and higher in potassium and phosphorus) for the first watering or two. Your need to water will certainly have to be monitored for a longer period of time. Do not become complacent about watering during the first year, even if the plants you are establishing are thought of as "drought tolerant." Moisture needs to exist below the root ball for the roots to extend downward. Too often, we do not water deep enough to make this a reality. Watering only the up-

Root systems become established much slower in shade than in sunny locations. Competition from existing roots makes it even more difficult. Take special care to water newly planted specimens often and deeply for at least the first six months.

per surface keeps the plant alive because the surface roots are kept moist. What we don't see is that the deeper roots are dying because they are in dry powdery soil. We need to keep the entire root ball moist once we plant something new, and we need to make sure to keep the area beneath the root ball moist enough to have those deeper roots extend downward. All of this is even more critical in the shade because root growth is slower regardless of moisture. Once fully established, most plants will do fine in the landscape without supplemental watering if we have selected the right plant for the place we have put it in.

Plants in shade may be more susceptible to certain diseases than plants in sunnier locations; especially those that attack the foliage. In part, this is because plants in shade have less energy to ward off certain problems, but largely it is the result of the increased humidity and reduced air movement that occur beneath a woodland canopy. Powdery mildew, certain rusts, and various rots and wilts are fungal problems and all are exacerbated by moisture; especially when foliage remains wet overnight during times when daytime temperatures are warm and nighttime temperatures are cool. You can't really prevent this when the water comes down from the sky as rain and fog, but often the problem comes from misplaced watering. Avoid watering from late afternoon through the evening when foliage is least able to dry off sufficiently. If you need to water, do it early in the day when the excess moisture is most likely to evaporate from the foliage and stems. Avoid watering the foliage completely, if you can, by using a soaker hose or something similar that puts water on the soil and not in the air.

Plants in the shade also do not recover as fast from pest damage. It is true that shady areas often have fewer pests than sunny ones, but pests do occur. Snails and slugs may be more abundant, for example, and wildlife such as rabbits and gray squirrels will visit. Stems that are clipped or otherwise fed on, will not recover as quickly in shady locations. I have noticed this in my own landscape where cottontail rabbits frequently visit. For the most part, they confine the bulk of their feeding to my sunny front and side yards, but

Plants grown in shade recover much slower from being fed on by rabbits, insects, and other herbivores than plants grown in the sun. These leaves are being fed on by leaf-cutter bees.

when they venture into my backyard woodland, their feeding is noticeable and it takes many more weeks for the damage to disappear. Plants fed on for extended periods will suffer far more than they would in the sun and they may not be able to recover. Over time, I have lost some of my violets in that part of my woodland because of regular rabbit damage. The same plants, closer to the woodland edge that receives more sunlight, have fared better.

There are many advantages to discover in a shade garden. It's not all about dealing with the challenges. Because plants grow slower in the shade, unwanted plants grow slower too and are much easier to control. Gardeners in Florida quickly discover that they have more weeds to deal with than they ever thought possible. I challenge anyone anywhere in the state to turn over a spot of soil and water it and not have a legion of weeds appear. The problem is significantly reduced in shady landscapes. For one, there are fewer weed species to contend with. Not that many of these can't become significant problems, but the diversity of shade-loving nuisance plants is lower and these plants grow slower too. For the most part, it is easier to keep the nuisance plants out of your shady landscape. You need to be vigilant, but you can take a few more days off each week than you can in a sunnier location.

Because plants grow slower in shade, they are also easier to maintain if you are a gardener who likes to shape and prune. Infrequent and light pruning is all that is needed to maintain plants in the shape and height that is desired. In fact, you may find that you can put your hedgers and pruning shears away completely.

Plants in shade need less fertility. Much of what shade-grown plants need can be obtained from the soil, and much of that can be obtained by the natural decomposition of the leaf fall. That is the reason why your mulches should be derived from nonwoody plant materials. Decaying leaves and small twigs release significant amounts of essential nutrients and create organics that hold moisture better; their decay promotes the development of a soil fauna that speeds the decay and the release of even more nutrients.

Healthy woodland soil is created by the addition of organic mulches that decay easily. It is retarded by the addition of mulches that are not designed to do so. Mulches should not be thought of as aesthetic top dressings. Woody mulches, like pine bark and cypress, do not decay easily. They require more energy to decompose, and they end up releasing very few nutrients into the soil. Nonorganic mulches, such as pea gravel and limestone do nothing positive for your plantings, and may actually cause more harm than good. Shady

Organic mulches decompose; this process enriches the soil and creates conditions that are invaluable to your plants.

landscapes are best mulched by the leaves generated by the canopy. Allow this mulch to fall to the understory below. If you are not getting sufficient mulch because your canopy is not well established, add leaves generated by your neighbors. Around my neighborhood, many of my neighbors still rake and bag their leaves. When they set them out on the curb to be picked up, I ask their permission to pick them up myself. This was very important in developing the soil of our landscape when Alexa and I first planted it.

Leaf mulches are not created equal. Large, thick, and leathery leaves do not decompose as easily or as quickly as others, and they may actually smother small understory plants if they are applied too thickly. Southern magnolia combines all of these undesirable traits and should be used with caution. Trees such as sycamore (*Platanus occidentalis*) and tulip tree (*Liriodendron tulipifera*) have very large leaves, but they are relatively thin and decompose much faster than southern magnolia. The leathery leaves of live oak are small, but they do not decompose quickly. Our shady landscape was designed around several live oaks left by the developer. The leaves they generate often take several years to decompose. This is not true for the thinner leaves of our turkey oak and southern basswood (*Tilia americana*).

Shaded soils also do not dry out as quickly as soils in sunnier locations. Both the shade and the layer of mulch retard evaporation. Once your soil is moist, it will stay that way much longer, and you will find that your need to supplement natural rainfall with irrigation is significantly reduced. Shady landscapes make being a water-wise gardener a much easier task.

This doesn't mean that you can ignore the need for water. Many of your shade-tolerant plants are likely more adapted to moist soils than to dry ones and, though shady areas lose soil moisture much slower than sunny ones, it may take more water to rehydrate them if they are allowed to become dry. Your canopy that serves to shade this landscape also intercepts rainfall. When we receive a typical Florida thunderstorm with all its fury, a good share of that water makes its way to the plants and soil below, but less intense rain events do not distribute the water equitably. Rain drops are caught by foliage in the canopy. Some of it eventually drips off these leaves, but some of it is guided down the petiole (the leaf stem), to a small branch, to a larger branch, and down along the trunk. In this way, canopy trees take water for themselves and prevent it from reaching their neighbors. Do not assume that a light rain is watering your plantings uniformly. It likely isn't. During periods of drought, check your soil moisture at least 6–12 inches below the surface and feel if the soil is moist or if it has become powder dry.

The other major issue with watering your shade garden is root competition. This is an especially significant issue if you are adding plants to an established canopy. Established plants have developed the root systems they need to thrive where they are planted. None of these roots are superfluous and, for the most part, they have divvied up all of the available space around them with their existing neighbors. Adding new plants to this community, with a small rounded root ball formerly confined to a pot, is difficult. New plants have to find space to muscle their way in and they have to strong-arm some of the soil moisture for their own use. Both of these tasks are difficult, especially considering that root growth is slower in the shade than in the sun. New plants need to be given plenty of water during establishment to compensate for what gets lost to the well-established root systems of their preexisting neighbors. You can't just chop a hole into existing surface roots to install a new plant and expect that hole to remain available forever. Existing plants will recover lost roots far quicker than a new plant will outmuscle them for the space. They will have to find a new equilibrium, but for that to happen there has to be enough water for everybody.

Root competition is always a significant concern when you add new plants to an established garden. Because roots establish themselves even more slowly in shady areas, new plants take even longer to adjust fully.

The final issue I will address is something Larry Hodgson discusses in his wonderful book, *Making the Most of Shade*: the challenges and the advantages tied to your personality as a gardener. Larry divides gardeners into two main types. I have to admit that I am a Type A gardener. I like to be out in my garden, fussing about. I like to see my plants change quickly during the course of the season. I like to have something to do. I enjoy my shady garden, but I spend more time in the sunnier areas of my landscape because there is more to do. Type B gardeners prefer the relaxed pace and reduced workload of managing a landscape in shade. They don't mind sitting beneath the canopy in a hammock or recliner reading a good book or scanning the canopy with binoculars looking for songbirds. What you consider to be work and what you consider to be enjoyment will color your concept of what truly constitutes the challenges and benefits that await you in a shade-dominated landscape, but when all is said and done, as long as we enter into this with our eyes wide open, we have a good chance for success.

3

Creating Shade

If you already have established shade, you may wish to skip this chapter, but if you are starting from scratch or wanting to expand the amount of shade you have, please read on. Most landscapes in Florida have at least some shade. Shade trees are either preserved by the developer or added as soon as the home is constructed because trees enhance the aesthetics of a home and significantly increase its property value. According to the Council of Tree and Landscape Appraisers, a mature tree can have an appraised value between $1,000 and $10,000. The difference in value will depend on the species of tree planted, its health, and its size. Not all trees are created equal, and that inequality will vary further over time depending on how well you take care of them.

There are many options to consider before you select a shade tree. Time spent in selecting the right tree(s) for your site will reward you many times over as your landscape matures. Shade trees are a lifetime investment. They are likely to outlive you, they will form the landscape foundation that everything else gets built upon, and they will take years to fully meet your objectives. If you fail up front, you will lose many precious years before you can rectify your initial mistake or you will simply be condemned to live with it. Weigh your choices intelligently. Don't be afraid to spend a few extra dollars up front to get what you truly want and don't settle for something less simply because what you want might be more difficult to track down and purchase. The right tree in the right location is the most important decision you will make throughout the entire process of creating any kind of landscape. Choose wisely.

I believe that the most important decision is the one made between selecting a deciduous or an evergreen species. The simple difference between

Deciduous trees allow sunlight to reach the understory during the critical winter and early spring months. This solar energy is what enables these plants to bloom and set seed.

whether your tree will be leafless during the winter and early spring or whether it will keep its foliage year round will make a greater difference to your understory plantings than anything else you will do. Deciduous trees let significant amounts of sunlight through their canopy for up to four months during the winter and spring. Evergreen trees maintain a constant and predictable level of shade year round. Nothing else you do will influence the rest of your shade garden more than this choice.

As I discussed in an earlier chapter, a deciduous canopy is the best choice for a landscape designed around spring blooming ephemerals (wildflowers) and spring blooming shrubs and subcanopy trees. The display of color seen beneath the canopy of a north and north-central Florida woodland is the result of sunlight generating that flush of growth from late winter until the canopy closes in midspring. During that brief period of unfiltered sunlight, magic ensues; violets and columbines (*Aquilegia canadensis*) emerge and flower, viburnums (*Viburnum* spp.) and blueberries (*Vaccineum* spp.) bloom and set fruit, and dogwoods (*Cornus* spp.) and redbuds (*Cercis canadensis*) set the woods ablaze with color. If your landscape occurs anywhere north of semitropical south Florida, this approach is possible, *if* you create a mostly deciduous canopy.

Live oaks (*Quercus virginiana*) are among the most commonly used canopy trees in Florida.

A deciduous canopy has other benefits as well; it cools your home during the months it is most required, but it lets sunshine in to warm your home, your gazebo, and your garden bench at a time when a bit of extra warmth might be desirable. In fact, you can save money on your home energy bill by shading your home in the summer and letting the sunshine in during the winter.

There has been a significant body of research on this question. One such study, conducted at Auburn University, found that for every 10 percent of shade coverage, the average home electricity consumption was reduced by more than 1.25 kWh/day and that dense shade in the summer reduced daily electricity consumption by more than 9 percent. This same study also ex-

Evergreen trees provide shade year round. Plants grown beneath them, like this wild coffee (*Psychotria nervosa*), must be adapted to relatively low light throughout the year.

amined the value of having reduced shade during the winter. It found that a one-percentage-point increase in average shade during the winter months increased electricity consumption and that average daily electricity use was about 6 percent higher per month in winter than for a house in full sun. Deciduous shade allows you to have this flexibility. If you use evergreens for shade, use them on the north side of your home.

An evergreen canopy is dependable and the best choice for landscapes where shade is desirable year round—extreme south Florida, for example. Evergreen trees also provide cover for songbirds and other wildlife during the winter months, when it is often more critical, but they limit the number of plants that will perform well beneath them. Understory plantings in evergreen shade tend to rely more on foliage than flowers for their beauty. Many ferns, for example, do well in evergreen shade. It will change your landscape approach, but it doesn't necessarily reduce aesthetics; it's just a different aesthetic.

There is no reason why you cannot mix these approaches if you want both, just be careful as you develop your landscape plan. If you want evergreen and deciduous trees, do it in patches large enough to accommodate the needs of your understory. If you desire some spring color, the patches of sunlight need to be designed large enough to truly put that part of the understory in the sun during the winter and early spring. That means using just a few evergreen trees and placing them north of the deciduous ones.

That is exactly what Alexa and I have done in our backyard. When the home was constructed in 1980, the builder left a small grove of young live oaks in the northwest corner of the lot. Today, these trees are large and they provide a beautiful evergreen canopy to that section of our landscape. Beneath it, we have our patio and our bench swing and we spend many wonderful hours there. When we also fell in love with the many wildflowers and subcanopy trees more common to north Florida, we extended our woodland south along our property line using deciduous trees so that we could accommodate them. At first, we were really only successful with our ephemeral spring color at the edge where the two woodlands met, but we have been expanding them as the deciduous trees mature. It will take a good many more years before it is everything we want, but we have a good start because we designed for it.

Another approach is to create two separate woodlands in different areas of your property. This is possible even if you live on a standard-sized lot. Just take into consideration where you want permanent shade and where you want sun in the winter. Design the evergreen shade to the north of your home and the deciduous shade to the south. In that way, you'll always have shade where you need it and the benefit of sun-driven warmth on colder days.

It is not enough only to consider the evergreen/deciduous nature of the trees you will plant. Canopy trees have a great many attributes that also must be considered. A significant one is canopy height. The taller the tree, the wider the shadow it will throw beneath. Truly large trees, like tulip tree and sweet gum (*Liquidambar styraciflua*) can reach heights greater than 80 feet. They will have a much bigger impact on the plants beneath than trees that normally reach a mature height of 50 feet or less. In fact, you might wish to consider using a subcanopy tree, like a flowering dogwood (*Cornus florida*) or fringe tree, for your canopy in small spaces. Your shade garden does not have to be dominated by large trees to have shade. Some of the most attractive shade gardens that I have seen have been designed around small trees and in confined areas. Sometimes, you might even be able to fit a bench beneath it all.

In addition to canopy height, trees differ in canopy width. Southern mag-

Live oaks (*Quercus virginiana*) produce a very wide crown as they mature and cast far more shade beneath them than trees with narrower crowns.

nolia and live oak are famous for their wide-spreading crowns. While this often makes a majestic landscape statement, it also creates expansive areas that are influenced by this shade. In small areas, it can be problematic, or at least challenging, to plant effectively beneath trees like this, and given that both of these trees are also evergreen, it requires that all of the plants used beneath this canopy be adapted to low light throughout the year. Not every canopy tree tends to send its upper branches horizontally like those two trees do. Elms (*Ulmus* spp.) tend to produce a candelabra shape with the major branches held at about 45° angles from the main trunk, and because of this, they throw far less shade for their height. Other potential canopy trees, like turkey and bluejack oaks (*Quercus incana*), have even narrower crowns for their height than elms.

Canopy width can be adjusted by judicious pruning, but fighting its natural growth form is a forever battle that can get expensive as the tree matures. Good arborists can reduce crown width by selectively trimming the outer branches, but the tree's inherent genetics will always want to recover its natural shape. If you need periodic pruning, however, do not attempt to do it "on the cheap." Use a licensed arborist, certified by a professional arborist association. These professionals know how to prune so that the tree's health is maintained and they understand the importance of your under-story plantings. The guy in the truck who offers to cut you a deal may cause permanent health issues to your valuable canopy trees and too often drops the limbs wherever they happen to fall—smashing sensitive plants beneath.

Canopy width can also be modified by the distance you space your trees apart. Most trees reach their fullest canopy width when grown in the open, without competition. When confronted with a neighbor, they will first at-tempt to grow up and then over it. As they stretch for the sunlight and even-tual dominance, they will forgo adding a lot of lateral branch width. If you plant several trees side by side that have about the same mature heights, all of them on the inside will stay narrower than normal. Of course, there is a limit to how close together you should plant canopy trees for them to remain healthy. It is a balancing act for sure, but adding several species together in a

You can force your canopy trees to reduce their natural crown width by planting them closer together. We have done this in our small backyard woodland by planting this tulip tree (*Liriodendron tulipifera*) and winged elm (*Ulmus alata*) ten feet apart.

planting will increase diversity, and this will make your woodland better for wildlife and more aesthetically interesting. As a rule of thumb, you should plant large canopy trees no closer than 15 feet apart if you want them to grow "normally." If you don't have that kind of room and wish to force them to remain narrower, do not plant them closer than 10 feet. Planting trees closer than 10 feet apart will cause them to grow at angles to each other instead of growing upright. For small trees, this can make an interesting landscape effect, but for large canopy trees, it can make them susceptible to falling over during extreme storm events, and when that happens they can cause significant property damage.

If you are creating shade where none currently exists, it is especially important to consider the growth rate of your potential canopy-tree choices. That said, do not be impatient and decide to use only species that mature rapidly. In our fast-paced modern society, we seem to want everything instantly. This often leads us to foolish decisions and, when selecting trees, this is true more often than not. In nature, trees that mature quickly are usually weeds because that is their inherent quality. Weeds take quick advantage of gaps in the forest canopy; they colonize them rapidly and fill the hole in as fast as possible so that other competitors cannot outmuscle them for the space. Trees that grow and mature quickly also often die at an earlier age and do not invest a lot of energy into making dense wood that will serve it over many centuries. Quick-growing trees are almost always weak and suffer significant damage during extreme weather events. They also rarely live more than 50–60 years before showing their age and declining in health.

If gardening is the ultimate expression of an optimistic mind, then planting canopy trees as saplings is the ultimate expression of gardening. In all likelihood, it will take several decades for these trees to reach a size that will actually shade you, and maybe a lifetime before they are fully mature. Alexa's small grove of young live oaks is now a cluster of large trees that forms the foundation of our shady back yard, but it has taken more than 30 years since the home was built for these trees to reach that size. The deciduous canopy that I have been working on since our marriage is still only 15 feet high after 7 years. The shade it provides is too open for many of the woodland plants I intend someday to plant beneath them. I am not a very patient person, but I am serious about planting the trees I want. Having that patience will pay off over time. That is the optimism of gardening.

Gardeners are also often fooled into thinking that they can speed up the process appreciably by using larger plants to start with. It seems to make sense and it does, in fact, work to some extent if you start with well-grown specimens, are willing and able to pay for them, and have the ability to water them well for extended periods of time. Canopy trees that are 30 gallon-size or larger can make a dramatic impact instantly in the landscape, but they are also difficult to establish. Often, the root systems of very large trees are not sufficient to maintain the top portion without a lot of extra watering for a great many months. And while they are getting established in their new landscape, they are incapable of adding more top growth. All of their energy is going into making roots.

Trees grown in smaller containers often reach the size of the larger trees in less than a year, and their root systems establish more quickly. As a rule of thumb, a 1-gallon tree will reach the size of a 3-gallon tree after one growing season; a 3-gallon tree will equal a 7-gallon tree in the same time; and a 7-gallon tree will equal the size of a 15-gallon tree within two growing seasons. Given that the price of a well-grown tree nearly doubles each time it is "stepped up" to the next pot size, you can save a great deal of money if you have a bit of patience.

Of course, this is all predicated on the assumption that you are purchasing a well-grown tree. This is not always the case. Most plant purchases are made by looking at the condition of the above-ground portion, but the most important part is the root ball. Plants can correct a great many defects in their stems; they cannot correct defects in their roots without a great deal of work. Roots that have become wound around themselves in a pot or grow bag will always remain tied up in a knot, and as they grow they will add girth and strangle the above-ground stem. The only way to rectify this is to cut off a portion of the root ball and force the plant to make a new root system that grows in the right direction. This stops all top growth for an extended period and requires you to water it extensively. There are no instances of "good deals" on trees if that "deal" is based on getting a large tree in a small pot at the small pot price. Do not fall for this. The overgrown tree will never reach its full potential. Pay a good nurseryperson for what it takes to have grown it well. The small cost difference will be more than made up in the life of the plant. Almost always, the difference in growth rate between two plants of the same species planted in the landscape at the same time is a difference in root structure at the time of planting. Pay attention to the roots when you pull the plant out of the pot. If they are wound around tightly in a ball along what was the outside of the pot, return the plant to the nursery and get another that is not pot bound. If you are keen to keep it anyway, use a sharp knife and make 3–4 half-inch cuts horizontally evenly around the root ball and cut the bottom half inch off completely.

If you have a well-grown tree, how fast or slow it grows is largely relative. What is the measure by which we judge the speed of growth? If we are gardening with wildlife in mind, we are interested in the age it takes for our trees to provide food and shelter. Most oaks and hickories (*Carya* spp.) do not produce nuts until they are about 20 years old. That is old for most shade trees. Elms and maples (*Acer* spp.) may reach that benchmark at 10 years. Hawthorns (*Crataegus* spp.) do not flower until they are about 7 years old; redbuds can bloom many years younger. Regardless, the time it takes a tree

It always pays to purchase well-grown specimens from your nurseryperson. Most "good deals," large plants in small pots, will have root systems that are severely coiled and in need of serious root pruning if the plant is ever to achieve its full potential.

to reach some measurable stage of maturity is not uniform. Good growing conditions will speed the process a bit, but most of it is determined by the inherent genetics of the species. If you are starting a shade garden purely from scratch, with no shade tree to serve as an anchor, it might be best to use at least a few species that are moderately fast and not rely purely on the slower ones.

Just because you do not have instant shade does not mean you cannot effectively plant the understory; it merely means that your initial understory may be more adapted to higher light levels than the one you will eventually have. If you wish eventually to use wildflowers and ferns that need protection from the summer sun, exercise a bit of patience and add them later. As your canopy begins to develop, use wildflowers that prefer higher light. There may even be ferns that will perform satisfactorily for the first few years. As the site gets more shaded, some of these may start to fade. When this happens, begin to insert the species you were originally planning for. Alexa and I have had to do this in our developing deciduous back yard. The trees are in place and developing a canopy. They had to go in first. The understory is largely composed of drought-tolerant native wildflowers that can handle the present conditions on the ground. They are not what I envision for my final design; they are placeholders, but they are attractive placeholders, and when they die from too much shade, I will not mourn their passing but laud their contribution.

Being a Floridian means that you have a great many possible choices when considering which canopy trees to purchase. Assuming you have already made some decisions about whether you want evergreen or deciduous species, how tall you want the trees to be, and whether you want trees with wide or narrower crowns, you still have dozens of good species to pick from that meet these requirements. The table below is meant to help you refine your list, but ultimately what you select is a personal decision and you must be happy with the trees you choose. No list can make that decision for you.

If you live in extreme south Florida and never experience freezing winter temperatures, you will want to stick to those canopy trees native to your zone. The vast majority are semitropical, evergreen species. A few, like live oak, cabbage palm (*Sabal palmetto*), and red maple (*Acer rubrum*) also occur in north Florida, but the majority are confined only to this region. Many semitropical native trees are rather slow growing, but there are exceptions.

Commonly Used Native Canopy Trees

Common Name	Latin Name	Evergreen/Deciduous	Height[1]	Canopy Width[2]	Root Depth[3]
NORTH/CENTRAL FLORIDA					
Red maple	Acer rubrum	Deciduous	60–70	40–50	Y
Sugar maple	Acer saccharum	Deciduous	50–70	30–40	N
Pignut hickory	Carya glabra	Deciduous	60–90	40–75	N
Mockernut hickory	Carya tomentosa	Deciduous	60–90	40–75	N
Sugarberry	Celtis laevigata	Deciduous	60–80	40–50	N
American beech	Fagus grandifolia	Deciduous	70–85	30–40	N
Green ash	Fraxinus pennsylvanica	Deciduous	60–90	40–55	N
American holly	Ilex opaca	Evergreen	35–50	15–25	N
Southern red cedar	Juniperus virginiana	Evergreen	30–50	20–30	N
Sweet gum	Liquidambar styraciflua	Deciduous	60–75	40–50	Y
Tulip tree	Liriodendron tulipifera	Deciduous	70–90	40–50	N
Southern magnolia	Magnolia grandiflora	Evergreen	60–80	30–40	N
Sweetbay magnolia	Magnolia virginiana	Evergreen	40–50	20–30	Y
Red mulberry	Morus rubra	Deciduous	40–60	40–50	N
Tupelo/Black gum	Nyssa sylvatica	Deciduous	60–90	30–40	Y
Red bay	Persea borbonia	Evergreen	40–60	20–30	N
Sand pine	Pinus clausa	Evergreen	40–60	25–35	N
Slash pine	Pinus elliottii	Evergreen	60–90	30–50	N
Longleaf pine	Pinus palustris	Evergreen	60–90	30–50	N
Loblolly pine	Pinus taeda	Evergreen	60–90	30–50	N
Sycamore	Platanus occidentalis	Deciduous	75–90	60–85	N
Carolina cherry laurel	Prunus caroliniana	Evergreen	30–40	20–30	N
Black cherry	Prunus serotina	Deciduous	60–80	35–50	N

Common name	Scientific name	Type	Height	Width	Shallow
White oak	*Quercus alba*	Deciduous	60–90	30–50	N
Southern red oak	*Quercus falcata*	Deciduous	50–75	50–70	N
Turkey oak	*Quercus laevis*	Deciduous	30–40	15–20	N
Laurel oak	*Quercus laurifolia*	Deciduous	50–70	30–40	Y
Swamp chestnut	*Quercus michauxii*	Deciduous	75–90	35–50	Y
Water oak	*Quercus nigra*	Deciduous	50–70	30–45	Y
Shumard oak	*Quercus shumardii*	Deciduous	60–90	40–55	N
Bluff oak	*Quercus sinuata*	Deciduous	50–65	35–50	N
Live oak	*Quercus virgininana*	Evergreen	60–80	60–120	N
Cabbage palm	*Sabal palmetto*	Evergreen	30–50	10–15	N
Bald cypress	*Taxodium distichum*	Deciduous	50–75	20–25	Y
Southern basswood	*Tilia americana*	Deciduous	50–75	35–40	N
Winged elm	*Ulmus alata*	Deciduous	45–70	30–50	N
Florida elm	*Ulmus americana*	Deciduous	60–80	25–40	Y

SOUTH FLORIDA

Common name	Scientific name	Type	Height	Width	Shallow
Gumbo limbo	*Bursera simaruba*	Evergreen	30–50	30–40	N
Pigeon plum	*Coccoloba diversifolia*	Evergreen	30–50	15–20	N
Buttonwood	*Conocarpus erectus*	Evergreen	35–50	20–35	Y
Strangler fig	*Ficus aurea*	Evergreen	45–60	35–50	N
Wild tamarind	*Lysiloma latisiliquum*	Evergreen	35–60	30–45	N
Royal palm	*Roystonea regia*	Evergreen	70–85	15–25	N
Mastic	*Sideroxylon foetidissimum*	Evergreen	50–70	35–45	N
Florida mahogany	*Swietenia mahagoni*	Evergreen	40–60	30–45	N

Notes: 1. Average mature height in feet.

2. Average crown width in feet.

3. Mature root system typically shallow (Y) or not (N).

If you live in the northern tiers of counties and you get regular freezing winter temperatures below 20°F, you will want to use the great diversity of trees common to north Florida and the rest of the Southeast Coastal Plain. These are the trees most of us consider "southern" as they also are common to states adjacent to us such as Georgia and Alabama. Most of these are deciduous, and many get quite tall over time.

In between these two zones is the vast majority of Florida and what you choose to plant is more open ended. Much depends on your microclimate: the subtle nuances of soil moisture, fertility, sunshine, and so on that characterize your specific planting area. If you live near the coast and have winter temperatures that do not generally go below about 26°F for extended periods, you may be able to plant some of the south Florida specialties. On the opposite extreme, you may do well with many of the north Florida natives if your site is not in full sun and your soils and moisture are somewhat similar to the top tiers of Florida counties. Of course, you always have the option of using trees that already occur naturally in your area. For any zone, this should always be your first consideration.

Alexa and I live in southern Pinellas County, not far from the coast, and our winter temperatures rarely dip below the mid-20s°F. Because Pinellas is a peninsula, we remain warmer than most counties several tiers south of us and inland. We have experimented quite successfully with a few semitropical shade trees, like Florida mahogany (*Swietenia mahogani*), but in all likelihood we will someday get another truly cold spell as occurred in 1989 and these temperatures may severely damage it. I considered this possibility in my landscape plan. My canopy is not designed around this tree; it is just a small part and its loss would not appreciably change my shady woodland landscape. I do not recommend using the semitropical canopy trees outside their normal range except as accents. Global climate change does not mean that Florida winters will be warmer; it means that our extremes will be greater.

Alexa and my landscape draws far more influence from trees that are native north of us, and most have fared quite well south of their normal range. Many north Florida species perform adequately farther south if they are given some protection from the full sun of summer and if the soil temperature and moisture levels are not extreme. We have built our poor soil up over the years by using leaves as mulch and allowing them to decay and form a better organic layer. We have watered the trees in sufficiently to establish their root systems, and we added them to the edge of our existing live oak grove. North Florida species, planted well south of their normal range, never perform quite as well, however, as they do further north. They do not get the same vivid fall colors unless there is an early cold snap, they do not bloom as fully unless there is sufficient winter cold, and they sometimes do not set fruit as well. That said, if there are trees that you truly desire and they are not quite within your geographic range naturally, do a bit of research and see if they might be one of those species that can be "pushed" a bit south. I, personally, get great pleasure from my silverbells (*Halesia* spp.), downy serviceberry (*Amelanchier arborea*), red buckeye (*Aesculus pavia*) and the like even if they are not likely ever to be quite as dramatic as they are farther north.

4

Working in Existing Shade

In the previous chapter, I assumed that we were starting with a blank slate, that we were creating shade in a location that was not shaded or, at least, expanding the extent of existing shade into areas currently in full sun. Most of us, however, have shade in some form and our real dilemma is how to use that shade more effectively so that our landscape provides more function. Working in existing shade can be a challenge for a significant number of reasons besides the dilemma of choosing the right plants.

Shaded areas, beneath existing canopy trees, can be tough to plant in because the trees overhead have already developed their root systems and

Adding new plants beneath the canopy of existing shade is difficult and requires extra care and management.

these systems are extensive. Understanding these root systems is important. Roots are the least understood portion of a plant, because they are not visible. Canopy trees initially send out a taproot that probes its way downward to anchor the young tree in the soil. This root remains for the life of the plant and becomes more extensive over time, but as any engineering student would tell you, that model would fail without extensive lateral roots nearer the surface to provide stability. The taproot is the anchor, but the laterals provide the balance necessary to keep the tree upright through storms, soggy soils, and high winds. Some trees do not produce significant taproots, but all trees develop significant lateral systems, often extending outward by as much as three times the canopy width. All roots gain girth as well as length each year.

In wetland trees, lateral roots hug the soil surface or occur just beneath it. This allows them to also help the developing tree breathe in oxygen-starved, saturated soils. Common home landscape trees that are naturally adapted to wetland soils (e.g., laurel oak [*Quercus laurifolia*] and red maple) will develop extensive lateral root systems regardless of where they are planted. It is genetic. As these trees age, their lateral root systems become more extensive; therefore, they are very difficult to plant under if you wait until they are mature. If at all possible, plant the understory beneath them while they are very young.

Trees also need a root system to effectively absorb water and dissolved nutrients. As soil is more fertile near the surface than deep underground, large trees develop an extremely complicated system of feeder roots off these laterals, just beneath the soil surface and mulch layer. If the main roots are the arteries and veins of a plant's external circulatory system, the feeder roots are the capillaries; they are the part of the system most significant to absorbing water and nutrients.

If you wish to add a plant beneath an existing canopy, you are battling the existing extensive and important root system. As you bisect the feeder roots and go a bit deeper, you quickly meet the established network of lateral roots. More often than not, these laterals will be too large to easily cut with a shovel and you will have to use a lopping shears or something similar to create a hole large enough to plant a new plant. Forcing a hole into the existing root system harms the existing trees. It cuts off structural and life-providing elements that the tree depends on for its health and well-being. Do not go about chopping holes into this system haphazardly. Feel your way about first

In existing shade, root competition is especially great. When adding a new plant, search carefully to avoid damaging the larger roots and cut a hole larger than the pot diameter to reduce root competition while the new plant becomes established.

and try to find gaps between the larger lateral roots. If you have to cut roots, cut the smaller ones and avoid damage to the largest.

Realize also that the hole you cut is only temporary. Shortly after you make these cuts, the severed root system starts to take action to recover. As these roots have been there far longer than those of your newly planted specimen, they have a huge advantage in refilling this newly created gap. By the time your new plant has realized that it can escape the root ball it was once confined to by its pot, the original roots you have severed have taken back what was once theirs. This battle for space gets more difficult to win the older and more established the canopy is that you attempt to plant beneath. For this reason, it is far better to plant beneath your canopy trees when they are relatively young than when they are decades old.

The second important consideration is providing sufficient water. An unbelievable amount of competition for water and nutrients is going on beneath the ground surface. The vast network of feeder roots from every plant in the area competes daily for this resource. The strong survive and the weakest lose out. Newly planted specimens in the understory have a distinct disadvantage in securing their fair share of what's available. Over time, they often establish their territory, but it's extremely important that you help them while they are getting established. Most significantly, they need lots of water during the initial months. If rainfall is not regular, you need to supplement newly planted specimens by providing a deep watering several times per week. If your soil fertility is below average (by Florida standards), you should also consider giving them a bit of extra fertilization targeted directly at their root ball—a formulation low in nitrogen made specifically for roots.

When planting below an existing canopy, use smaller specimens whenever possible, especially in places where it is difficult to create planting holes. It will be easier to cut smaller holes in an existing root system and smaller plants establish much quicker. I rarely plant anything larger than 1-gallon specimens underneath my existing oak grove, and I choose quart-sized plants whenever possible when using herbaceous species such as ferns and wildflowers. Small specimens are not nearly as needy as larger ones. They have less top growth to maintain so their root systems do not have as great a burden to provide for it. They can expend more time establishing their root systems and fighting for the space they ultimately need.

Well-grown specimens in 1-, 3-, and 7-gallon pots. Small plants require less soil disturbance than larger plants and establish themselves more quickly. Purchasing larger plants allows you to have a more mature landscape in less time, but it requires more work to establish them. Deciding which way to go is a balancing act.

Planting is also best done when it is easiest for your new plants to get the resources they need. In Florida, that means planting in the winter or during the summer rainy season. Do not plant into an existing canopy during periods of water stress. In most Florida locations and during most years, that translates to April, May, and early June. These may be wonderful planting months up north, but they are absolutely the harshest months to plant in Florida. Winter planting makes good sense. Deciduous trees are no longer photosynthesizing, so their water budget is extremely reduced. Nearly 99 percent of all water withdrawn from the soil by any plant is lost from the leaves during photosynthesis. When large trees are leafless, their need for water comes only from their need to maintain core metabolic functions. Even evergreen canopy trees use far less water during the winter. Photosynthesis and core metabolic needs slow down in lower temperatures, so the need for water is reduced. Freezing temperatures do not affect the establishment of newly planted specimens *if* those specimens are adapted to our climate. Native plants, used in the appropriate zones, will not be harmed or even slowed by winter freezes.

Though I greatly prefer to plant during the winter, summer can also be good *if* you wait until afternoon thunderstorms have become regular. Since water and dissolved nutrients are the limiting factor during establishment, wait to plant until natural watering can play a bigger role. In most summers, regular rains keep the soil relatively moist, and this moisture extends deep into the soil column. Summer conditions seem harsh, but in a shady garden area experiencing regular afternoon thunderstorms, establishing new plants is far easier than you might guess.

Your new plants will also face significant competition for nutrients. All of the essential elements required by plants, except oxygen, hydrogen, and carbon, arrive in soluble form with the water absorbed by the roots. The roots of new plants are often wound up in a ball, they have never had to fight with others for the water and nutrients they need, and they have not likely formed the associations with soil bacteria and mycorrhizal fungi necessary to function most efficiently. Because they are planted in the shade, they will develop these systems more slowly than plants grown in higher light levels, so it is necessary to water them well for longer periods of time to get them adequately established. A good rule of thumb is that it will take a year for your plants to become fully adjusted and this is true even for native Florida plants. When adequate rainfall is present, watering may not be required, but pay special attention to these plants during periods of drought. It doesn't take much to kill off a significant portion of a plant's root system and it takes a lot to get it reestablished. Water your plants before they wilt and before the soil becomes completely dry. Eventually, supplemental watering should not be necessary and that is our goal, but it is penny-wise, pound-foolish not to get your plants off to a healthy start so they can fend off the adversities of nature without you later on.

There is some debate as to whether you should start with larger or smaller specimens when planting into existing shade. I have argued mostly for smaller plants as I find them easier to insert into the holes chiseled within the existing root structure. Those who argue for using slightly larger plants do so because they feel the larger specimens come into the landscape competition with larger root masses, and this gives them a better competitive advantage. In reality, both arguments are correct. The real unknown in this equation is the healthy root ball. A healthy root ball, regardless of the size of the pot, is what you need to look for, and it is just fine to inspect it before making your purchases. Just be careful as you do so. Hold the plant upside down and inspect the drainage holes at the bottom and sides

The best time to plant in Florida is when the prevailing weather conditions make it easier on the plants to become established. A good time to plant is during the summer when afternoon thunderstorms are somewhat predictable.

of the pot to see if the roots are visible. If you cannot see any roots as you turn the pot around in your hands, it means that the plant has likely been recently repotted and you are paying for a pot size above what the plant really deserves. Moving plants up to larger pot sizes is necessary and means that your nurseryperson is doing the right thing, but I would recommend that you either wait to make your purchase for a few weeks, or buy it now and wait a few weeks until the roots become visible before installing it into the shade garden.

Alternatively, if large roots are extruding from the bottom or side holes and you can see that they are curving around the sides of the pot, it means that this plant is pot bound and should have been moved to a larger-sized pot before this was allowed to happen. I would recommend not purchasing

The roots of this tree have been confined too long in a pot that is too small. They will never straighten out and grow properly without some severe pruning followed by extended watering while they recover.

The root system is even more important than the trunk for the long-term health of your tree. Before you purchase a tree, make sure it has a healthy root system. These new roots have just reached the sides of the pot and have not become a tangled mess.

such plants, but if you truly want it and cannot find a better specimen, you will need to do some root pruning to get it ready to plant into your shade garden. Roots, like stems, have "memory." They do not straighten out over time; they keep their shape and add girth. Roots that wind around each other increase in girth as the plant matures and this strangles the plant in much the same way as if it were an animal's windpipe. If the major roots of your newly acquired plant are winding around each other, score the sides of the root ball, perpendicular to it, about ⅓ inch deep in three to four locations and cut about ½–1 inch off the bottom. Repot this plant, fertilize it with a root-stimulating fertilizer at the recommended dilution, and water it well for 3–4 weeks before trying to add it to your landscape.

If the roots are visible but the larger ones are not sticking out of the pot, it is likely safe to carefully remove the plant with its root ball from the pot. Holding it upside down, tap the pot and pull on it gently. It should come out easily after a few taps. The root ball should hold the dirt in place if it is well established in the pot. The larger roots should be visible, but should not wind around themselves. They definitely should not have reached the bottom and then been forced to grow upward. The finer roots, the ones that will actually feed the plant, should be bright white and should extend in all directions through the soil. If you see healthy roots, you know that you are purchasing a plant with the greatest possible chance of winning the battle for water and nutrients once installed into the preexisting landscape. Roots are the most important link to success, not top growth.

Root competition will be the biggest challenge in getting your new plants established, but it isn't the only one. Shade is a challenge to overcome, even in a shade garden. As I discussed previously, plants adjust and grow slower in shady environments. Even shade-tolerant plants often find the existing conditions too shady to get well established. This is often not a problem for plants adapted to deep shade, but many of the plants you select are likely better adapted to partial shade, and they may have been grown in nurseries where they were given higher light levels than they will find in your land-scape. While such species should eventually become accustomed to more shade, it may be prudent to do some selective pruning of the canopy to temporarily let more light in at the time of planting.

There are two distinct pruning methods to reduce the degree of shade be-neath your trees, raising the height of the crown by limbing lower branches and thinning the crown by reducing the density of the canopy branches. Both can have dramatic results on the health of your understory while improving the condition of the canopy trees as well, but only when done correctly. Incor-rect pruning methods will stress your trees and can cause them permanent injury. There is a right and a wrong way to prune. Sadly, many of the door-to-door "arborists" that cruise my neighborhood have not been trained in proper pruning methodology. You can tackle the smaller jobs yourself, but leave the large canopy work to experts. It will be worth your investment to hire a certi-fied arborist to climb through the canopy, taking off just the right branches to create the light gaps you desire.

Correct pruning is done by taking the branch off just above its union with the larger one. This junction is pretty obvious and is known as the collar. When you cut just above the collar, the tree will quickly seal up the wound and grow around it. Just like animals, plants form "scabs" and protect them-selves from "bleeding" to death and from getting infections. They just do it a bit differently. If you cut a limb too far above the collar, the wound will fester

When pruning a limb, make sure you make the cut immediately above the "collar"—the junction where the limb meets the larger limb it is growing out of. Correctly pruned limbs allow the tree to heal quickly and thoroughly without a significant risk for disease.

for a longer period, and the wood between the cut and the collar will slowly die, putting the plant at greater risk from insect pests and disease. If you make the cut below the collar, the wound will not heal properly and the tree will be at significant risk for additional injury. Approach pruning the same way you would approach hiring a surgeon for yourself; use an experienced and knowledgeable person, use the right tools, and make sure the edges of those tools are clean and sharp.

Limbing up a tree involves removing the lowest branches. In very small trees, you should avoid this completely because their growth rate is dependent on photosynthesis, and removing photosynthetic surface area will slow their growth rate. As trees get a bit older, however, lower limbs may be trimmed away if the shade they produce is not desirable. Simple geometry will tell you that a tree's trunk will throw far less shade than its lower branches. For most trees, these lower branches are eventually shed anyway so speeding this process a bit will not negatively impact the future form of your tree. Just do it judiciously and never remove more than one-third of a tree's limbs. Limbing should only very rarely be considered for cosmetic/aesthetic reasons, but should be done for the health of your plantings. A few words to the wise: never prune a limb above your head without some sort of protection, and understand that even medium-sized limbs will be much heavier than they appear. If you can't do the job safely, you should hire someone who can. Finally, if you are cutting from the top down, the weight of the branch will often cause the limb to tear away from the main stem. When a limb tears away, it leaves a sizable wound that takes a long time to heal. To ensure a clean cut, make a shallow cut first along the bottom of the branch, beneath where you will make the top cut. As you cut downward toward the lower cut, the branch will not likely tear but will cut cleanly.

Reducing the density of the crown takes a bit more work, especially if the crown is 60 or more feet above the ground. For this, I recommend the work of a certified arborist unless you have access to specialized equipment. Not all limbs are created equal, and sometimes certain limbs actually cause harm to the tree. Thinning a crown should begin there. Poorly formed and dead limbs should be the first to go. Next should be limbs that may be rubbing against others. These should be taken off at the most appropriate collar. Once these are removed, attention can be given to reducing the breadth of the crown if it has grown to exceed the width desired. In my own yard, this became necessary as my newer trees began to reach the edge of the older live oak canopy. Reducing the breadth of the oak canopy allowed the other trees to develop better canopies of their own and it allowed more sunlight to reach the understory.

If the canopy becomes too dense, it is also possible to remove some of the larger branches to create gaps for the light to shine through. Never remove more than one-fourth of the existing canopy of a tree, and be careful only to remove those branches that will make the difference you are looking for. Creating gaps does not necessarily mean creating places where the light will reach the understory unimpeded. Normally, what is desired is to have the light less filtered so that a higher portion reaches the plants below.

This limb was not pruned properly. Cutting only the upper portion of the limb caused it to tear, and its weight created a much larger wound than should have occurred. This wound will take a much longer time to heal and produces a far greater risk that disease may enter the tree.

Light intensity is measured in foot candles. Increasing the amount of foot candles that reaches the ground layer can markedly increase the health and growth of most shade-tolerant plants. Small changes in light levels can have dramatic results as long as the light levels are not increased to somewhere near full sunlight.

5

Planting Site Considerations

Now that we have discussed the concepts of creating shade and planting into existing shade, it is time to discuss the other site factors that need to be considered before you actually purchase your plants. These factors are important to all landscapes regardless of sunlight, and ignoring them may well cause your landscape to fail regardless of how well you select for plants with shade tolerance.

Once you have established shade, the most important consideration is your soil. For many of us, soil is merely "dirt," something we can work around simply by adding chemicals and water, but this is woefully misguided. Soil is a great many things. If you understand it, you can improve it or at the least, effectively cope with what you've been given. You must match plants to your soil, so that they thrive over time instead of struggling to their eventual demise. Understanding soil is of paramount importance.

Soils are composed of four main components: inorganic particles of varying sizes broken down from parent rock, air spaces, moisture, and organics derived from the decay of plant and animal material. Most soils are approximately 45 percent inorganic particles, 50 percent water and air, and 5 percent organic material. This changes very little from landscape to landscape.

Soil structure is largely based on the composition of the inorganic soil particles. By definition, rocks are not part of the soil as they are too large to play a role in a plant's needs, though they certainly affect our ability to garden. Rock is anything larger than 2 mm (a bit less than 0.1 inches). Even in Florida, rock is a common component of our overall soil. It influences drainage and it affects the ability of roots to burrow into the soil column. It just doesn't have much influence in providing nutrients.

Soil scientists describe soils based on the inorganic particles no larger

Much of Florida's landscape soils are naturally sandy with very little organic matter to help with moisture retention.

than 2 mm. Sand is particles 2–0.02 mm in size, silt is 0.02–0.002 mm, and clay is less than 0.002 mm. Only sand grains are visible as individual grains to the naked eye. Silts are like flour; we see it, but we can't make out the individual grains. Clays are far too fine to differentiate at all. You would need an electron microscope for that. When soils are "loamy" (40 percent sand, 40 percent silt, 20 percent clay), they are considered perfect for most vegetation, however, loamy soils are not a common occurrence in Florida. We have developed our rich diversity of native vegetation on soils that are often much higher in sands.

The size of the soil particles does not affect its fertility, only its drainage. Fertility comes from the parent rock and is influenced by the soil's pH (something we will discuss a bit further on). Sandy soils are not necessarily infertile. If the parent rock was composed of the essential elements all plants need, elements such as iron, manganese, potassium, and phosphorus, these elements should be available regardless of particle size. Of course, Florida's parent rock material comes from a wide variety of prehistoric sources, so different parts of the state have different inherent fertility that must be considered. Most of our truly sandy soils originated in the Appalachian Mountains and washed down here from the north due to erosion over millions of years. Underneath that sand is limestone put down at an even older age. When that limestone is near the surface as it is in extreme south Florida or in places such as the Brooksville Ridge, the inherent composition of inorganic elements will be different, not necessarily infertile, just different.

The pH of a soil is a measure of its acidity based on the presence of free hydrogen ions (H^+). By convention, a neutral soil has a pH of 7. Soils with a pH less than 7 are considered acidic; soils above 7 are considered basic. All of this is important because pH affects the availability of elements essential for plant growth. When soils are acidic they cause elements like iron to be released from the inorganic soil particles. To a certain level, this is good. Plants need iron and leaching it from the sands, silts, and clays of the soil makes it available. The problem arises when soil pH becomes highly acidic. When this happens, too much of a good thing can occur. It's like taking vitamins; getting the recommended amount is good for us, going overboard can cause toxic reactions. Soils that are basic have the opposite problem. When the pH is high, many essential elements are there, but unavailable to the plants in sufficient quantities.

Over time, plants have evolved ways to cope with the vagaries of soil pH. Some, like those in the blueberry/azalea family, have adapted to highly acidic soils and actually require them. Others, like most of the subtropical plants found in extreme south Florida, thrive best on soils that are basic. Many simply "go with the flow." Knowing your plant's ability to cope with pH and having measured it within your landscape soils is critical to developing a plant palette that will succeed.

It is nearly impossible to significantly alter the soil structure and pH of your soil over time. These are characteristics that we, as gardeners, have to work with in harmony with what we've been given. Most amendments, designed to alter soil pH are only temporary influences. If your soil is acidic, it will quickly neutralize the lime you add, for example, making it necessary for you to periodically add more for the life of your landscape. For the most part, it is simply easier to play with the deck you've been given.

While the parent material comprises about 45 percent of your soil and influences pH and soil fertility, the 50 percent composed of water and air spaces may be the most significant to the success of your landscape. We all

Mucky soils occur when moisture is nearly constant and large amounts of leaf litter decay at the surface.

understand that plants need water, but we often fail to grasp how important the air spaces are. Because of this, we drown plants as often as we kill them for lack of water. The balance between water and air is a critical dance that directly influences a soil's ability to support different plants, regardless of particle size and pH.

Water is required by all plants regardless of their tolerance to drought. The ability of a plant to photosynthesize is dependent on sufficient water. Most of the essential elements are dissolved in water and enter through its roots. Water is required for plant cells not to collapse; like a water balloon, each cell needs enough water to maintain its shape. Water also is necessary for most of the essential chemical reactions that keep a plant alive.

Too much water, for too long a period, however, will kill a plant just as surely as lack of water will because plant roots also need air. Gas exchange between a plant and its environment is just as critical as it is for us. Plants take up carbon dioxide from the air through their leaves and stems for photosynthesis, but they also respire and release carbon dioxide back into the environment. A critical portion of their respiration is done through their

In extreme south Florida and in various locations in central and north Florida, the limestone that underlies all of our state lies near the surface, creating soils that have a high pH.

roots. When soils are saturated, their roots cannot "breathe"; they suffocate and die. When I first became interested in native plant landscaping, I mistakenly believed that the plants most adapted to excessively drained soils would die given too much water. What I learned is that they die given too little air. It may seem the same, but it isn't. All plants need water, some just need more air—the kind provided by larger soil particle sizes and good drainage. When grown in excessively drained soils, these plants survive being watered daily by afternoon thunderstorms.

The part of the soil we have some influence over is the organic component; the remaining 5 percent. Organics, by themselves, do not necessarily indicate fertility, but they release nutrients in various amounts as they decompose. Organics also hold water and slow its percolation downward through the soil column. This can be good or bad depending on the type of soil you have. Too often, we equate organics with soil improvements, especially here in Florida. When done correctly, adding compost and other organic material can improve difficult soils, but we need to understand what we are doing and why before we can amend our soils effectively.

To be useful in increasing soil fertility, the organic material needs two important things: it has to be fertile to start with and it has to be decomposed thoroughly. This might seem a simple matter, but it is all too forgotten by many whose landscapes I visit. Organic material does not magically become fertile on its own. It can only release what it already has stored inside, so we need fertile organic material and we need to use it in a landscape rich in decomposers.

For this reason, woody mulches are not satisfactory for landscapes deficient in organic matter. Wood has inherently little fertility. Plants do not sequester large amounts of essential elements in their wood as they do in their "greener" portions. Wood also does not easily decompose. Whether it is sawdust, chipped limbs from a yard-waste recycling program, or chopped bark, wood provides the least satisfactory means of adding meaningful organics to your soil. Wood products in general can sometimes even tie up nitrogen in the soil and cause nitrogen deficiency in plants. Because of this, garden experts often advocate the use of nitrogen fertilizers in planting areas where wood-based mulches are used, violating the reason for adding organics in the first place. The best organic materials to mulch with are plant materials that decompose quickly and have naturally high amounts of essential elements. If you top dress your planting areas with leaf mulch, for example, it will generate far more soil fertility over time than using something derived from wood.

None of this matters, however, if your soil does not have a healthy assemblage of decomposers. The living part of your soil comprises everything from fungi and bacteria to earthworms, ants, and termites. These microfauna are the key to releasing the nutrients locked up in the organic matter and increasing the soil's fertility. In a native forest soil, there may be thousands of decomposer species all working toward this goal in various ways. In typical developed landscapes, most are nonexistent or severely reduced in numbers. Soil microfauna are especially active in the upper few inches of the soil column, the stratum most affected by our use of herbicides and insecticides. We cannot expect these organisms to thrive and do their work for us when we are constantly poisoning the soil they live in.

Once organic matter sheds its nutrients through decomposition, this fertility is either taken up by the plants or leached into the soil column, below the depth where plant roots can use them. You cannot think to increase soil fertility in any meaningful way by adding it to the planting hole. Such

Plant roots require mycorrhizal fungi in the soil to maximize their ability to absorb water and nutrients. A healthy soil is not a sterile soil.

organic material will decompose in a relatively short period of time and the fertility will be gone. A much more effective method is to constantly top dress the planting area with high quality organics and encourage the decomposers.

Organic matter also increases the ability of sandy soils to hold moisture. When water comes into contact with organic matter, it is absorbed as if the organic matter were a paper towel. The organics slow the movement of water downward through the soil column. This also prevents the essential elements dissolved in that water from leaching as well. Soils that have a healthy percentage of organic matter remain moister longer after a rain and hold essential elements longer so that they can be absorbed by plant roots.

The flip side is that organics can prevent water from percolating through the soil in the desired manner, and this is especially problematic if the organics dry out completely. It takes water to rehydrate organic particles. When they are completely dry, they repel water initially. If you have ever watered a portion of your landscape when the soil is powder dry, and watched the water mostly run off the surface, you have seen the influence of dry organic matter. Water does not do that in pure sand. It takes water to initially rehydrate the surface of the organic particle so that it can absorb more. While that is happening, a good deal of water is not penetrating the soil column, but running over the surface.

When organics comprise a large portion of the upper soil column, they can impede water from percolating to the deeper root zone. Because they tie up water and hold it for later, surface roots benefit, but when conditions get dry, they do this to the detriment of the deeper roots. I've seen this many times in my own yard. When I water portions of my landscape in times of extreme drought, I often find that the water has only penetrated the upper six inches of soil; even after an hour the region below remains powder dry. When this happens, the plants survive by using their feeder roots to absorb water, but the deeper roots, the ones needed to keep the plants alive in droughty times, suffer. The organic matter in your soil is a significant component of your landscape's potential, but you need to understand its role and take care not to let it dry out completely before you water during times of extreme drought.

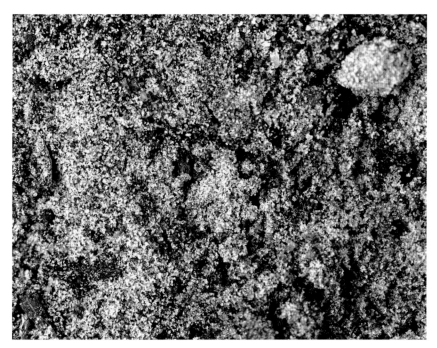

Organic matter in soil is the result of plant and animal matter that has decayed. It is most evident as the dark flecks scattered in a handful of mineral soil grains.

Hydrology, the way water moves and remains on your landscape, is also important. In modern developments, homes are constructed above the average level of standing water that occurs during normal rain events. Modern development codes generally keep homes from flooding during the summer rainy season or during extreme weather events. This does not mean, however, that all portions of the landscape are elevated in this way.

Hydrology can vary significantly, even within a single-family lot. Some properties have been designed purposely to direct water away from the home into another section of the yard. Such areas receive significantly more water and can remain flooded or saturated for long periods of time. Understanding how water moves across your landscape should influence your plant choices. Not all plants can survive inundation or even saturated soils, while others thrive in it.

Many landscapes simply have naturally low areas that sit closer to the water table. Even if you never see it, the depth of the water table, especially when it is at its annual highest, affects plants. Plants adapted to sending down deep root systems will intersect the water table as it rises during the summer rainy season. If this happens with plants that are not adapted to saturated soils, they will die. If your landscape does not sit atop a former ridge, it would be useful to have some understanding of how deep the water table tends to be during the peak of the wet season. Just because your home doesn't flood does not mean that your plants won't be affected by a high water table, especially the larger trees and shrubs.

Setting Goals and Objectives

Too many of us want to start projects without a clearly formed plan. We are impatient and we seem to believe that everything will magically take shape as we get things underway. Landscape projects, regardless of light or shade, fail more because of poor planning than anything else. As my mother used to remind me, "an ounce of prevention is worth a pound of cure." Nothing could be truer when contemplating a landscape project. We see plants and purchase them on a whim, figuring we will find them a place in our land-

Native plants are the plants that occur here naturally and are adapted to Florida's growing conditions without additional gardening inputs.

scape when we get home. I am not immune to impulse plant purchases so I understand this well. It's just not an effective strategy and it will result in failure if done too often.

Planning a landscape is more than making a list of the plants you want. It begins by defining your objectives and prioritizing them. Your landscape has many possible objectives and more than one of them will be important to you. We are only considering plants native to Florida in this book so we have already set that as an objective in our shade garden. If you are not restricting yourself to native plants, you will have a larger plant palette to choose from initially. Just make sure that your plant selections are species adapted to Florida life. A great many non-native plants, beautifully photographed in other shade-gardening books, will not prosper in Florida's climate. We know that Florida plants already occur here. Not every one of them is adapted to every location, but we know that all are adapted to some part of the state. You will need to narrow your plant palette to include only the species adapted to your site, your unique type of shade, your soils, and your hydrology.

Besides wanting to use plants that will thrive in your location, your objectives could include factors such as aesthetics, wildlife value, and the conservation of natural resources. The relative importance of these should be carefully considered and then honestly ranked according to their importance to you. All of these are important, but they can sometimes be in conflict with each other. By developing an honest plan for your shade garden and ranking the relative importance of each of these sometimes-competing objectives, it becomes easier to settle on a final planting scheme.

No one wants a landscape that is ugly. While it can be said that beauty is in the eye of the beholder, ugly is ugly. No one should be satisfied with an ugly landscape even if it is accomplishing every other objective you have. The problem is that for far too long we have *only* looked at beauty as our ultimate objective. I could fill a bookcase with the landscape books I have purchased over the years that consider nothing other than the aesthetic beauty of the final landscape design. Beauty does not have to be sacrificed for function. There are a great many beautiful plants that are also good for wildlife and the conservation of natural resources. If beauty is your primary purpose, it will overshadow the other concerns when you are selecting plants, but not necessarily preclude other considerations. You can have more than one objective.

All plants look best in a landscape when they are cultured. A great many native plants have such intrinsic beauty that it requires very little effort to bring out their best in a landscape.

I believe that landscapes should have an ecological purpose as well as an aesthetic one and that we are wasting a significant opportunity to benefit the rest of the living world by ignoring this. Nowhere more than Florida is the imprint of development more damaging. Florida is one of the fastest-growing states in the nation, and a significant portion has been altered by pressure from development. These lands are not all covered by blacktop and concrete; the portions that exist as urban and suburban landscapes do not have to be written off as ecological wastelands. It is an easy task for us to use plants that provide habitat *and* beauty. Often, it is merely using one shade tree instead of another, switching from one flowering hedge to another, or adding more diversity into our plant palette than is currently the norm.

The greatest change, however, involves limiting the amount of turf grass we use to only those areas where it is needed. Though turf grass is what we have come to accept as normal (and in some areas what is required by law), it uses huge amounts of water, energy, and chemicals just to survive, and it gives us little in return. Turf most certainly gives us a surface for recreation and entertaining, but elsewhere we would do much better to use plantings that give something back to the environment, especially in the shade where turf grasses perform poorly. I have previously written extensively on the topic of using native plants to improve habitat for birds, butterflies, and other wildlife. I will not repeat myself here except to write that Florida is home to thousands of beautiful native plants, and we should be using them to replace sterile turf grass areas that have no physical or ecological purpose. If wildlife and natural resource conservation are important to you, these objectives will be added to your list of landscape priorities. How high up your list these objectives stand will help you make honest decisions when you finalize your plant palette. A plant can be pretty but useless for wildlife. It can also provide valuable food and cover for songbirds but be aesthetically uninteresting to you. Most of us want to strike a balance between the two extremes, and Florida has a great many beautiful, but functional native plants to satisfy those various demands.

If wildlife is an interest, you will choose plants that provide food in terms of fruit and insects. Small fruit, like those of wild coffees (*Psychotria* spp.), feed a great many birds throughout the year, but are especially important

Turf grass requires a lot of maintenance in a landscape and often gives back far less than it takes. Reducing turf to only those areas where it is truly needed and replacing it with a living landscape can reap great rewards for both you and the environment.

during the winter months when many insect-eating songbirds switch their diet to one that relies more on fruit. Most flowering plants produce some sort of fruit during the year, but not all fruit is created equal. As songbirds do not have teeth, they are restricted to fruit they can swallow whole. Fruit size is a limiting factor for songbirds but not for mammals. Taste is also a consideration. Not every fruit is palatable to birds, just as with humans.

Insects are a major component of a living landscape, and they are attracted in several ways. Most significantly, insects are drawn to flowers that are designed to be pollinated. Insects account for more than 75 percent of all flower pollination, and 80 percent of all plants produce flowers. This figure is a bit lower for shady habitats but is still a noteworthy percentage. Insects are required for most plants to produce seeds, fruits, and nuts. They also are an important food for birds, toads, frogs, and other wildlife. Flowers are not created equal in regard to pollination. Many cultivated flowering plants have been bred to form complicated flowers that pollinating insects can't navigate. To the nursery trade, such plants are advantageous. They are not supposed to set seed and reproduce in your landscape; they are grown by tissue culture or cuttings and pollination never takes place. When these plants die, you are supposed to purchase new ones. Some non-native plants

Landscapes that rely primarily on native plants provide better habitat for songbirds, butterflies, and other wildlife, and a living landscape provides significant interest and enjoyment.

simply don't have their pollinators with them here in Florida. They are in Asia, South America, or Africa, where the plants originated. Native plants are most likely to attract the greatest diversity of pollinating insects, and are thus the best choices for feeding our native wildlife.

Plants also attract insects by having scaly bark instead of smooth bark. When you are in a woodland, watch the birds and pay attention to where their feeding activity occurs. More often than not, birds are working the trunks and branches of woody plants, poking under the bark looking for insects. They also work the leaf litter. Good wildlife landscapes have areas like these where everything is not completely manicured and smooth.

There is a considerable body of research showing that insect diversity increases with landscape diversity. Landscapes, native or otherwise, that rely on just a few plant species, repeated over and over, harbor few kinds of insects compared to those that use a broader mix. Landscape diversity, holding everything else constant, creates insect diversity, and since different wildlife feed on different insects or on the products of their pollination, it seems obvious that diversely planted landscapes will harbor more wildlife.

Last, and most significant, insects will be present when landscapes are not routinely treated with pesticides. We have been conditioned to believe that having insects in our yards is a bad thing. To me, it means that my landscape is alive. The vast majority of insects are beneficial and interesting. Only a few cause actual damage. If the leaves of my plants are being eaten, it means I am doing something right, not that there is something wrong. Plants are adapted to being chewed on. Plants with "perfect" foliage and nothing "out of place" are not real. Such attitudes scare me. The widespread use of pesticides has caused so much harm to our living environment that it is impossible to catalog sufficiently. Native plants used appropriately in landscape settings should not have to be sprayed to survive, birds and other insect predators should help take care of problems as they arise, and only the rare and real problems should be addressed selectively.

Landscapes that harbor life are becoming more important to us over time. We seem to have grown more aware of how important this is and how enjoyable it can make the time we spend in our gardens. I have included wildlife considerations in the plant descriptions I provide in the chapters ahead in hopes that this will enable you to make better decisions when selecting the plants you wish to use if wildlife is a priority.

Most insects are beneficial and interesting neighbors in their own right. Insects provide invaluable pollinating services and food for songbirds and other wildlife.

Of course, we will want to manage our shade gardens in such a way as to conserve resources. That is the primary reason I have restricted the plants in this book to those that are Florida natives. We should strive to use plants adapted to our site so that we do not have to use irrigation and fertilizers once our plants have become established. This makes economic sense as much as it makes ethical sense. Not every native plant will be well adapted to your landscape and not every non-native one will be ill adapted, but overall, native plants will achieve the ecological goals you set (including providing for wildlife) far better than a landscape derived from species gleaned from other continents. How important it is to you to save water and not resort to using fertilizers and pesticides will also dictate the plant list you ultimately choose.

We all want everything, but that is never truly possible in the real world. Our landscape will be a compromise based on what's most important. Some of the plants Alexa and I have planted are not super showy, but we love them for the wildlife value they contribute. I have witnessed friends who have essentially let good plants die because conserving water was their greatest priority and they felt that if the plant could not survive on its own it didn't have a place in their landscape. While I respect their principles, I favor diversity, and I am not opposed to using my hose a few times a year if it means keeping a treasured plant in good condition. Water conservation is important to me; it's just not my highest priority when confronted with the need to choose.

Setting priorities needs to be done from the start of your planning phase. How can you make plant choices when you haven't defined your priorities? If you have to choose between two plants, do you select the one that most appeals to your aesthetic sense or the one that will provide the most wildlife benefit? Rarely are they identical. Sometimes beauty will win over function and sometimes the choice will go the other way. Ultimately you will want to achieve your landscaping goals to the fullest extent possible, and that is done by setting priorities.

As you review the plant choices provided in this book, you will find that

Your landscape plan requires that you set realistic priorities that consider all of your interests.

you have a great many to select from. Each will add something to the whole. It is not necessary that every plant provide for all of your objectives. Some may simply appeal to your senses. That is perfectly fine. I have those plants in my own landscape. They bring me joy, and they make my time spent outdoors more enjoyable. The entire community of plants you install should be designed to accomplish your goals and make your landscape enjoyable to be within.

As you plan, consider using a variety of plant species. Diversity is a good thing, but balance your eagerness to add everything you admire. Refrain from the Noah's Ark approach. You do not need to take one of everything with you on your personal landscape voyage. Sometimes having one of a great many things makes sense, but oftentimes it makes for a hodgepodge of species that never quite functions as a community or a landscape. Some species, like the coffees, function best planted in clusters in the understory. Some understory subcanopy trees, like flatwoods plum (*Prunus umbellata*), make a more significant impact when planted in small groupings. These are considerations each of you should be taking into account as you develop your plan.

7

Natural Shady Habitats

I believe that there is no better place to look initially for landscape direction than nature, especially since this is a book on native plants for shady areas. Florida has many native plant communities designed around the presence of shade. For the most part, these communities are referred to as "hammocks." Though you might guess that this word originated from the fishnet structure frequently strung between two trees, it is really a corruption of

Typical Florida hammock. Devil's Millhopper Geological State Park, Gainesville, Florida.

the word "hummock" and refers to the fact that many broad-leaved canopy trees that form this plant community occur on slightly raised areas near lake edges. These hummocks of forested land became known as hammocks.

Hammocks are communities of plants dominated by hardwood canopy trees; unlike so many other communities in Florida dominated by pines (i.e., softwoods). Hardwoods include many trees familiar to us in the Florida landscape. Live and laurel oaks as well as southern magnolia are ubiquitous throughout the state. These, and a great many other hardwood trees, reach heights of more than 60 feet and form a canopy above the other plants resident to these communities. The largely unbroken canopy of these trees creates shade below them.

Hammocks change dramatically from north to south Florida because of climate and soil differences, but the most important change comes from the relative percentage of evergreen trees in the canopy. North Florida woodlands are mostly dominated by deciduous trees. By the time we reach the counties farthest south, the canopy is replaced by evergreens. Somewhere, in central Florida, these two significantly different forests merge and intermingle.

Hammocks also vary based on hydrology. Historically, most developed in association with wetlands, and these provided some protection from the frequent wildfires that are part of our natural heritage. Fires swept across Florida each summer, triggered by the lightning embedded in afternoon thunderstorms. Such fires burned thousands of acres and were extinguished most often by their encounter with large wetlands, lakes, and rivers. Hammocks formed in these "fire shadows" and fostered conditions that also impeded future fires, specifically, moist soils and damp leaf litter. As Florida became developed, wildfires were largely contained and hammocks also developed in dry places. These "xeric hammocks" are dominated by many of the same canopy species, but the understory diversity is limited by droughty soils as well as shade. Xeric hammocks tend to have fewer plant numbers and species than moister hammocks.

Florida hammocks also change based on their position relative to the coast. The need to tolerate salt, both as spray in the wind and as surface water during extreme storm events, limits coastal hammocks to a subset of species. Hammock plants in the Florida Keys must have some salt tolerance. Coastal hammocks farther north are less likely to encounter hurricanes on a regular basis, and some plants are more salt tolerant than others. Dealing

American holly (*Ilex opaca*), spruce pine (*Pinus glabra*), and southern red cedar (*Juniperus virginiana*).

What separates northern hammock forests from other regions of the state is the presence of a subcanopy forest of shorter spring-flowering trees. Many of these are popular landscape species that can be planted in the open for their beautiful blooms. Many can also be used to form a canopy for shade gardens designed for small spaces. In nature, these subcanopy trees often occur beneath the higher canopy of a deciduous forest, and they set the woods ablaze in color before the taller trees leaf out. The most widely recognized members of this group are flowering dogwood, redbud, fringe tree, and southern crabapple (*Malus angustifolia*), but others should be more widely used, especially the silverbells, various hawthorns (*Crataegus* spp.), flatwoods plum, downy serviceberry, and silky camellia (*Stewartia malacodendron*).

North Florida hammocks also contain many spring-flowering shrubs. These are multistemmed woody plants that rarely reach the heights of the subcanopy trees described above, but they share the attribute of blooming profusely before the canopy above them completely fills out. Many of our

Also abundant beneath the deciduous canopy of a north Florida hammock are spring ephemeral wildflowers, such as these butterweeds (*Packera glabella*).

most popular landscape shrubs are really native to north Florida communities. This group includes most of our native azaleas and viburnums, as well as mountain laurel (*Kalmia latifolia*). Common to north Florida hammocks are the evergreen trunkless palms; especially dwarf palm (*Sabal minor*) and needle palm (*Rhaphidophyllum hystrix*).

Because of the influx of winter and spring sunlight, north Florida hammocks contain a huge diversity of ephemeral wildflowers, as well as a high diversity of ferns and grasses. There are too many species to be listed here, but they include commonly used species like violets and phlox (*Phlox divaricata*). Most spring wildflowers do not normally fare well in landscapes dominated by evergreen trees, but they can be used, even outside their natural range, if given some winter sunshine followed by protection from the strong summer sun.

SOUTH FLORIDA HAMMOCKS

On the opposite end of the state are unique hammocks that contain elements also found in the Caribbean. This region is generally confined to the southern two tiers of counties, but some elements extend farther north, hugging the coast where winter temperatures rarely dip below freezing. Development pressure has replaced most of these forests, but beautiful remnants still exist in protected areas such as Dagny Johnson Hammock Botanical State Park in north Key Largo, Matheson Hammock in Miami, and Mahogany Hammock in Everglades National Park.

South Florida hammocks are semitropical and composed of evergreen species. Unlike the hammocks of north Florida, these species are not confined to blooming in the spring, and flowers and fruit can appear in just about any month. The canopy of these subtropical hammocks is generally no taller than about 60 feet, and the structure of the understory is often simpler. Most forests are composed of a diverse tree canopy with a less diverse shrubby understory. The deep shade precludes the development of a rich wildflower flora, and there are fewer ferns and native grasses than are evident in north Florida.

The real beauty lies in the rich tapestry of greens in the foliage and the diverse structure of form inherent to the canopy. Many have their own color, generated by bark, fruit, and flowers. Though there is no real season for this color as there is farther north, there is always something happening in

Typical south Florida hammock. Lover's Key State Park, Fort Myers Beach, Florida.

this community, and the use of these plants creates year-long interest in the landscape.

South Florida hammocks contain live oak, sugarberry, and cabbage palm, but the rest of the community is unique to this region. The most commonly encountered canopy trees include gumbo limbo (*Bursera simarouba*), mastic (*Sideroxylon foetidissimum*), pigeon plum (*Coccoloba diversifolia*), strangler fig (*Ficus aurea*), black ironwood (*Krugiodendron ferreum*), and paradise tree (*Simaruba glauca*), though a great many other species are present. Florida mahogany (*Swietenia mahagoni*) is common to the hammocks of the Florida Keys and is widely planted outside this range.

Beneath this canopy are mostly evergreen trees and shrubs; often with narrow crowns. One exception is the deciduous beautyberry (*Callicarpa americana*), found statewide in a wide variety of habitat types. True stoppers (*Eugenia* spp.) and Simpson's stopper are perhaps the most widely planted of this group in Florida landscapes, but many others have also found favor including myrsine (*Myrsine cubana*), marlberry (*Ardisia escallonoides*), white indigoberry (*Randia aculeata*), and the wild coffees. South Florida counter-

Because the canopy of south Florida hammocks is evergreen, less sunlight reaches the plants beneath it, and the diversity of the subcanopy and ground covers is limited.

parts to more northern species include Krug's holly (*Ilex krugiana*) and West Indian cherry (*Prunus myrtifolia*).

South Florida hammocks have very little ground cover diversity and much of the soil is covered by a thin layer of leaf litter, not the ferns, grasses, and wildflowers found in the north. Sword ferns (*Nephrolepis* spp.) are widely distributed, however.

CENTRAL FLORIDA HAMMOCKS

The region south of the Citrus-to-Volusia County line and north of Collier-to-Broward Counties is a mixture of the two extremes. Most hammocks in this region share a near-equal combination of evergreen and deciduous trees in the canopy, which creates conditions that reduce the diversity of the understory, especially for wildflowers and grasses. Generally, the percentage of evergreens in the canopy increases from north to south. For example, deciduous oaks such as shumard and swamp chestnut extend into the north-

Central Florida hammock. Hammock Park, Dunedin, Florida.

ern half of this region, but the evergreen live oak, and the nearly evergreen laurel and water oak (*Quercus nigra*), extend well into the southern half; hickories, ashes, and elms are present throughout, but all of the deciduous magnolias are absent.

Few of the truly showy spring-flowering understory trees and shrubs are common, and these too decline from north to south of this region. Ultimately, they are replaced by mostly evergreen species like yaupon holly (*Ilex vomitoria*), Florida privet (*Forestiera segregata*), and several of the wild coffees.

Some of the showier vines, such as coral honeysuckle (*Lonicera sempervirens*) and Carolina yellow jessamine (*Gelsemium sempervirens*), produce flowers in the canopy, and several wildflowers (depending on the amount of spring sunlight) are common to the understory. Common species include violets, lyre-leaved sage (*Salvia lyrata*), frostweed (*Verbesina virginica*), and giant ironweed (*Vernonia gigantea*). Basketgrass (*Oplismenus setarius*) and several species of witch grass (*Dicanthelium* spp.) are also widespread, and the diversity of ferns is intermediate between north and south Florida. Common ferns to central Florida hammocks include the shield ferns (*Thelypteris* spp.), chain ferns (*Woodwardia* spp.), sword ferns, and some of the spleenworts (*Asplenium* spp.).

As we look to nature to help define our personal landscape plan, we need to be mindful that landscapes need not be wholly confined by the natural environment. Landscapes are not identical to the wild places surrounding them, and our ability to monitor and maintain our gardens allows us some leeway in mixing species that might not normally occur together. The microclimate surrounding our homes is not the same either. We might have subtle differences in temperature and moisture that require consideration and adjustments in our potential plant palette. Nature can supply the overall design concepts, but it is up to us individually to draw the final plan, working with our site conditions and understanding the growing limits of the species we most desire to use.

8

Expanding Your Possibilities

Landscape Amenities

All too often, I meet gardeners who tell me they would like to add plants to their landscape but can't because of the conditions present on their property. While some things are difficult or even impossible to modify, other obstacles are quite easily removed. We are often too quick to limit ourselves. Native plant landscapes should work with nature, but that does not mean having to accept every landscape condition you inherit with the property. There are things you can amend or work around.

As I discussed previously, you can take steps to improve the fertility and water-holding capacity of your soil. In a shaded landscape, this is even more important than in a sunny one because most of the plants you will want to use benefit from these conditions. The easiest way to rebuild the types of damaged soils common to developed areas is to use organic mulches that decompose naturally instead of inorganic or wood-based mulches that do not easily decompose. In nature, shady landscapes receive organic material almost daily. In deciduous landscapes, they also receive a huge amount in the fall. As the leaves lie on the ground, they are instantly assailed by a host of decomposers that break them down into an organic fertilizer useable by plants. Soil fungi, bacteria, nematodes, earthworms, ants, termites, and other invertebrates all take twigs and leaves and render them useful. Over time, this cover forms a rich layer of humus and releases nutrients that plants require. If you venture into any woodland with an intact leaf layer, you will find that it is moist where it comes into contact with the soil and that tiny feeder roots extend throughout it. From the outset, plan on using organic mulches. If you have an existing canopy, it is likely already producing sufficient leaf mulch. Embrace it, and don't rake it off. If you have been using commercial woody mulches, stop.

Organic mulches decompose, and this process encourages extensive root growth just beneath the leaf litter. It also attracts invertebrates, such as earthworms.

If you do not have an established canopy, you will want to mulch heavily with leaves obtained elsewhere until your own trees can take over that role. In my neighborhood, far too many people spend hours each fall raking leaves off their lawn grass. They bag the leaves and set them on the curbside for someone to haul away. In the early days, that someone was me, not the folks with the refuse companies. At first, Alexa and I felt a bit strange hauling away other people's hard work, so we asked permission. Except for a few raised eyebrows, no one ever denied our requests, and eventually we came to realize that no one cared as long as someone hauled it off their curb. Every week across every neighborhood in America, folks work to remove valuable leaf litter instead of using it to make their landscape beds more productive. If you use yours, you will see the difference almost immediately, and you will be saving limited landfill space for things that are truly refuse. As you plan your shade garden, you may also wish to initiate a program to compost your organic leftovers. A composter, used properly, can generate a large amount of valuable humus in a relatively short time. This can be worked directly into the soil or raked into the surface layer of leaf mulch. Mulches can be added after your plants are installed, but I like to jump start the process by laying out the planting bed ahead of time and mulching it immediately.

When you go to plant something into the bed, simply move the mulch away until the plant is installed. You can go overboard with mulches too. Do not bury your plants deeper than 12–18 inches with leaf mulch. Add more over time if it breaks down. Once the whole landscape gets established, you will likely find that your trees and your understory reach a status quo in terms of mulch and mulch depth.

Alexa and my yard occurs on a former xeric pineland and our soils are sandy and well drained, but we wanted to use a number of wetland plants in our landscape that could never grow there naturally. Many of us face similar situations and simply resign without a fight. Creating wetland conditions is not a difficult problem to solve. In fact, it is far easier to create a wet area in your landscape than it is to create a dry one. Throughout our landscape, we have altered our natural conditions in a variety of different ways so that we could use moisture-loving plants in a way that does not require a great expenditure of water.

We created a seasonally wet prairie in our side yard using very simple materials. For years after the home was built, water poured off the back corner of our roof and eroded the soil beneath it. Attempts to use plants or

You can create a small wetland in your landscape with very little effort.

rocks to soften the blow were not very satisfactory. The sheer force of the water beat on the plants and affected their growth and the rocks merely made the area devoid of vegetation. Our solution was to capture that water and direct it to an open, partially shaded area we wanted to landscape. We captured the water by creating a linear "stream" using plastic pool liner material and river rock. The liner was installed just beneath the soil surface from the edge of the roofline to the area of our landscape that was to become our wetland. Lime rock and river rock were then used along the length of this "stream" to make it more aesthetic and to prevent vegetation from clogging it up. A shallow grade change allowed the water to flow slowly down this stream and into the area where we then constructed the wetland. Our wetland is approximately eight feet in diameter. In this area, I dug a hole three feet down, lined it with a heavy plastic pool liner, and refilled the hole. As most wetland plants have shallow root systems, and ours includes only herbaceous plants, this depth has worked well.

The liner precludes water from soaking into the aquifer so that the only water loss comes from evaporation. Each time it rains, the area receives all the water that used to erode the soil beneath our roof, and this moisture keeps everything wet enough to preclude our watering except in extreme drought conditions. Like most wetlands, the area fluctuates in how wet it becomes. Our plants have prospered, and our need for supplementary water is negligible.

We also created much smaller wet areas in our landscape using large pots and small plastic pools that hold water. These fill up whenever it rains and this water evaporates slowly, especially in the summer when humidity levels are highest. We then set slightly smaller clay pots inside them that are filled with soil and planted with wetland plants. Because of the drainage holes in the planted pots, water is wicked upward from the water-holding pots or plastic pools beneath them, and this keeps the soil moist to wet. You can regulate the depth of the planted pots to simulate the water depth to which you want to expose your plants. Some plants prefer to be in shallow water while others do best in wet soil that is not completely saturated. Over the past few years, we have used this method extensively in sunny and shady locations, and we have been successful in growing many species of wildflowers that would have formerly been impossible. We have also found that we rarely need to water these systems. When additional water is occasionally needed, we are watering a pot instead of an entire landscape.

Alexa and I took an area in our yard that was prone to erosion and created a "dry" stream that now directs water to our created wetland.

This created wetland in our landscape was simply constructed by excavating a hole about three feet deep, lining it with a polyurethane pond liner, and then filling the hole with the original soil.

Small wetlands can also be made by simply putting a planter pot inside a larger pot that does not have drainage holes. Rain fills the pot beneath and keeps the planted pot wet.

Using large pots in our landscape has also allowed us to use native wildflowers that are not adapted to our soil conditions, especially north Florida wildflowers that we previously had no success with in the ground. For some, our soil is simply too droughty and infertile. We match the soil in our pots to the needs of our plants, and we water them only when necessary. Landscape pots also can be moved to meet each plant's light requirements. This approach has significantly increased the diversity of our understory and enabled us to enjoy many wonderful species that bring us joy and attract pollinators. Unlike petunias and pansies that last a few months and need to be replaced, our pots hold perennial native wildflowers that function annually as part of our landscape. The only difference in having them in pots is they sit on top of the ground instead of growing out of it. The bees, butterflies, and hummingbirds do not discriminate.

Well-designed pots in the landscape also add an additional aesthetic. They provide a sort of lawn art that exceeds the beauty of the plants themselves, and they can draw attention to features in the landscape that warrant it (an interesting tree trunk for example) or add color to a spot that needs it. Your shade garden will be mostly shades of green for much of the year, regardless of where you reside. Pots come in every shade of the color spectrum and the end result will reflect your individual sense of color and style.

Not every plant you may wish to use will adapt to your growing conditions. Many, like these Walter's violets (*Viola walteri*) and Indian pinks (*Spigelia marilandica*), can be kept as perennials by growing them in a large landscape pot.

Creating better drainage is a tougher problem to resolve, but it isn't impossible to overcome. For one, you could use landscape pots filled with soil that drains more quickly than the soil of your landscape. Though this approach can be effective for certain herbaceous species native to droughty soils, well-drained soils need to be watered frequently. This is difficult to do long term with pots because we sometimes forget to water or we leave on vacation. Over the years, I have had marginal success growing wildflowers this way, and I no longer attempt it. The approach I *have* taken is to alter the soils and elevation of a planting bed to increase drainage. This can't be done well on a large scale and it does not work well for woody plants with deep and extensive root systems, but I have had great success using it for herbaceous species in limited planting areas.

For areas that do not drain rapidly enough, it is often possible to excavate the first several feet of topsoil to reach a deeper soil layer that is sandier. This topsoil can be used elsewhere in your landscape, offered to your neighbors for their landscape projects, or given to a local landscape supply company that sells fill. Once the upper layer of soil is removed, you can backfill the hole with coarse sand or mix coarse sand with a portion of the original soil.

If part of the problem is elevation, you can mound this area of your landscape to create a slope. Very few shade gardens will require better drainage, however.

Whether your final design is purely natural or includes elements of art and whimsy, you will need to ensure your final design has ample paths throughout. Simply put, you need pathways both to enjoy and to manage your landscape. Though weeds are less aggressive in shade gardens than they are in the sun, you will still get invaders that need to be pulled. You will need to replace something that dies, and you will want a closer look at something of interest. Pathways are places that preclude the use of plants so we sometimes shun them, but they are vital to access places in the landscape without causing damage.

Pathways are a feature that should be designed to meet the individual needs and aesthetics of the gardener. In places where it seems best to use a natural approach, a simple path mulched with leaves and kept free of plants can suffice. By winding it a bit, however, this simple walkway will appear less

If your site does not drain sufficiently well to use plants that require deep sandy soils, you can increase drainage by removing native soil and replacing it with coarse sand. We have done this in small portions of our landscape to encourage certain scrub plants that we could not grow otherwise.

Pathways are important to a landscape. Make them aesthetically interesting, and make sure they allow you access to perform the necessary garden management.

artificial and more inviting. In other situations where a bit more formality seems warranted, paths of brick or stone can be quite effective. We use both in different parts of our landscape and have tried to match each approach to its context. The important key to any approach is providing enough access to reach every corner of the landscape and allow for its exploration and maintenance.

Sitting areas are also important, especially in a shade garden. Part of the pleasure of shade is the opportunity to relax in it. Something as simple as a bench will allow you to sit and take in the spectacle of your landscape. Adding a slightly larger seating area allows you to entertain in the shade. Alexa and I have a small deck at the edge of our shade garden, and we use it extensively to relax, watch birds, and enjoy a glass of wine with friends.

9

The Plants

Now that we have discussed the considerations necessary for planning a successful shade garden in Florida, it's time to review the actual plants. These are plants native to Florida, adapted to shade, and attractive when used in the correct location. As previously mentioned, no plant is adapted to every setting statewide. I have arranged this chapter by regions to make it a bit easier for you to narrow your choices to those that will perform best where you live. Many north Florida plants can be used well into central Florida, so I have combined these under one heading and make special note of those that cannot be pushed too far south of their natural range. Some south Florida plants perform well when used north of their natural range, though many are susceptible to cold temperatures when they dip below the mid-20s°F. Plants naturally restricted to south Florida are specifically identified as such, and those that can be pushed a bit north of their natural range are identified.

For the purposes of this book, I have also separated the plants by growth form. Understory trees are those that typically grow beneath the canopy of taller ones. They are single-trunk woody plants that typically do not exceed 40 feet in height at maturity. Shrubs are woody plants that typically have multiple stems instead of a single trunk. Shrubs can sometimes reach the same heights as understory trees. What differentiates them from each other is the growth form. Vines are mostly woody species that climb into the canopy to access sunlight. Plants that are not woody are herbaceous, and these types of plants typically comprise the ground cover layer. Herbaceous ground covers include ferns, grasses, and wildflowers. I have separated each into its own category and, where appropriate, further separated them by regions of the state where they can be grown. Wetlands are unique areas with their own unique flora. I have included a separate section for shade-tolerant herbaceous plants that require wet soils.

Nearly all of the plants featured in this book are available commercially. Some may be difficult to locate at this time, but demand creates supply and the many talented nursery growers in Florida that specialize in native plants will quickly respond to a demand created by eager landscapers. All of these plants are species I have personally grown in my landscape or in landscapes I've designed. The information is, therefore, supplemented by my experience, and the plants' inclusion in this book indicates that they can be obtained if you are willing to search a bit for a source. I have included a list of current sources of plant material at the end of this book. I hope this list will quickly become outdated as more interest is generated in using native plants, and more growers discover that providing for this market makes financial as well as ecological sense.

If you are tempted to grow your own plants, be aware of the laws governing the collection of plant material from the wild. Plants are the property of the landowner, regardless of whether the species is common or exceedingly rare. It is illegal to collect any part of a plant (seeds, cuttings, etc.) without permission of the landowner. Even with permission, never collect more than what you actually need, and do not collect more than a small fraction of what is there. It is also illegal to collect from city, county, state, and federal parks and preserves. Plants listed as threatened or endangered cannot be collected and transported without a permit issued by the Division of Plant Industry, Florida Department of Agriculture and Consumer Protection (FDACS), or the U.S Department of Agriculture if the plant is federally protected, even if the landowner has given you permission. Do not collect something you do not know everything about. Identify it, know its growing requirements, ascertain its legal status, ask permission, and know what it will take to propagate it successfully. There have been times when I have had to grow something I wanted myself because I could not find another grower who was propagating it. I prefer to encourage the native nursery business, however, and the best way to do that is to purchase their plants.

UNDERSTORY TREES

Because understory trees typically grow beneath the canopy of taller species, they are shade tolerant. In deciduous forests, they tend to leaf out before the canopy closes and they often produce showy flowers in early spring. Understory trees at all latitudes form a second layer beneath the canopy that provides valuable nesting habitat for many birds and foraging and hiding cover for all wildlife. In small landscape areas, they can be used to great effect without a taller canopy above, as most also tolerate relatively high light levels. In larger landscape settings, understory trees create interest and a sense of fullness that is not possible using only shrubs and ground covers.

Trout lilies (*Erythronium umbilicatum*) are a classic ephemeral woodland wildflower, blooming in early spring before the forest canopy has leafed out and disappearing beneath the leaf litter once shade has been restored.

North and Central Florida

Red buckeye (*Aesculus pavia*)

Red buckeye is our only native buckeye and is naturally found throughout north Florida, south to Sumter, Lake, and Orange Counties in the north-central area of the state. In this region, it occurs in moist woodlands with fertile soils, frequently near riverine bottomlands and almost always in deep shade from late spring to fall. Thankfully, it is rather adaptable in cultivation and performs quite well in average landscape settings once established. It should be shaded, however, during the summer and fall or it may drop its leaves.

Red buckeye is a wonderful addition to a mixed woodland setting, even in small landscapes. Its narrow crown allows it to fit into relatively small spaces, and it grows slowly, only reaching its mature height of about 30 feet after many years. Red buckeye has attractive foliage. Like other members of this genus, it has palmately compound leaves with five leaflets per leaf, much like the way your fingers extend off the palm of your hand. The leaves turn golden yellow in the fall, given adequate chilling temperatures.

What makes red buckeye special, however, is its crimson red tubular flowers in the spring. Flowers are produced even in young specimens, and mature, well-grown plants produce numerous flower spikes in mid-spring, each with more than a dozen blooms. They open from the bottom of the stem upward

Red buckeye (*Aesculus pavia*)

over several weeks and produce a beautiful show, attracting the attention of hummingbirds, butterflies, and other pollinators. The first time I encountered this tree in bloom, I was drawn to it by the great activity of sulfur butterflies flitting around it. Pollinated flowers produce nuts that provide food for squirrels. The nuts are toxic to people if chewed and ingested.

I have used red buckeye with success in Pinellas County and it has done well, though never quite achieving the full potential seen in its natural habitat. Water it well during the first year; it is drought tolerant once fully established. I like red buckeye as an accent tree, used with other spring-blooming understory trees and shrubs, but it is also dramatic when planted in small clusters of 3–5 specimens in larger settings. This species is widely propagated by nurseries specializing in native plants and is not difficult to find.

Downy serviceberry (*Amelanchier arborea*)

Downy serviceberry, or shadbush, is one of my favorite understory trees and is far too infrequently used in Florida home landscapes. A narrow-crowned tree with deeply furrowed bark, it often "disappears" into the woodland understory when not in bloom but is impossible to ignore when it is.

Downy serviceberry
(*Amelanchier arborea*)

Downy serviceberry naturally occurs in woodland understories in Florida from the central panhandle region westward. Here, it attains a mature height of about 30 feet. It typically has a very narrow crown with thin branches. The oval leaves have small teeth along the edge and turn yellow in the fall. Its common name comes from the fact that these leaves are silvery "hairy" as they emerge in very early spring.

Downy serviceberry is in the rose family and blooms profusely in the spring, well before most other woodland trees and shrubs. The flowers are arranged in panicles off the end of each stem and the five pure white petals are elongated and dangle downward. The blooming period is fleeting, rarely more than one week, but the effect is spectacular at its peak. Like all roses, the flowers attract a wealth of pollinators.

The pollinated blooms produce clusters of blue-black fruit that resemble blueberries. They are edible and voraciously consumed by birds such as cardinals and mockingbirds. Because the fruit ripens in early summer, downy serviceberry is an especially valuable food plant in a home landscape for fruit-eating wildlife.

I have had success with this beautiful small tree in my Pinellas County landscape, but it performs best in north Florida where it gets more winter cold. It is adaptable and quite drought tolerant once established, but give it water during the first year and mulch it well with leaf litter to ensure its best growth. Downy serviceberry can also tolerate moderate light levels, but its narrow crown and brief blooming season lend its best use to a mixed understory and not as a specimen tree. This wonderful tree is only rarely propagated by commercial sources at this time but can be found with a bit of searching.

Blue beech (*Carpinus caroliniana*)

Blue beech (aka musclewood, ironwood, American hornbeam) is actually a birch, not a beech, and it naturally occurs throughout north and central Florida in a variety of moist shady woodlands. In nature, it prefers the bottom of slopes, near rivers and streams where the soil is occasionally flooded, but it is extremely adaptable in the landscape and performs well in nearly any woodland setting.

Blue beech is a small deciduous tree that reaches a mature height of about 30 feet. Its narrow crown makes it easy to fit into nearly any landscape setting and its rapid growth allows it to assume its stature within a few decades. Like other birches, the leaves are oval with sharply toothed margins. Each leaf is

Blue beech (*Carpinus caroliniana*)

typically less than 1 inch wide and asymmetrical in shape. They turn a brilliant orange-yellow in fall when given enough chilling temperatures, and this feature may be its greatest aesthetic appeal. Blue beech has a smooth bluish gray bark and the trunk assumes a rippled appearance, somewhat like the arms of an experienced body builder; hence its two most commonly used names.

Blue beech produces catkins in the early spring that are relatively inconspicuous. The female catkins form papery bracts in summer that enclose several hard seeds. These are consumed by some birds, though its best wildlife use is as a nesting tree.

Alexa and I love blue beech for its simple elegance. It can be used effectively as a specimen or to form a canopy in small settings where a taller tree wouldn't fit. It also works extremely well beneath the canopy of taller trees, in shade for most of the year. Despite its widespread occurrence in Florida and its adaptability, it is not widely available from commercial sources. It may take some planning to locate a nursery with a high-quality specimen.

Redbud (*Cercis canadensis*)

Redbud is one of the most popular flowering trees for Florida landscapes. In Florida, it occurs in upland settings from extreme north Florida to Hillsborough and Polk Counties in the central portion of the state. It is very adaptable throughout this region but does not tolerate salt or wet soils.

Mature redbuds reach heights of about 25 feet. When grown in the open,

Redbud (*Cercis canadensis*)

they produce a spreading crown that may extend that wide, but in the understory they remain much narrower. Like many members of the bean family, redbuds grow quickly but are not long lived. They also are somewhat brittle and susceptible to wind damage if grown in the open.

The simple heart-shaped leaves of redbuds are attractive and make this a beautiful foliage tree. They turn a rather dull yellow in the fall before adding to the leaf litter below. Like the downy serviceberry, described above, redbud is one of the earliest trees to bloom in the spring. In fact, the two bloom together, along with flatwoods plum and southern crabapple well before anything else has given it consideration. Redbuds bloom profusely, producing large numbers of soft pink blossoms in clusters at the end of each branch. Pollinated flowers develop into small thin beans that eventually split and shed their seeds. These seeds are not widely consumed by most wildlife, except ground foragers such as mourning doves.

Redbud can be used to form a canopy in small landscape settings, or it can be used beneath a deciduous canopy formed by taller trees. It is exceptionally adaptable and easy to establish throughout north and central Florida, but it will not bloom as profusely if given too much shade during the winter and early spring. Do not use it under evergreen shade. Redbud is one of the most widely grown native trees in Florida and can be found in most nurseries. Take care, however, to use only specimens grown from Florida stock. Many out-of-state nurseries ship redbud to large commercial brokers. These trees are poorly adapted to Florida's climate and often fail to bloom and leaf out properly. If you live near the southern end of its range, it is best to use stock native to your location as even north Florida specimens may not perform well.

Fringe tree (*Chionanthus virginicus*)

I have a special affinity for fringe tree and have planted it in every yard I have lived in since moving to Florida. The simple elegance of its tasseled flowers in midspring bring me joy and I revel in its beauty when I find a well-grown tree in full bloom. To me, fringe trees in bloom mean spring has fully arrived.

In nature, fringe tree occurs throughout north and central Florida in a wide variety of woodland settings. It has a moderate growth rate, but new growth occurs only in the spring. The new buds swell, the stems elongate and the ends of every branch, including the tip of the main trunk, rapidly add 6–12 inches of new growth before stopping for another year. In the open, fringe tree is often wider than it is tall, but in a woodland understory it stays narrower. Mature heights of about 30 feet take several decades to achieve, but even very young trees produce flowers.

Blooming occurs in late spring, after most other understory trees have finished. Panicles of flowers are produced at the tip of each stem, usually before the leaves are formed. Each flower has four petals that dangle nearly one inch below the stem, covering the entire crown of the tree and creating a sort of snowstorm of white that moves with each breath of wind. Fringe trees are dioecious, meaning they bear male and female flowers on separate trees, but both produce nearly identical flowers. Female blooms that are pollinated eventually produce egg-shaped deep-purple fruit that is eaten by birds.

Fringe tree
(*Chionanthus virginicus*)

Although fringe tree is a spectacular flowering tree, it has limited aesthetic appeal the rest of the year. Its branches are thin and the elliptical leaves are produced only at the tips, leaving the rest of the branch bare and somewhat uninteresting. For this reason, I like to use it in mixed woodland settings where it can "hide" a bit during the year when not in bloom. Do not attempt it in locations where it will get shade during the winter and early spring as it will bloom too sparingly. In a small landscape, use it as a specimen where it can be easily observed. If you have more expansive grounds, sprinkle this small tree throughout the landscape and allow it to dazzle you every spring.

Fringe tree is not a difficult tree to find from commercial growers. Although it blooms when only a few feet tall, it is best to use specimens that are somewhere in the 3- to 7-gallon size range unless you have a lot of time and patience. It is an easy, pest-resistant, drought-tolerant tree, but water it well during the first 12 months to ensure it is well established before leaving it completely to nature.

Flowering dogwood (*Cornus florida*)

Perhaps no flowering tree, native or not, is more representative of southern landscapes than flowering dogwood. Throughout the South, it is used nearly everywhere as a specimen tree in the open landscape or as an understory planting beneath a taller canopy. Flowering dogwood occurs naturally in a

Flowering dogwood (*Cornus florida*)

wide variety of open and shady upland habitats from the Florida border south to most of central Florida. Flowering dogwood is adaptable, but requires well-drained upland soils to thrive. In north Florida, it thrives in open areas, but near the southern end of its range, it seems to prefer a bit of shade during the summer and fall. It is not salt tolerant and will perish if kept too moist.

Flowering dogwood has great aesthetic appeal. Well-grown specimens attain a mature height of about 35 feet, and they attain this rather quickly. The branches come off the main trunk in "layers," giving it a distinctive shape that is easy to identify even when the trees are leafless in winter. The foliage is oval and light green in color, which, overall, makes it an attractive foliage plant.

What sets flowering dogwood apart from its competitors, however, is its flowers—more accurately, the showy white bracts (there are pink forms too, but none are native to Florida) that surround the tiny heads of green flowers. These large showy bracts are really modified leaves designed to draw the attention of pollinators to its inconspicuous blooms. It works. Dogwood flowers are widely visited by bees and butterflies, and these pollinated flowers eventually ripen into showy red berries that are consumed by a great diversity of birds and other wildlife in late fall. Flowering dogwood is an excellent wildlife plant.

Flowering occurs in midspring, but the blooming period can extend for many weeks because individual trees in the same setting often bloom on their own schedules. Because the showy bracts are not really flowers, they remain attractive before the flowers have opened and long after they have withered. Flowering dogwood, therefore, adds color to the landscape for many weeks each spring.

For much of its range, flowering dogwood can be used to create a canopy of summer shade in landscapes where space is at a premium. Throughout its range, it also works well beneath the canopy of taller deciduous trees. It tolerates alkaline as well as acid soils, but needs good drainage, reasonable air movement, and moderate fertility. This is simply a beautiful tree that can be used in nearly any setting of a woodland garden.

Flowering dogwood is easy to locate from commercial sources, but like the redbud discussed above, care should be taken to use only Florida native stock. Specimens grown by out-of-state sources are unlikely to persist long in our climate and rarely thrive. If you are at the southern end of its natural range, it is especially important to use plants grown from stock near your latitude. Flowering dogwood is not a long-lived tree and is susceptible to a variety of diseases that can cause it harm; most common are fungal problems such as powdery mildew and anthracnose. Such problems are exacerbated when it is attempted in less-than-ideal growing conditions using stock from outside Florida.

Hawthorns (*Crataegus* spp.)

Hawthorns are a widely variable genus of small deciduous trees that rarely reach a mature height greater than 30 feet. As members of the rose family, they have beautiful displays of white blossoms in the spring, followed by crops of apple-like fruit (i.e., "haws" or "hips") in the summer or fall. As the name implies, these species are also thorny, but thorniness is variable both between species and even within them. It is not unusual to find "thornless" varieties in nature, and sometimes this trait is selected by horticulturalists looking to please homeowners who wish to avoid the spines. Of course, the beauty of thorniness lies in the eyes of the beholder, and *always* is a plus for songbirds looking for a place to nest and hide.

Hawthorns give plant taxonomists fits because they are not easily separated into distinct species. Many form local populations, sharing unique traits that give them their own local identity. Some taxonomists give these clonal populations separate species status while others consider them to be local varieties of more-widely distributed species. Therefore, the "splitters"

Hawthorns (*Crataegus* spp.), like this parsley haw (*C. marshallii*), are members of the rose family. Though thorny, they produce showy displays of white flowers in the spring and small apple-like fruit in the summer or fall.

list dozens of native species for Florida; the "lumpers" consolidate that number down to about one dozen.

While I tend to side more with the "splitters" when it comes to hawthorns, I have not done so here, and I include only those that are widely accepted and, of course, only those adapted to the shade garden.

Hawthorns are susceptible to cedar-apple rust, a fungal disease that is transmitted between eastern red cedar and haws. Cedar-apple rust causes lesions on the surface of the leaves that can interfere with growth and forms strange-looking cankers on the fruit. Some species are more resistant than others, but it is never wise to plant haws within a quarter mile of a red cedar.

May haw (*C. aestivalis*)

May haw is one of the better-known species of hawthorns in Florida, due in no small part to the jelly commonly made from its ripe fruit throughout the Deep South. This is an irregularly shaped small tree with light-colored bark and deep green foliage. The leaves are sometimes lobed like a small mitten and sometimes without lobes, but they are always deeply toothed along the margin. Flowering occurs in early spring, before most other hawthorns, and the ½-inch-long bright-red fruit ripen in May; hence its common name. May haw fruit is the only native species with enough citric acid to warrant its use as food. The relatively large size of the fruit, however, limits its use by birds.

May haw occurs naturally only in north Florida, south to Levy County

May haw (*Crataegus aestivalis*)

near the north end of the peninsula. In this region, it is most common at the edge of wetlands where soils are frequently saturated. Despite this, it is a highly adaptable hawthorn for home landscape use. Specimens I installed more than 20 years ago in Pinellas County in upland conditions have thrived, and I harvest fruit from them annually to make wine. Why make jelly?

May haw is not the showiest hawthorn for the shade garden, but it makes a beautiful addition to a mixed understory, especially in landscapes that are roomy enough to accommodate its broad crown and thorniness. The white flowers are large for the genus (about ½ inch across) but occur singly on the stem or in very small clusters. It is often available from commercial nurseries in north Florida. If you choose to add it to your landscape, water it well for the first year to ensure it becomes established. After that, it should not require any additional attention.

Parsley haw (*C. marshallii*)

Parsley haw is one of the most distinct hawthorn species in Florida, easily recognized by its highly scalloped leaves that look a bit like Italian parsley. Native to moist forest understories, its natural range extends from north Florida to Hillsborough and Polk Counties in central Florida.

Parsley haw has several traits that lend it appeal for the home landscape.

Parsley haw (*Crataegus marshallii*)

For one, it is diminutive and rarely exceeds 20 feet in height. Often with multiple trunks, each bends and curves enough to give it great aesthetic interest in the landscape, and the bark on mature specimens often peels away exposing a coppery inner bark that is especially attractive. Parsley haw blooms in midspring about the time it puts on new leaves. Many clusters of small flowers are produced at the ends of each branch. The flowers when newly opened have red anthers. Pollinated flowers form clusters of small red fruit in the late fall. If not eaten immediately by wildlife, they persist well into the winter and become an especially important food source for American robins and cedar waxwings looking to stock up before their annual migration north.

Though parsley haw is by nature a wetland tree, it performs wonderfully in most landscape settings. I like it best set back a bit from the trail, just close enough to admire it when in bloom and during the winter when it is leafless and in fruit. Parsley haw is regularly available from a small group of commercial native plant nurseries.

Beautiful haw (*C. sargentii*)

Beautiful haw is one of those species that taxonomists never seem to agree on completely. Frequently referred to as *C. pulcherrima* in other texts, beautiful haw is a variable species that occurs in upland woodlands in the central panhandle south to Alachua County near Gainesville. As the name implies, this

Beautiful haw (*Crataegus sargentii*)

haw has attractive foliage, somewhat resembling the leaves of a sugar maple, and attractive small clusters of white flowers in midspring.

As an upland species, beautiful haw should be adaptable to most landscape settings in north and central Florida, but it is only very infrequently sold by commercial nurseries and made available to the public. Should you desire to add this haw to your shade garden, you may have to look extensively to find one. If you do, use it much the way I have recommended for others in this genus. The fruit ripens in late summer and is not held on the plants through winter. The color of the fruit is variable, but the relatively large size makes it only marginally useful to most birds.

Littlehip haw (*C. spathulatum*)

Littlehip haw is easily one of my favorite trees in Florida. Found naturally here only in four counties in the central panhandle, it occurs in the understory of well-drained upland woods. This is a narrow crowned, upright tree that can be extremely thorny. The trunks of mature specimens often are rippled, and the reddish bark frequently peels away, providing great aesthetic interest. The foliage slightly resembles parsley haw, but as if the leaves were stretched to be twice as long as wide.

I particularly like littlehip haw for the massive display of blooms it produces each spring. While most haws have small to medium-sized clusters of

Littlehip haw (*Crataegus spathulata*)

bright white flowers in the spring, littlehip haw takes it to a higher level, producing so many that mature trees often seem to be draped in a white curtain. Each tiny flower that is pollinated produces a small haw that turns bright red by fall. Many of these persist through the winter while the trees remain leafless, making it a valuable songbird plant.

Littlehip haw is adaptable to most landscape settings throughout north and central Florida. Three trees I planted more than 20 years ago in Pinellas County are mature and thrive without any supplemental care. At present, it is not an easy species to find from commercial nurseries but can be found with some sleuthing. Use it in small clusters instead of as a solitary specimen. Keep it away from trails and walkways because of its thorniness but close enough to admire its beauty.

Green haw (*C. viridis*)

Green haw naturally occurs in wet woodlands from the panhandle south to north-central portions of the peninsula. It is often a multitrunk tree with light-colored, slightly peeling bark, and its branches are quite thorny.

The foliage of this species resembles that of beautiful haw with variable lobes and toothed leaf margins. Flowering occurs in midspring; each cluster of blooms consists of about 10 flowers. The ripe fruit turns reddish orange by late fall and persists well into winter.

Alexa and I planted a green haw many years ago in our landscape in typi-

Green haw (*Crataegus viridis*)

cal soil and moisture conditions, and it has thrived. I suspect it could be used in most landscapes throughout north and central Florida if given some care during the first year to establish it. Its spreading crown, however, makes its best use in landscapes where sufficient space is available. Green haw is an attractive tree that is only rarely offered by commercial sources at this time.

Silverbells (*Halesia* spp.)

Silverbells are deciduous trees native to the understory of north Florida woodlands. Both species, described below, are similar in aspect and differ mostly by the shape and size of their flowers. They are narrow-crowned, crooked-single-trunked trees and reach a mature height of about 25–30 feet. Their foliage is oval, greenish yellow, and finely toothed along the leaf margin. In the fall, these leaves turn a rather dull yellow before falling to the ground.

What makes silverbells special is their beautiful flowers. In early to midspring, the trees are covered by a mantle of white bell-shaped blooms. The floral show lasts just a week but can be spectacular. Trees of both species bloom at an early age, but not nearly as profusely as mature plants. Large, dry elliptical seeds ripen in the fall and are not a significant wildlife food. As their common names imply, two-winged silverbell and Carolina silverbell differ by the number of prominent ridges (i.e., wings) along the edge of their seeds.

Neither species is widely propagated by commercial sources, but two-winged silverbell is more easily available. I like them best when used in a mixed understory with other spring-blooming trees and shrubs. They are not especially attractive foliage plants, so put them in the middle of the planting bed where their spring blooms can be admired, and then allow them to disappear into the woods for the rest of the year. In large planting areas, use several, but scatter them throughout the bed.

Carolina silverbell (*H. carolina*)

Carolina silverbell occurs throughout the panhandle and south to Citrus County in the northern peninsula. It occurs in a variety of upland habitats throughout this region, sometimes at the edge of wetland floodplains. Besides having different seeds, Carolina silverbell has smaller blooms with fused petals that resemble bells in structure. Each is about ½ inch long, but large numbers are produced in April.

Carolina silverbell is sometimes offered by commercial native nurseries just north of Florida but is extremely hard to find within the state. This is dif-

Carolina silverbell (*Halesia carolina*). Photo by Gil Nelson, with permission.

Two-winged silverbell (*Halesia diptera*)

ficult to understand, given its beauty and adaptability for the shade garden. I grew my specimens from seed I collected in north Florida, and my young trees have done well in my Pinellas County landscape. Though it is a bit less showy than two-winged silverbell, it is an attractive flowering tree that should be more widely used.

Two-winged silverbell (*H. diptera*)

Two-winged silverbell is the showier of the two species native to Florida. It often occurs in the same woodlands as Carolina silverbell, but its distribution is more restricted statewide; two-winged silverbell is naturally found only in the panhandle counties west of Jefferson County. Two forms are recognized; the typical form occurs throughout this region and a larger-flowered form (*H. diptera* var. *magniflora*) is found around Torreya State Park near the Apalachicola River. Not surprisingly, the large-flowered form is the one most frequently offered in the nursery trade. The petals of two-winged silverbell are not fused as far down the floral tube as those of Carolina silverbell, so the flowers are not as bell-shaped and the petals dangle a bit like those of fringe tree.

Two-winged silverbell can be used well into central Florida if care is taken to provide it with the right conditions and additional water is supplied, as needed, during the first year to get it established. The two trees I have in my Pinellas County landscape have done well over the past five years, flower in the spring, and set viable seed in the fall.

Florida anise (*Illicium floridanum*)

Florida anise is a small evergreen upright tree that rarely exceeds 20 feet tall. A member of the star anise family, its foliage and seed capsules are highly aromatic, as is indicative of this mostly Asian genus. Florida anise has a restricted range in our state. It occurs in moist forest understories in scattered locations within the central and western panhandle. In locations where its growing needs are met, it often forms large colonies.

Florida anise is most often a narrow-crowned tree with short branches. The leaves are elliptical, deep green and glossy, which makes it a beautiful foliage plant, but the spring blooms are what separates this wonderful tree from its competition. Sometime in late March to early April, Florida anise produces large numbers of bright crimson flowers. Each is characterized by having several dozen spidery petals. A well grown plant, in full bloom, is a spectacular sight and demands attention from even the most plant-blind visitor to the landscape.

Although Florida anise has a restricted range in north Florida, it is relatively adaptable into central Florida landscapes if care is given to provide for its habitat requirements. In north Florida, I have seen it grown in open areas, but further south it needs partial to full shade during the summer and fall. It adapts to a variety of soil conditions, but performs best if given extra fertility and moisture. Mulch it well with leaf litter and water it well for the first year until it is fully established. I have found it quite forgiving if such care is taken initially. Florida anise cannot, however, tolerate fully saturated soils for more

Florida anise
(*Illicium floridanum*)

than brief periods. Do not plant it in areas that frequently flood. Because of its great beauty, Florida anise is widely propagated and relatively easy to locate from commercial sources.

Ashe magnolia (*Magnolia macrophylla* var. *ashei*)

Ashe magnolia is unique to Florida, extremely rare in nature, and found only in the central and western counties of the panhandle in rich woodlands. Some taxonomists consider it a unique variety of the more widespread bigleaf magnolia (*M. macrophylla*), but it is unique enough to consider separately here. Ashe magnolia is a diminutive deciduous member of this genus of large canopy trees. It often occurs as a crooked single-trunk tree, reaching mature heights of less than 20 feet. The individual leaves are huge (often three feet long or more) and shaped somewhat like a shoe. The underside of each is silvery.

Blooming occurs in late spring. Extremely large crystalline white flowers,

Ashe magnolia (*Magnolia macrophylla* var. *ashei*). Photo by Gil Nelson, with permission.

with purplish markings near the base, are produced in great numbers. These eventually form the cone-like follicles indicative of this genus and the bright red fruit dangle from them in summer, providing birds with an important food source.

Despite its great rarity in nature, Ashe magnolia is widely propagated by commercial sources and is far more adaptable than might be expected. I do not recommend its use too far south into central Florida, but I have seen it grown successfully in north-central counties, and it is widely grown throughout north Florida landscapes. Do not plant it in evergreen shade, provide it protection from summer sun, and give it a bit of extra soil fertility by mulching it well with leaf litter.

Southern crabapple (*Malus angustifolia*)

Flowering crabapples are widely used in landscapes across North America because of their showy spring blooms and their attractive form and foliage. In Florida, our native southern crabapple is no exception. Native only to the panhandle counties, it occurs most commonly in the understory of deciduous forests and in hedgerows and woodland edges. As such, it is adaptable to varying degrees of sunlight and can be used as a specimen tree in the northern portions of the state.

Southern crabapple (*Malus angustifolia*)

Southern crabapple is a somewhat crooked deciduous tree that rarely stands taller than 25 feet. When planted in sunny locations, it forms a wide crown, but this is more reduced when it is used as an understory subcanopy tree. Its branches are nearly horizontal to the main trunk, zigzag as they grow outward, and have numerous short spur branches that give it a rather thorny nature. This is a short-trunked tree. The bark is gray, but streaks of the reddish inner bark become exposed as the tree matures. New branches are also cinnamon brown in color. The foliage is typical of most apples; the deep-green oval leaves are slightly toothed, about 1½ inches long, and occur in clusters along the stem.

What makes southern crabapple a prized addition to the landscape, however, is the mass of light-pink, fragrant flowers produced along its branches in spring. This showy display also attracts the attention of pollinating insects, especially bees and butterflies. By late summer, the flattened one-inch apples are ripe. They are yellowish green with a slight pink blush. Their size limits their value to only the largest songbirds and to mammals, and their lack of tartness does not lend itself well to jellies and wine.

Southern crabapple is a short-lived (maybe 50 years) tree, susceptible to many of the diseases common to other apples. Do not use it in deep shade or in areas with restricted air movement. I like it best when used as a subcanopy tree, mixed with other early spring-blooming species—especially the white-flowered flatwoods plum and downy serviceberry. It will prosper in most typical landscape soils and can be used into central Florida if provided light shade during the summer months. Because of its beauty, southern crabapple is widely propagated by north Florida native-plant nurseries.

Eastern hop hornbeam (*Ostrya virginiana*)

Eastern hop hornbeam is a close relative of blue beech and they are often found growing together. It has a more limited natural range in Florida, however, occurring throughout the northern counties, south to about Hernando County in north-central Florida. Eastern hop hornbeam is a narrow-crowned tree, but it can reach a mature height of about 50 feet. It is almost always found in the understory of upland deciduous forests, but tolerates more sunlight if planted in the open.

Eastern hop hornbeam has elm-like foliage and bark that peels off the trunk in thin sheets. Its common name comes from the papery bracts that surround the ripened seeds. They look decidedly like the hops used to brew beer. This is an attractive tree but not as showy as most described in this book. Perhaps its showiest feature is its bright yellow leaves in autumn.

This tree is widely propagated but may take some time to find commercially. I like it best when used in expansive mixed woodland plantings, scattered in the distance where it can blend in a bit behind showier spring-blooming species.

Eastern hop hornbeam (*Ostrya virginiana*)

Plums (*Prunus* spp.)

Plums are members of the rose family and characterized by their profusion of white flowers in the spring. Plums are favorite landscape plants around the world, and Florida is home to four species. Two of these, described below, tend to occur in the understory of deciduous woodlands and are excellent choices for a shade garden. Native plums produce large numbers of white flowers that attract a wide assortment of pollinators and tart fruit that can be made into jelly if picked when fully ripe. Wildlife also relish the fruit, but most birds find them too large to consume easily. They are short-lived, deciduous, fast-growing species.

American plum (*Prunus americana*)

American plum occurs in scattered upland locations in north and north-central Florida. Typically an irregularly shaped, wide-crowned tree, it reaches a mature height of about 30 feet. The bark is coppery in color and shaggy on mature specimens. The foliage is narrowly ovate with noticeable teeth along the margins. Blooming occurs in very early spring before the trees leaf out. The five-petal flowers are large for the genus and often turn pinkish as they age. In full bloom, they are spectacular, but they remain in flower for only about a week. The nearly 1-inch rounded plums ripen in early summer.

American plum is an adaptable, beautiful understory tree but is difficult

American plum (*Prunus americana*)

to find commercially. If you plant this plum, be aware that it may sucker and form small colonies over time.

Flatwoods plum (*Prunus umbellata*)

Flatwoods plum is perhaps the best choice for the shade garden in north and central Florida. A narrow-crowned tree that rarely exceeds 15 feet at maturity, it is a common component of woodland understories throughout this region and is adaptable to nearly every site condition typical to home landscapes. Flatwoods plum performs best if used beneath deciduous canopies as it blooms only sparingly if not given good light in the late winter and early spring. Flowering occurs in very early spring. Though the flowers are a bit smaller than those of American plum, well-grown specimens are covered in a mantle of white and always draw attention.

Flatwoods plum can tolerate high light levels and can be used in small shade gardens where a larger canopy is inappropriate. They also perform well beneath taller deciduous trees. Use it as an accent tree or scattered throughout a more expansive mixed forest understory. Flatwoods plum does not produce suckers and spreads only by wildlife eating and planting their seeds. This plum is frequently propagated by commercial nurseries that specialize in native plants.

Flatwoods plum (*Prunus umbellata*)

Wafer ash (*Ptelea trifoliata*)

Wafer ash is a rather nondescript small tree, resident to the understory of deciduous hammocks from north Florida well into the central peninsula. At maturity, it rarely stands taller than 20 feet. The thin trunk, reddish brown in color, is characterized by having few stiff branches that are not wide spreading. The foliage is distinctive. The leaves are composed of three leaflets (sometimes five), palmately compound in structure, attached to the branches on long stems (petioles). As a member of the citrus family, the foliage is aromatic when bruised or crushed. These aromatic oils attract the attention of giant swallowtails and these beautiful butterflies seek this plant out to lay eggs. As such, wafer ash is most commonly used in the landscapes of butterfly enthusiasts and this has fueled its limited availability around the state from commercial growers. The leaves turn an attractive yellow in fall.

Wafer ash flowers in the spring. The small greenish four- to five-petal flowers are not showy and are produced in clusters along the ends of the branches. Plants are often dioecious, but others may have flowers of both sexes on the same plant. If pollinated, the female flowers produce clusters of flattened, winged seeds that are not especially useful to most wildlife.

Wafer ash fits well beneath the canopy of a shade garden because of its small size and narrow crown, but it also has a tendency to sucker and form small colonies. These attributes do not make it a top choice for most shade

Wafer ash (*Ptelea trifoliata*)

gardens, except those of avid butterfly gardeners. Though giant swallowtails use a wide variety of citrus family trees as host plants for their caterpillars, I have found wafer ash to be their top choice when given a broad selection of possible choices. For that reason, it will always be available in limited supplies throughout north and central Florida.

Carolina buckthorn (*Rhamnus caroliniana*)

Carolina buckthorn has a naturally scattered distribution from north to south-central Florida in the understory of deciduous forests in both alkaline and acidic soils. Never common and often absent from places it seems well adapted to, it can form attractive colonies in those places it does occur.

Carolina buckthorn is a nonthorny deciduous member of the buckthorn family. It can attain a mature height of 30 feet but has short branches and never forms a wide canopy. The leaves are simple, elliptical in shape, and deep green in color. The young twigs are covered by brown "hairs." All of these features make it an attractive foliage plant.

Flowering occurs in late spring. The tiny whitish blooms are inconspicuous and borne in small clusters along the stems. Carolina buckthorn is monoecious so each plant produces the dark oval ⅓-inch-long fruit in late fall that are relished by songbirds and other wildlife.

Carolina buckthorn makes an interesting addition to a mixed understory

Carolina buckthorn (*Rhamnus caroliniana*)

designed to maximize wildlife value. Because of its growth form, it fits well into tight spaces. It also works well in larger settings. Use it near the middle section of the planting bed and allow it to "disappear" into the understory when its aesthetics are at their lowest. When its fruit are red and ripening to black in the fall, I think it is at its showiest.

Gum bumelia (*Sideroxylon lanuginosum*)

This genus was recently known as *Bumelia*, which is still the most widely used common name for members now lumped together as *Sideroxylon*. Most members of this genus perform best in open sunny habitats or occur as large trees. Gum bumelia is an exception.

Gum bumelia occurs as a small, irregularly shaped tree from north Florida to Pinellas and Hillsborough Counties in central Florida. It performs well in open woodlands where it gets nearly full sun but is most often found beneath the canopy of taller trees. The largest specimens I have encountered in Pinellas County receive very little direct light under the canopy of a mostly evergreen woodland. Gum bumelia is a deciduous slow-growing species; at maturity it may reach 30 feet tall, but that takes several decades. It has a narrow crown, but the short stiff branches are thorny.

I find gum bumelia to be an aesthetically interesting species. Its deeply fissured bark and its irregular shape provide a respite from other straight-

Gum bumelia (*Sideroxylon lanuginosum*)

trunked trees and shrubs that tend to blend together in a landscape. The small, dark green oval leaves are densely coppery beneath, and the small white flowers are especially fragrant and draw an extremely wide variety of pollinators to them in the spring. Pollinated flowers eventually form very dark ¼-inch fruit in late summer and fall that are eaten by many songbirds, including cardinals and mockingbirds.

Gum bumelia is an extremely hardy and adaptable understory tree with good wildlife value and aesthetic qualities; however, it is only infrequently propagated by commercial sources and may be difficult to locate. Because of its thorny nature, do not use it adjacent to trails or at the front of a shade garden. I like it best as an accent tree in a location where its unusual character will draw a visitor's eye to it and the plants nearby.

Silky camellia (*Stewartia malacodendron*)

Silky camellia is one of the most beautiful flowering understory trees native to Florida, but has an extremely small natural range here and performs well only under a rather narrow range of growing conditions. Found from the central panhandle westward, it prefers moist, rich soils along riverine slope forests. Al-

Silky camellia (*Stewartia malacodendron*)

though it may act more like a shrub, silky camellia most often becomes a small tree to about 15 feet tall. The side branches are arranged in tiers, much like those of flowering dogwood, and the leaves are broadly elliptical in shape and slightly toothed along the margins. Its common name is derived from the fact that the new leaves are clothed in silvery silky "hairs." Silky camellia is deciduous.

These characteristics make silky camellia a beautiful foliage plant, but its most attractive attribute is its spectacular flowers, produced in late spring. These blooms are more than 1 inch across. The five petals are purest white in color and offset the deep purple filaments in the center and throat. The flowers occur in small clusters with each bud opening for several days and with the rest behind it to open later. In the peak of flowering, there are few native trees that can rival it for beauty.

Silky camellia is a bit more adaptable in the home landscape than might be suspected from its limited natural distribution. It can be used in relatively high light situations in north Florida, like flowering dogwood, to form the canopy of a shade garden in areas where space is limited. It can also be used as an accent tree beneath the canopy of taller deciduous trees. In such settings, I suspect it can be pushed well south of its natural range if care is given to provide the soil and moisture conditions it prefers. Silky camellia is propagated by a few native plant nurseries in north Florida and is not widely available for home landscapes. It can be found, however, with a bit of persistence. This is a slow-maturing tree, but it may be best to use smaller specimens and have patience than to attempt larger specimens too acclimated to life in a container.

Horse sugar (*Symplocos tinctoria*)

Horse sugar is so named because its foliage is a favorite of browsing wildlife and domestic animals. Native to upland and mesic forest understories from the panhandle to central Florida, horse sugar generally occurs as a wide-crowned tree between 20 and 30 feet tall at maturity. The leaves are shiny green, elliptical, and without noticeable teeth along the margins. Often, it blends into the rest of the understory.

Flowering occurs in midspring. The individual flowers are yellowish and rather small, but they are produced in clusters along the leafless branches of the previous year's growth, making them noticeable. They are very fragrant and draw the attention of many pollinating insects. Eventually, pollinated flowers produce small cylindrical greenish fruit that are only marginally important to wildlife.

Horse sugar
(*Symplocos
tinctoria*)

Horse sugar is tardily deciduous, holding its leaves into early winter. It can be incorporated into most landscape situations in north and central Florida, but it works best aesthetically when used in a mixed understory where it can blend in for much of the year. I like it best in more expansive settings where adding diversity is a priority. Horse sugar is only rarely grown commercially at this time and may be difficult to locate from commercial sources.

Florida yew (*Taxus floridana*)

Florida yew is a very rare endemic evergreen found naturally only in Liberty County in the bluff forests near the Apalachicola River. A remnant species of a climate that existed in Florida during the last Ice Age, it has held on to this narrow area where its climate needs can still be met. Fortunately, it seems more adaptable when grown in home landscape settings, and I have seen it used successfully in north and north-central Florida when provided with the conditions it prefers.

Florida yew grows slowly and eventually reaches a mature height of about 20 feet. It has an irregular growth form and wide-spreading branches. The needles are flat, flexible, and shiny green. Each is only about ¾ inch long and often has a twist along its length. Yews are dioecious, so only female plants bear the small nut-like cone surrounded by a bright red fleshy aril.

Despite its natural rarity, Florida yew is rather widely propagated by commercial sources in north Florida and is not difficult to find for home landscape purposes. It is a state protected endangered species, under consider-

Florida yew (*Taxus floridana*)

ation for federal listing, and no parts of this plant can be collected at any time without a permit and permission of the landowner. This species is a novelty in the landscape. Its evergreen nature and interesting shape and texture lend interest to expansive landscape settings as specimen plantings. They also provide excellent winter wildlife cover. Do not give it deep shade, provide it some elbow room from neighboring plants, and use it in average to moist soil areas protected from the heat of summer.

Sparkleberry (*Vaccineum arboreum*)

Sparkleberry is so named because of the profusion of bell-shaped flowers it produces each spring. As such, it is one of the most attractive understory flowering trees available for home landscapes throughout north and central Florida. Sparkleberry is most abundant in the understory of deciduous woodlands. It is, however, very tolerant of soil and light conditions and can perform well under high sunlight and nearly every soil type except extreme wet.

This is a very slow-growing tree. As it ages, it develops a highly irregular shape with a twisted trunk and coppery peeling bark that is all but unique to this species. Mature specimens are never identical in form but are always exceptionally interesting to behold. The leaves are small, rounded, and leathery. They are a deep green during much of the year and turn red to purple-red in very late fall to early winter.

Sparkleberry
(*Vaccinium arboreum*)

Flowering occurs in midspring about the time that flowering dogwoods are done. Mature specimens are completely covered by small, bright-white, bell-shaped flowers. They are fragrant and attract large numbers of butterflies and other pollinating insects. Pollinated flowers form small purple blueberries in the fall. Unlike other blueberries, they taste rather bitter and are not good for human consumption, but they are a wonderful food source for songbirds. Because the fruit often remains through the winter, migratory birds such as cedar waxwings and American robins feed heavily on it before making their migration northward.

Sparkleberry is widely propagated and can be used in a great many settings. It adapts slowly from pot culture, however, and requires additional watering for at least the first year. Once established, it is exceedingly drought tolerant and disease free. I like it best when used as an accent beneath the canopy of deciduous trees. Do not give it too much shade or it won't bloom properly. Place it in an area where its flowers (and nectaring butterflies) can be admired, and where its wonderful leafless form can be fully appreciated in winter.

South Florida

The understory trees included below are best used in the southernmost tiers of counties, basically the area southward from Lee County on the west coast to Palm Beach County on the east. In most years, the minimum winter temperature in this region is above 32°F and the flora here is more closely related to that found in the Bahamas and Bermuda than to the rest of the peninsula. There are many native Florida plants that occur statewide. There are others that occur well into south-central Florida. The ones discussed below are specialists that are best adapted to parts of the state that only very rarely experience temperatures below freezing. I make special note of those that I have experience growing into the mid-20s°F, because some can be used outside their natural ranges in home landscapes that provide them some winter protection.

Wild cinnamon bark (*Canella winterana*)

Wild cinnamon bark is one of my favorite semitropical south Florida trees. Its lush evergreen foliage and twisting trunk give it an aesthetic appeal that I never tire of, and its maroon-red flowers and bright red fruit add an entirely different dimension that is both beautiful and useful to wildlife. In nature, wild cinnamon bark is rare. It occurs only in a few hammock woodlands in Miami-Dade and Monroe Counties, as well as some of the far western Florida Keys. Here, it may reach a mature height of 40 feet but with a narrow crown.

Wild cinnamon bark (*Canella winterana*)

Though not related to the true cinnamons, wild cinnamon bark produces a similar fragrance when the bark is bruised. Though its natural range is quite restricted, I have used it in locations where winter temperatures routinely drop into the mid-20s°F and it has suffered no apparent damage. I like it best as an accent in a mixed semitropical understory. Place it where its form and beauty can be easily admired, and set it somewhat apart to draw extra attention to it at all times of the year. It is tolerant of most landscape conditions. Flowering often occurs in summer, and the fruit typically ripens in fall or early winter. The flowers occur in small clusters at the ends of the branches.

Stoppers (*Eugenia* spp.)

The four stoppers native to Florida are wonderful small evergreen trees often used in home landscapes. Named for their supposed value in relieving diarrhea, they are widely propagated by commercial nurseries in south Florida, produce large numbers of fragrant white flowers, and equally large numbers of small berries that are of great value to songbirds and other wildlife. Stoppers are easy to maintain in the landscape, susceptible to very few problems, and attractive year round. They tolerate high light levels and can be grown in full sun, but when grown under these conditions, they tend to stay shorter and do not produce the beautiful twisted trunks that I believe heighten their aesthetics.

White stopper (*E. axillaris*)

White stopper has the widest natural distribution of our native species. Found from coastal Levy County on the west coast to Volusia County on the east, and south through the Florida Keys, white stopper reaches a mature height of 25 feet. It is narrow-crowned with short stiff branches and smooth grayish bark. The foliage is oval and each leaf has a distinct point at the end. It is extremely aromatic. White stopper smells much like a skunk, and on warm days this aroma can be detected many yards away. Over the years, I have met people who love the smell and others who completely disdain it. I also know a few who have planted it as a buffer between their home and that of an unfriendly neighbor . . .

Flowering occurs most commonly in the summer. The large numbers of flowers eventually form black round fruit that are relished by birds and other wildlife. White stopper tolerates winter low temperatures in the mid-20s°F without any visible damage. Use it in small clusters to create a south Florida semitropical feel to the landscape. Because of its narrow crown, it can fit nearly

White stopper
(*Eugenia axillaris*)

any landscape setting and its wide tolerance of landscape situations allows its use nearly everywhere its minimum winter temperature can be routinely met.

Red-berry stopper (*E. confusa*)

Red-berry stopper is the most distinctive of the four species found in Florida. More often a shrub than a small tree, it rarely exceeds 15 feet at maturity. The limbs are thin and numerous, and they tend to bend downward in a weeping aspect. The individual leaves are small and ovoid, with long tapered tips. This gives it a decidedly distinct form that can be used quite effectively in the landscape. Red-berry stopper is rare in Florida and naturally known only from Miami-Dade County and the Florida Keys. It has far more tolerance to growing conditions than this range might suggest, however, and it suffers very little damage when minimum temperatures do not dip below 26°F. Do not attempt this plant in areas that experience lower temperatures because major stem damage will occur. Flowering takes place in early summer and the mass of white blooms eventually turns into bright red berries. Red-berry stopper foliage is not noticeably fragrant from a distance and this makes it a wonderful choice for homeowners who cannot tolerate the skunky smell of other stopper species. Use red-berry stopper as an accent plant in a mixed understory or to create a visual barrier to screen a neighbor's fence or other unsightly structure. It will screen plants behind it, so be careful to place smaller species in front.

Red-berry stopper (*Eugenia confusa*)

Spanish stopper (*Eugenia foetida*)

Spanish stopper (*E. foetida*)

Spanish stopper has a slightly smaller natural range than white stopper but often occurs in the same woodlands and has very similar characteristics. In nature, Spanish stopper occurs along the coast from Sarasota County on the west to around Cape Canaveral on the east. It rarely exceeds 15 feet at maturity, has grayish mottled bark and somewhat twisted trunks. The foliage is more rounded than white stopper, and the leaves are only about half as long. As its Latin name suggests, the foliage is very "skunky" smelling, though in my experience it doesn't quite rival that of white stopper. Flowers and fruit are quite similar to white stopper and its use in the landscape is, too. I like to combine both species in a mixed understory setting, planting each in small clusters that accentuate their foliage differences. Spanish stopper can withstand low temperatures into the mid-20s°F without noticeable damage.

Red stopper (*E. rhombea*)

Red stopper is the rarest of our four native species and occurs naturally only in a few locations within Miami-Dade County and the Florida Keys. This narrow small tree reaches a mature height of about 20 feet. The bark is smooth and light colored while the dark green leaves are oval with long, tapered tips. These are somewhat widely spaced on the short branches and give it a more open appearance. Though the foliage is similar to white stopper, its overall

Red stopper (*Eugenia rhombea*)

aspect is not the same, and the leaves lack the strong skunky fragrance present in the former. The white flowers, produced mostly in summer, become rounded fruit that turns red and ripens to black by late fall. Red stopper is not as widely propagated as the other species and has more limited landscape use. Light damage occurs in temperatures below freezing and significant damage is likely below 26°F. I like the look of red stopper and have used it as an accent in mixed understory settings. Protect it from winter winds, and use it individually or in small clusters where it can be admired.

Princewood (*Exostema caribaeum*)

Princewood is an attractive small tree or shrub native to southern Miami-Dade County and the Florida Keys. Rarely exceeding 20 feet in height, it has conspicuously jointed twigs and leathery, deep green elliptical leaves. The limbs are thin, but strong. Princewood is best known for its white tubular flowers that are produced nearly year-round on new growth. Each bloom is nearly 2 inches long and fragrant, and the plants remain showy for much of the year. Pollination is mostly accomplished by long-tongued moths in the evening. Eventually the fruit ripen into dark, woody capsules that are not

Princewood (*Exostema caribaeum*). Photo by Roger Hammer, with permission.

very useful to wildlife. I do not have experience with this species outside its normal range but suspect it should not be pushed too far north. Use it to form a screen in a mixed semitropical understory or as an accent in a more expansive setting where its fragrant white flowers can be appreciated.

Inkwood (*Exothea paniculata*)

Inkwood occurs throughout South Florida and along the eastern coast as far north as Volusia County. Its distinctive foliage, fragrant flowers, and wildlife value make it an interesting addition to shade gardens throughout the southern portion of Florida, but it is not widely propagated and may be difficult to obtain.

Inkwood is evergreen and the deep glossy leaves are compound, in twos or fours. Each leaf is oblong, about 4 inches long, and clustered at the end of the thin stems. The bark is dark gray in color. Mature specimens attain a height of about 40 feet. At this size, the crown is rather broad and irregular. Inkwood is normally dioecious, but monoecious specimens can occur. Flowering occurs in spring. Clusters of ¼-inch white flowers are produced on short lateral branches near the crown. Pollinated female flowers produce clusters of deep purple fruit that ripen by midsummer and are a food source for songbirds and other wildlife.

Inkwood is an adaptable tree that has good cold tolerance into the mid-

Inkwood
(*Exothea
paniculata*)

20s°F. Use it within a mixed semitropical woodland setting. Because it is often dioecious, make sure you plant both sexes to ensure you get fruit if wildlife are a concern.

Blolly (*Guapira discolor*)

One of my favorite south Florida small trees is blolly. Its tight light-colored bark, arching trunks, and glossy leaves make it an attractive foliage plant, while the bright coral-red fruit produced on female trees is both beautiful and highly prized by wildlife. Blolly occurs naturally in much of south Florida, and its range extends north along the east coast to Volusia County. It has excellent cold tolerance into the mid-20s°F and can be planted near the coast well into central Florida. Specimens I added to a Pinellas County landscape have thrived for more than 20 years.

Mature specimens reach almost 40 feet in height. This is a narrow-crowned tree that fits well in a mixed planting, but it has a tendency to twist and bend as it grows upward so its crown is rarely directly above its main trunk. The foliage occurs mostly at the tips of the thin branches. Each leaf is oval, 1–2 inches long, light green, and very glossy. Flowering generally occurs in mid-summer. Small greenish white tubular blooms occur in small clusters. These are visited by tiny pollinating insects, and fruit eventually ripens by fall. If a male plant is nearby, female plants produce large numbers of ⅓-inch shiny red fruit. Plants in fruit are extremely showy.

Blolly is widely propagated for the home landscape and is not a difficult

Blolly (*Guapira discolor*)

species to find from commercial sources. Because it is dioecious, use it in clusters of three within a mixed semitropical landscape setting. It is fast growing and normally produces fruit within about 5 years.

White ironwood (*Hypelate trifoliata*)

White ironwood is so named for its light-colored, extremely dense wood. Resident naturally to Miami-Dade County and the Florida Keys, it is most often found in the understory of semitropical hammocks, where it reaches a mature height of about 30 feet. This is often a shrubby tree with an irregular growth form. The foliage is trifoliate, composed of three small leaflets that are light green and glossy.

Clusters of tiny pale green flowers are produced in early summer. As the trees are monoecious, each eventually produces panicles of oval deep-purple fruit, about ⅜ inch in length. The fruit are sweet and fleshy, surrounding a hard pit, and they are eagerly consumed by birds and other wildlife.

White ironwood is only rarely available from commercial sources at this time and may take some searching to find for the home landscape. It is a useful addition to a mixed understory planting. Because of its relatively small size, it fits well into small settings and its adaptability and attractive foliage make it an interesting accent plant.

White ironwood (*Hypelate trifoliata*)

Krug's holly (*Ilex krugiana*)

Krug's holly is the only native holly restricted to the semitropical region of Florida. Its natural range here includes a small portion of Miami-Dade County in the Everglades; it is not present in the Florida Keys. This species is more closely related to some Central American hollies than to other Florida natives. At maturity, Krug's holly reaches about 30 feet in height. Its form resembles the very common Dahoon holly (*I. cassine*): upright, stout branches, and shiny green foliage. The leaves are elliptical, without teeth, and wavy along the margins.

Flowering occurs in late spring, and the fruit ripen by summer. Clusters of flowers occur along the stems, and the fruit ripen from orange-red to deep purple. Hollies are dioecious, so only the females produce fruit.

Hollies, in general, make excellent pest-free additions to home landscapes, but Krug's holly is not widely grown commercially and may be difficult to locate. I have no experience with this species in terms of cold hardiness, but its very limited range suggests that it should be used only in landscapes that do not experience freezing temperatures. It is best used in mixed plantings, and both sexes must be planted to ensure fruit production for birds.

Krug's holly (*Ilex krugiana*). Photo by Roger Hammer, with permission.

Black ironwood (*Krugiodendron ferreum*)

Black ironwood is so named because of its dark heavy wood, reputed to be the densest wood of any North American tree. It is so heavy that it sinks in salt water. It has a wide natural range in south Florida and extends up the east coast through Volusia County. Throughout, it is most often encountered in hammock understories.

Black ironwood is a narrow-crowned evergreen tree with a somewhat twisted trunk that reaches 35 feet at maturity. Its deep fissured bark and glossy green foliage make it an exceptionally attractive landscape specimen. The leaves are broadly oval and light green in color. They also tend to curl somewhat instead of lying flat. It is monoecious. Very tiny, greenish, fragrant flowers are produced in summer in large numbers. They lack petals and are inconspicuous, but they attract a variety of very small pollinators. By late summer, large numbers of sweet, edible fruit have ripened. They are especially attractive to wildlife, making black ironwood an excellent bird plant.

Black ironwood is cold tolerant into the mid-20s°F and is adaptable to a wide range of landscape conditions. It can be used an as accent tree to create shade in small landscapes or as an understory specimen in a mixed woodland. I like it best when used in the middle of a mixed species planting, but near enough to a walkway or trail for its fragrant flowers and attractive form to be admired. Black ironwood is routinely propagated by commercial nurseries throughout south Florida and should not be difficult to locate.

Black ironwood (*Krugiodendron ferreum*)

Simpson stopper (*Myrcianthes fragrans*)

Simpson stopper is the most widely used south Florida native for home landscapes in our state and can be used effectively throughout all of south and central Florida. Its popularity stems from its great aesthetic features, its adaptability, and its value to wildlife. Simpson stopper performs well in full sun, but it tends to develop more like a dense shrub than a small tree under these conditions. When used in less sun, in the understory of an evergreen hammock, it forms a trunk and the majority of its foliage is near the top and at the ends of its branches. In both situations, it has great landscape value.

For the shade garden, Simpson stopper forms a narrow-crowned small tree that eventually stands about 25 feet tall. The somewhat crooked trunk has coppery exfoliating bark that is quite attractive. I like Simpson stopper grown in shade for this reason. The leaves are leathery and rounded, about 1 inch wide, and aromatic when crushed. The trees are monoecious. Flowering occurs most often in late spring, but sometimes a second blooming occurs in early winter. The flowers are typical of the stoppers, bright white and numerous on the ends of the branches. As its Latin name implies, the flowers are also highly fragrant. Bright red, edible fruit ripen several months later. Birds, like mockingbirds, cardinals, and catbirds, are especially fond of them.

Simpson stopper is widely cultivated by commercial sources and is easy to locate. It tolerates winter temperatures into the low 20s°F without noticeable

Simpson stopper (*Myrcianthes fragrans*). Photo by Christina Evans, with permission.

damage and performs under nearly every typical home landscape setting. Do not give it too much shade, however, if you want fruit for birds.

Lancewood (*Ocotea coriacea*)

Lancewood is a bay family relative that naturally occurs throughout south Florida and portions of southern central Florida. Sometimes shrublike, it eventually develops into a small evergreen tree that reaches 40 feet in height. Like other members of this family, the leaves are highly aromatic when crushed, and it serves as a larval host for spicebush swallowtails.

Lancewood has simple, elongated lance-like leaves that can reach 5 inches long. They have a well-defined tip. Flowering occurs over a prolonged period between spring and fall; sometimes two distinct blooming periods occur during this time. The clusters of small white flowers occur on new growth near the ends of the branches. The fruit ripens by fall. Each fruit is deep purple, ⅓ inch long, and encircled by a bright crimson cup near the attachment at the stem. The fruit are eagerly eaten by songbirds.

Lancewood is adaptable to a wide variety of growing conditions but is susceptible to the same fungal disease, laurel wilt, that is currently decimating other members of this family—bays (*Persea* spp.), avocado (*Persea ameri-*

Lancewood
(*Ocotea coriacea*)

cana), and spicebush (*Lindera benzoin*), among others. The extent of its susceptibility to this disease has not yet been well determined. Until a remedy is discovered, its use in the home landscape should be carefully considered.

Darling plum (*Reynosia septentrionalis*)

Darling plum naturally occurs in only a few locations within Miami-Dade County and the Florida Keys. It can be shrub-like but can also be a small tree, eventually reaching about 25 feet in height. A close relative of black ironwood, it shares some of that species' wonderful attributes but is rarely grown commercially and may be very difficult to locate for home landscape use. It seemingly has less cold tolerance, and its use should be limited to south Florida.

Darling plum has stiff, thick leaves, oval in shape, and with a rounded tip that curves downward. Plants are monoecious, and flowering occurs on new growth in late spring and early summer. As in black ironwood, the flowers are small, without petals, and rather inconspicuous. Fruit ripen by late summer. They are purple, egg shaped, and edible. Birds favor them also.

Darling plum makes an interesting addition to a mixed south Florida hammock understory. If you can locate it, use it as an accent with other small trees, such as stoppers and black ironwood. This is a species that should have wider use in the home landscape.

Darling plum (*Reynosia septentrionalis*). Photo by Roger Hammer, with permission.

UNDERSTORY SHRUBS

It is sometimes difficult deciding if a plant is a shrub or a subcanopy tree because in nature many woody plants can grow as both. If it occurs with multiple trunks arising near the ground, it is shrub-like, and if it (more often than not) has a single trunk before branching out above the ground, it is treelike. Genetic diversity, browsing by wildlife, accidental loss of the top of the plant in its early life, and other factors can change the typical growth form, however, and it is not uncommon to see both forms growing in close proximity to each other. The species I've included below are those that I most often see occurring in nature as multiple-stemmed woody plants. Most of them can be "trained" to grow more treelike, if pruned that way. If you wish to keep a shrub from becoming multiple-trunked, select a main stem and prune off the others as they arise near the ground. As the plant matures, it will adopt that main stem as a trunk. The look you desire is somewhat in your hands, but realize that shrubs want to be shrubs, and there are many aesthetic, wildlife use, and structural reasons why shrubs are important. I believe both subcanopy trees and shrubs should be used in the shady landscape.

North and Central Florida

Pipestem (*Agarista populifolia*)

Pipestem occurs naturally within a relatively small region of north-central Florida, but it can be grown throughout north and central Florida if given some consideration for its habitat needs. In nature, pipestem is found in moist acidic soils, often near streams, and beneath the canopy of deciduous trees. In the landscape it can tolerate less than optimal conditions but will not truly prosper if kept too dry and/or unprotected from midday sun. Pipestem is a member of the azalea/blueberry family (Ericaceae) and shares some of those family traits. It acclimates very slowly after planting and should be watered well for at least the first year to get it established. The specimen Alexa and I have in our landscape is not in an optimal place but has fared well with no irrigation now that it is fully established.

Eventually, pipestem reaches a mature height of about 10 feet. Its many arching branches, clothed all year in shiny bright green elliptical leaves, make it always attractive as a foliage plant, but the large number of fragrant bell-shaped white flowers in late spring make it an exceptional addition to the shade garden.

Pipestem (*Agarista populifolia*)

The blooms attract a wide assortment of pollinators, but the dry seed capsules that follow are of little value to other wildlife.

I find pipestem to be most effective in the landscape when used as a specimen near trails, where its fragrance and beauty can be easily admired. Do not crowd it; give it plenty of room for its arching branches to grow unhindered, and do not plant it in evergreen shade or it will never flower effectively. Pipestem is widely propagated by nurseries that specialize in native plants and should not be difficult to find for the home landscape.

Beautyberry (*Callicarpa americana*)

Beautyberry is one of the most widely used native shrubs in Florida and easily one of the most adaptable. Occurring statewide in nearly every possible setting, it can be used in the shade garden if placed where it will get a bit of direct light during the day or high amounts of filtered light throughout. Do not plant beautyberry in deep shade or it will get leggy and will not bloom or fruit adequately.

Beautyberry grows quickly and reaches a mature height of about 6 feet within a few years. It is deciduous and produces many arching branches off the main stem. If allowed to grow naturally, well-grown specimens will be as wide as they are tall. The foliage should be a rich green; specimens given too

Beautyberry (*Callicarpa americana*)

much light are often yellowish. Each leaf is oval and sharply toothed. When bruised they are also aromatic. Flowering occurs in late spring and early summer, well after the leaves have formed. Small clusters of pale pink blooms encircle the stem and form along it for much of its length. By fall, large numbers of magenta berries, about ⅛ inch in diameter, are ripe. Beautyberry fruit are edible and can be made into a jelly, but I prefer to leave them to the birds. White-fruited forms are available and these produce white flowers.

Beautyberry can be planted in clusters to form a visual screen, but I prefer to use them as accents near the edge of the canopy or within a well-defined gap in the overhead canopy. Do not crowd this sprawling shrub or try to force it into a small landscape setting by keeping it pruned. Its beauty is its form and its fruit, and these features must have space to achieve their full potential. This is a commonly propagated species and should be easy to find from commercial sources. Of course, if you wait long enough, you might get one planted by a visiting bird.

Sweet shrub (Strawberry bush) (*Calycanthus floridus*)

Sweet shrub occurs sporadically in many north Florida counties but is listed as a threatened species. A deciduous understory shrub, it spreads by underground suckers and eventually forms small thickets of thin, straight reddish brown stems between 6 and 9 feet tall. The highly aromatic leaves are dark

Sweet shrub (*Calycanthus floridus*). Photo by Eleanor Dietrich, with permission.

green and oval in shape with prominent deep veins. Flowers are produced in spring. They are deep maroon in color and produce a strong fragrance somewhat reminiscent of ripe bananas and/or strawberries, hence its other common name. The fragrance is variable, however, and certain clones are commercially available that are grown specifically for this attribute. Early settlers used these aromatic flowers in their dresser drawers to keep their clothes smelling sweet. A somewhat fleshy fruit is produced in fall that has very limited wildlife value.

Sweet shrub is a somewhat difficult species to incorporate into a shade garden because it suckers (and looks best when allowed to). I like it best in expansive settings where it can be used as a screen. Use it near a trail, however, if you wish to admire its fragrant blooms. Once established, sweet shrub is adaptable to most typical landscape settings, but it requires cold during the winter to bloom and achieve its full growth. I have kept plants for more than 20 years in Pinellas County, and they have survived but never flowered. Provide it with a good woodland setting, filtered light during the summer, and lots of sun during the early spring. Many nurseries propagate this native shrub and various flower color and fragrance forms are available.

Dogwoods (*Cornus* spp.)

Most of us in the South are familiar with flowering dogwood, but the many wonderful shrubs that comprise the bulk of this genus have been largely ignored. Shrubby dogwoods are found in nearly every natural habitat in north and central Florida and they make wonderful additions to landscapes where color and attractiveness to wildlife are valued. They are deciduous and produce good fall color. In the spring, they produce many clusters of white flowers at the ends of each stem, and these ripen in late summer and fall into colorful small berries that are relished by songbirds. The two species described below are the most adaptable shrubby dogwoods for Florida shade gardens.

Silky dogwood (*C. ammomum*)

Silky dogwood is native to the understory of moist soil woodlands in a few north Florida panhandle counties. It is far more common to our north. Silky dogwood is a multistemmed shrub that may reach 15 feet at maturity. Each stem arches; the new branches are reddish and covered by silky "hairs." The foliage is ovate, wider than most other dogwoods, and without noticeable teeth along the leaf margins. Flowering occurs in spring. Rounded clusters of small white flowers are produced at the ends of each stem. These attract pollinators and the birds that feed on them. The fruit ripen in fall and form panicles of pale blue "plums," spotted by white dots, each ⅓ inch in diameter. The fruit are its showiest feature.

Silky dogwood is only rarely available from commercial sources in Florida, and stock originating from states to our north should not be used as it is likely

Silky dogwood (*Cornus amomum*). Photo by Gil Nelson, with permission.

to fail in our climate. Like many wetland plants, however, it is more adaptable to home landscape settings than its narrow natural range would suggest. The specimen I have in my Pinellas county landscape, for example, is thriving in my sometimes droughty woodland conditions. Just make sure it is well watered during the first year to adequately establish it. Use silky dogwood in small clusters (3–5) if you have adequate room because this most effectively shows off its best attributes. In smaller settings, it works well mixed with other spring blooming shrubs beneath a deciduous canopy.

Roughleaf dogwood (*C. asperifolia*)

Though some plant taxonomists have considered this shrub to be a variant of the more common swamp dogwood (*C. foemina*), it is unique enough to be given species status. Native to upland woodland habitats throughout north and north-central Florida, roughleaf dogwood is the most widespread and adaptable shrubby dogwood for home landscape settings. Mature specimens reach a height of 15 feet. The stiff stems are rough to the touch, as are the small lance-shaped leaves. Flowering occurs in spring. Flat clusters of tiny white flowers are produced at the tips of each branch. By fall, the ⅛-inch blue fruit are ripe and ready for the songbirds that have been waiting in anticipation.

Despite its adaptability and its overall landscape value, roughleaf dogwood is only infrequently available from commercial sources specializing in native plants, and it may take some sleuthing to find. Use this dogwood throughout

Roughleaf dogwood (*Cornus asperifolia*)

north and central Florida beneath the canopy of deciduous trees. It can take higher levels of sunlight in north Florida, but I think its best use is in a mixed landscape. Scatter it widely in a more spacious setting or as an accent where space is limited. This is not an especially showy species, but it provides some spring color, good fall color, and exceptional wildlife value.

Coral bean (*Erythrina herbacea*)

Coral bean is found statewide in nearly every conceivable habitat, from coastal dunes to the interior of shady woodlands. It performs best when given higher levels of sunlight, but it flowers and grows well with much less. This is a deciduous shrub that often produces many stiff upright branches from a short, thick woody stem. These stems are covered by prickly thorns. In north Florida, coral bean is often less than 6 feet tall, but in semitropical south Florida, it can reach mature heights of 15 feet. Elongated flower stalks arise from the ends of each stem in early spring, before the leaves, and these produce racemes of 1½-inch tubular red flowers that are extremely showy. Hummingbirds are especially drawn to them, but they also attract sulfur butterflies and bumblebees. The leaves are compound, in threes, each triangular in shape. In the fall, the pollinated flowers give rise to bumpy beans that split open to reveal coral red seeds. These are not poisonous (as I have sometimes read), but they have only marginal use to seed-eating wildlife.

Coral bean (*Erythrina herbacea*)

Coral bean is widely propagated statewide because of its showy spring blooms and value to hummingbirds. Because of its prickly nature, do not use it near walkways where you are apt to bump into it, but do not put it so deep into the landscape that you cannot view its spring flowering. I like coral bean when used as an accent in a small landscape or widely scattered in a more spacious one. Give it a little space and plenty of sunlight in the winter and spring. As a hummingbird plant, it is best used in north and north-central Florida where the ruby-throated hummingbird nests. In landscapes farther south, timing hummingbird migration with the coral bean flowering period is not always reliable.

Hearts-a-bustin' (*Euonymus americanus*)

Hearts-a-bustin' has been given a number of other common names, including strawberry bush and wahoo, and it is the most widely occurring native member of this genus in Florida. Found throughout north and central Florida, hearts-a-bustin' is resident to deciduous woodlands with adequate moisture and fertility. It produces many upright, somewhat spindly stems that attain a mature height of 6 feet. The elliptical leaves appear opposite on the stems, are shiny green, and have very fine teeth along the margin. They are deciduous late in the fall. Flowering typically occurs in March to early April. They occur on long thin stalks and are small and greenish. What gives this thin shrub its

Hearts-a-bustin' (*Euonymus americanus*)

many names and its landscape value are the fruit that ripen in late summer. The ripe seed capsules are somewhat spiky and resemble a strawberry. Once they are fully ripe, they split open and this exposes the bright red seeds that dangle on thin threads until eaten by birds or falling to the ground.

Hearts-a-bustin' is an interesting accent to a mixed woodland understory. It is adaptable to typical landscape settings, but should be used under a deciduous canopy to ensure sufficient sunlight to flower and set fruit. Use it in small clumps in the middle of a landscape so that it can make its presence known in fall but be inconspicuous the rest of the year. This species is commonly grown by commercial sources and should not be difficult to locate for home landscape use.

Privets (*Forestiera* spp.)

Florida is home to several privets that make valuable additions to the home landscape, adaptable for use in a shade garden but also for sunny locations. Flatwoods privet (*F. ligustrina*) and Godfrey's privet (*F. godfreyi*) are wonderful deciduous shrubs for north and north-central Florida landscapes, but they are only rarely available commercially and will not be specifically addressed in this book. They offer nothing additional to the more widely grown Florida privet, described below.

Florida privet (*F. segregata*)

Florida privet is an exceptionally adaptable shrub, naturally found in every coastal county in peninsular Florida. It can be used statewide, however, from open sunny settings to areas with shade. It will not perform well, however, in dense evergreen shade. Florida privet is tardily deciduous; it keeps its leaves through winter and loses them for a brief period about the time it flowers. The leaves are elliptical, small, and bright green in color, making this a wonderful foliage plant and screen in areas where an otherwise unappealing view needs to be blocked. Florida privet stays denser when given higher light levels. It can be sheared regularly to maintain a preferred height and density, but when left to grow unchecked, it will reach a mature height of 9 feet.

Flowering occurs in early spring. The flowers are small and greenish but quite fragrant. The fragrance is appealing to some and not so to others, but it attracts a huge assembly of pollinating insects, including many pollinating flies. Florida privet is dioecious so only the female plants bear fruit. The small olive-shaped purple fruit are highly prized by mockingbirds, cardinals, and

Florida privet
(*Forestiera segregata*)

other fruit-eating birds, especially because they ripen in very early summer when such fruit is rare in nature.

Florida privet is a valuable addition to the landscape where birds are desired and in situations where a screen is also wanted. Otherwise, it is not exceptionally showy and does not make a dramatic landscape statement. It will not flower well or grow as full if planted in too much shade. Use Florida privet (or the other two species mentioned above) at the edge of a woodland landscape to provide a hard break between the shade garden and sunnier areas. Florida privet is widely grown commercially and should be relatively easy to locate.

Witch alder (*Fothergilla gardenii*)

One of my favorite plants in our shade garden is our witch alder. Witch alder is a beautifully different native shrub that adds color to the spring and fall shade garden. Native to only four counties in the central panhandle, it is listed as a state endangered species. Within this narrow region, it occurs in low woodlands, near water, but never in saturated soil. Despite all this, it shows far more adaptability in the home landscape and can be successfully grown

Witch alder (*Fothergilla gardenii*). Photos by Gil Nelson, with permission.

into central Florida, once well established. Witch alder is a small deciduous shrub that rarely exceeds 3 feet in height. Its new growth is reddish and the foliage is rounded; each leaf has a crenulate edge with pointed teeth along the margin. In the fall, these leaves turn beautiful shades of orange and golden yellow. These attributes make it an attractive foliage plant, but it's the flowers that make it an exceptional one. Flowering occurs in spring. Elongated "fingers" of flowers emerge from the ends of each stem, each comprising many tiny bright-white flowers, tinged in pink. These "bottlebrush" racemes of flowers make it the center of attention, regardless of everything else that might be blooming around it.

Because of its small size, witch alder is a wonderful shrub to use in mass near the front of the shade garden or along trails. It can be used effectively as an accent in a small garden setting but looks best when massed in clusters of at least three. Protect it from too much sun, but provide ample sunlight in winter and early spring or it will not bloom well. Witch alder is only sporadically available from commercial native nurseries in Florida but is well worth the hunt. Although it has very limited wildlife value, its beauty is hard to duplicate.

Witch hazel (*Hamamelis virginiana*)

Witch hazel is a close relative of witch alder but shares few of the other's attributes except for the shape of its foliage. Witch hazel is a large deciduous shrub that can reach 20 feet or more at maturity. Its many branches grow in a zigzag manner. In Florida, witch hazel occurs in the understory of deciduous woodlands with average moisture from the northern border into the north-central peninsula. It is well adapted to most landscape settings to south-central Florida, but needs protection from summer sun when grown farther south.

Witch hazel makes an attractive foliage plant for the shade garden during most of the year but is exceptional in the late fall when its dull green leaves turn brilliant gold. Flowering occurs in late fall to early winter. Each bloom comprises four thin "spidery" twisted yellow petals. Though not exceptionally showy, they are interesting and add color at a time when little else is generally happening in the landscape. Pollinated flowers form seed capsules that have little wildlife value.

Witch hazel has a long and storied history as a medicinal plant, and extracts from its bark have long been used to treat a wide variety of maladies among Native Americans and early settlers to today. It is not widely available from commercial sources in Florida. You may have to hunt a bit to add it to your Florida shade garden.

Witch hazel (*Hamamelis virginiana*)

Oakleaf hydrangea (*Hydrangea quercifolia*)

Though hydrangeas are used throughout North American landscapes, only the native oakleaf hydrangea is adaptable enough to be used in much of north and central Florida. The closely related wild hydrangea (*H. arborescens*) is a beautiful shrub but reaches its southern limit in the Florida panhandle and is not adaptable to most landscape settings in the state. In nature, oakleaf hydrangea is largely confined to limey soils but can be used well outside those parameters in the home landscape when provided the proper growing conditions. It becomes a large (to 12 feet) multistemmed specimen with arching branches and peeling orange-brown bark. The leaves appear in spring and are large, deeply lobed, and toothed along the margins. Though the Latin and common names suggest otherwise, I believe they look more like maple than oak leaves. They turn a rich wine-red in late fall. Like other hydrangeas, snowball clusters of white flowers are produced in late spring to early summer. Papery covered seeds ripen several months later that have little wildlife value.

Use oakleaf hydrangea in semishade; never in deep evergreen shade or it will slowly expire and rarely bloom. It is adaptable to soil pH and moisture, once established, but is one of the few woodland shrubs that excels near a foundation of a concrete block home. Because single plants are robust, it makes an excellent accent plant near the back of a small woodland planting or

Oakleaf hydrangea (*Hydrangea quercifoli*

in the middle of an expansive one. It also makes an effective hedge or screen. Oakleaf hydrangea is widely propagated and should be relatively easy to find from commercial sources.

Hollies (*Ilex* spp.)

Hollies are a wide and varied group and many have been traditionally incorporated into home landscapes. They can be evergreen or deciduous, but all are dioecious. Only females produce fruit, but a male should be planted nearby to ensure pollination. Most nurseries do not sex their hollies, so it may be necessary to purchase them in threes or more to stack the odds of getting at least one of each sex. If you can, purchase your plants in the spring when they are flowering. Look for the small anthers that produce pollen when choosing the male. Female plants will have a vase-like structure at the base of each flower and a small needlelike structure above it for the pollen to stick to. For wildlife and color, it is best to maximize females and minimize males in your landscape. Plants with fruit, purchased later in the year, are females, but plants without fruit can be either. Many hollies require high light levels to perform well. The ones described below make good additions to shady landscapes. All of these produce red fruit, though yellow-fruited forms are available for some.

Carolina holly (*I. ambigua*)

Carolina holly occurs in nearly every upland habitat of north and central Florida, from the full sand and sun of Florida scrub to relatively moist fertile woodland understories within hammocks. It performs best in sunny locations but will do well in shade if given high light levels in winter and spring and/or good indirect light year round. I like Carolina holly a lot. Its Latin name comes from the fact that it doesn't really look like most hollies—at least foliage-wise. Its deep coppery stems and deep-green slightly serrated leaves make it look a bit like a cherry. Normally, it remains below 10 feet tall, with a crooked trunk and many thin spreading limbs. This is a deciduous holly, and the leaves turn a dull yellow in late fall. What I like best about this holly is its fruit. Female plants produce large numbers that ripen by fall. They are a brilliant, almost translucent, coral red; they remain on the plant well into winter and are especially visible because the leaves are absent.

Carolina holly is adaptable but needs good drainage and cannot tolerate too much moisture for extended periods. Use it in small clusters near the middle section of a mixed woodland. Because it is deciduous, it does not make

Carolina holly
(*Ilex ambigua*)

a good screen, but it provides great wildlife nesting cover and food value in a landscape where this is important. This holly is not widely available commercially, but there are always a few that keep it in the trade and a few that sex their stock.

Possumhaw holly (*I. decidua*)

Possumhaw holly is another deciduous holly, native throughout north and central Florida. Unlike Carolina holly, it is most often encountered in moist soil habitats but can tolerate average landscape conditions once established. Water it well during the first year and it is unlikely to need supplemental watering afterward. Possumhaw holly reaches a mature height of about 30 feet. Its light-colored trunk is crooked and it produces many stiff branches that form an irregular crown. The foliage is oval in shape with wavy margins and rounded teeth. Female plants produce many bright red fruit, a bit deeper in color and somewhat larger in size than Carolina holly. They are held well into the winter months, if birds don't eat them sooner, and these may be its best landscape feature.

Possumhaw holly (*Ilex decidua*)

Though possumhaw holly is widely used in landscapes to our north, it is only sporadically propagated in Florida. I like it best when used in small groupings in a woodland setting near water. If you wish to add it, do not purchase your plants from sources outside Florida because these plants are unlikely to flower and fruit well.

Yaupon holly (*I. vomitoria*)

Yaupon holly is extremely adaptable and the most widely grown native holly in Florida. Common to a very diverse collection of native habitats, it occurs on back beach dunes as well as the understory of woodlands. In too much shade, it will become leggy and not flower and fruit well, but it will perform just fine if used in high levels of filtered sun or beneath the canopy of deciduous trees where it will get full sun in winter and early spring. Yaupon holly occurs throughout north and central Florida. Its light-colored trunk is often crooked and it produces many stiff crooked limbs, like possumhaw holly. It is evergreen, however, and its deep green, narrow leaves have a simple wavy margin. Many forms occur in nature, and these have been selected and propagated by commercial nurseries. Hence, it is possible to select compact and dwarf forms, as well as varieties with distinctly weeping branches. Most, except the dwarf forms, reach a mature height of 20 feet.

Yaupon holly makes an ideal screen for upland sites. Its dense foliage provides excellent cover for songbirds and other wildlife and the bright red fruit

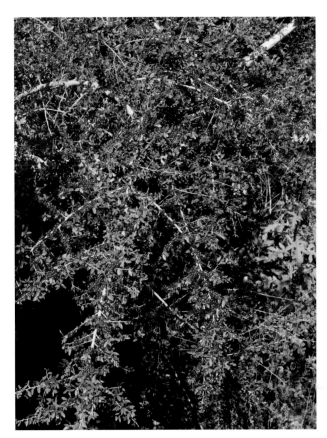

Yaupon holly
(*Ilex vomitoria*)

on female plants are an excellent wildlife food, especially in late winter and early spring. Yaupon holly responds well to shearing and its rambling growth form is often enhanced by a bit of judicious pruning. The weeping forms make interesting accent plants for sunny locations. In the shade garden, I prefer the compact forms as they remain denser and highlight the beautiful foliage of this species. The Latin name comes from its use by Native Americans during religious ceremonies. A tea made from its roasted leaves has caffeine, and this was drunk to excess at times to help generate visions.

Yellow anise (*Illicium parviflora*)

Yellow anise is endemic to a few counties of the central peninsula along wetland edges, though it is used throughout north and central Florida in a wide variety of landscape settings. I have seen it used well in parking lot medians, for example, in full sun and poor soil, but it looks best when grown under shade and provided a bit of extra moisture. Unlike red anise, which acts like

Yellow anise (*Illicium parviflora*)

a small tree, yellow anise produces many weak stems that tend to arch under the weight of the foliage. Over time, most plants become wider than tall, reaching a height of about 15 feet. Though it is possible to prune this plant to take up less space, the weeping aspect is destroyed if it is pruned too severely. Like other members of this genus, yellow anise has elliptical thick shiny leaves that are extremely fragrant when bruised. As it is evergreen, this beautiful foliage is present year round. As the Latin name implies, the flowers are small and almost inconspicuous. Each is yellow and produced in the late spring.

Yellow anise is very adaptable but a bit too sprawling for small landscapes. Use it as a screen in larger settings and keep it lightly pruned if it begins to crowd out its neighbors. Plan for the room it needs so that your pruning is not overly severe. Alexa and I have maintained our yellow anise for more than 10 years in our woody understory with no supplemental irrigation, and it has prospered; just give it some additional water the first year to make sure it has time to adjust to its new home.

Virginia willow (*Itea virginica*)

Virginia willow is not a willow at all, but a member of a separate small family with quite different characteristics. The common name is likely the result of its affinity for wetland conditions, and unlike many wetland plants, Virginia willow cannot be used in dry upland sites with any real success. This species

Virginia willow (*Itea virginica*)

occurs throughout Florida. For much of its range, it is deciduous, but in extreme south Florida it is nearly evergreen. Mature specimens eventually reach a height of 6 feet, but it is a thin-stemmed species with arching branches that rarely stand taller than about 4 feet. The leaves are elliptical, noticeably toothed along the margin, and several inches long. They turn a maroon red prior to leaf fall. Virginia willow's best feature is its flower stalks, produced in spring, at the tips of each stem. Racemes of small white, sweetly scented flowers make it quite showy for several weeks. Light pink flowered forms are also available commercially. Pollinated flowers ripen into small hard capsules with little wildlife value.

Virginia willow is best used in moist to wet soil, in areas where it will receive adequate light in the winter and spring. If planted in deep evergreen shade, it will fail to flower and eventually weaken and die. It also tends to sucker and form colonies over time. Give it plenty of room or be prepared to prune the suckers repeatedly. I like to use this species along the edge of ponds and other water features, in expansive settings where it can spread. In mass, it is a beautiful plant.

Mountain laurel (*Kalmia latifolia*)

I would consider moving to north Florida to use mountain laurel in my landscape. It is one of our most beautiful native shrubs but not an easy one to use outside its native range in Florida. For the most part, this is an Appalachian

Mountain laurel (*Kalmia latifolia*)

species that has continued to reside in a few places within the central and western panhandle. In these woodlands, it receives slightly cooler temperatures and somewhat richer soils than the norm. Mountain laurel is an evergreen shrub that can eventually reach a mature height of 25 feet. It produces many branches off the main stem and the leaves are thick and elliptical, much like the rhododendrons (*Rhododendron* spp.), which are its close relatives. For much of the year, mountain laurel is a rather nondescript, wide-crowned shrub. This changes dramatically, however, when it comes into bloom in spring. The rich pink, cup-shaped flowers are borne in clusters across the top of each plant. They attract the attention of every pollinator in the neighborhood, as well as every human who chances to see it. Eventually, the pollinated flowers form dry seed capsules that provide very little food value to wildlife.

Mountain laurel is one of the most prized native landscape plants in the Southeast, but it requires the right location to prosper. This is a resident of deciduous woodland slopes. It cannot tolerate too much moisture for even short periods, so never plant it where the soils might get soggy. It also requires high light levels during the late winter and early spring to flower adequately. Never put it in evergreen shade or in deep shade. Mountain laurel prefers filtered or early morning sun even during the summer and fall. Despite its delicate looks, it also abhors too much "fussing." Select the right spot for it, plant it, make sure it receives water during establishment if needed, and then leave it alone. Mountain laurel is killed more often by too much care than by neglect.

If you wish to attempt this beautiful shrub, purchase your plants from Florida stock. Small specimens may establish quicker than larger ones; larger specimens tend to need more water and time to become established and a higher percentage do not make the transition from the nursery pot to the ground. Mountain laurel makes a splendid specimen plant in a small landscape and a breathtaking mass when planted in small groupings of three or more.

Dog Hobble (*Leucothoe axillaris*)

Dog hobble is another member of the azalea/blueberry family but is far less known than mountain laurel and its other close cousins. It occurs naturally in much of north Florida and sporadically into central portions of the state, mostly near streams, springs, and other moving water bodies and always beneath the shade of deciduous trees. It is an evergreen shrub, rarely reaching 4 feet tall, with a thin main stem and a tendency to arch. The leaves are a deep glossy green and elliptical in shape. Overall, this is an attractive foliage plant that fits well into a border along trails and edges. Flowering occurs in early spring. Like many other members of this family, short racemes of white bell-shaped flowers adorn the ends of each stem. In many specimens, the white blooms are edged in pale pink. Pollinated flowers give rise to dry seed capsules that ripen in the fall.

Though dog hobble is a wetland plant, it can tolerate average soil conditions adequately once established. Like pipestem, water it well during the first

Dog hobble (*Leucothoe axillaris*)

year and during extended droughty periods to ensure its roots have extended beyond the original root ball and well into the soil. I like this attractive evergreen shrub best when used in mass near trails and the front of the shade garden, where its flowers can be most admired. Dog hobble is grown by several commercial native plant sources and is normally not difficult to locate.

Shiny lyonia (*Lyonia lucida*)

Lyonias are also members of the blueberry/azalea family and include a number of beautiful shrubs deserving of landscape use, but only shiny lyonia is well adapted to the typical conditions present in a Florida shade garden. Others, like coastalplain and piedmont staggerbush (*L. fruticosa* and *L. mariana*, respectively) are best used in sunny locations. Shiny lyonia occurs statewide in a wide variety of growing conditions. It can be found in shallow standing water beneath the canopy of bald cypress (*Taxodium distichum*) and in full sun at the top of a sandy ridge. This adaptability allows its use in a shade garden setting as well.

Shiny lyonia is an evergreen shrub with a thin twisting trunk and numerous short, weak branches. Mature specimens reach 10 feet in height with a very narrow crown. Its leaves are shiny, light green, and elliptical. Overall, this is an attractive plant, but not especially distinctive. The major source of its beauty is its spring flowering. Shiny lyonia produces many racemes of pink

Shiny lyonia (*Lyonia lucida*)

to almost rose-colored bell-shaped flowers at the tips of its branches. They are excellent nectar sources for butterflies, bees, and other pollinators, but the ripened dry seed capsules have little wildlife value.

This adaptable shrub would not be my first choice for the landscape, but it works well in adding diversity to a mixed understory setting. Use it in the middle to rear portion of the understory in small clusters. Water it well for the first year to make sure it's established; after that it should require little care. Shiny lyonia is widely propagated by commercial native plant nurseries and should be easy to locate.

Wax myrtle (*Myrica cerifera*)

Wax myrtle is so commonly used in home landscapes in Florida that it's easy to forget it's a native plant. Occurring statewide in a variety of upland and wetland locations, it is exceptionally adaptable, quick growing, but not especially long-lived. It is evergreen with a strong central stem and many thinner side branches. Mature specimens can attain a height of 35 feet, but most are about 20 feet tall. In sunny locations, mature wax myrtles are dense and wide-crowned, but in shadier sites they tend to be thinner and less effective as screens and bird nesting sites.

Wax myrtle is often used in landscapes simply for its attractive foliage and adaptability. Its flowers are nondescript, but its gray waxy berries are signifi-

Wax myrtle (*Myrica cerifera*)

cant. The waxy outer covering of these fruit have been used for centuries to make bayberry candles and the fruit itself is an important food source for many wintering birds. As wax myrtle is dioecious, only females produce fruit. For this reason, it is worth the effort to plant it in multiples of at least three and to maximize the number of females to the extent possible. One male for every dozen females is sufficient for good pollination.

In shady settings, wax myrtle is less effective as a screen, but it still is best used for that purpose and not as a specimen. Routine pruning increases density and is advised for this species when grown in deeper shade. When possible, use wax myrtle in filtered sun or in locations where it will receive at least a few hours of direct sun daily.

Needle palm (*Rhaphidophyllum hystrix*)

Florida has many native palms, but surprisingly few are routinely used in home landscapes. One of the best for shady areas is needle palm. Needle palm occurs throughout north and central Florida, beneath the understory of larger trees and often in moist soil. As a trunkless palm and one adapted to low light, it makes an interesting addition to a landscape, especially in those where the look of palms is desired. Needle palm can reach a mature height of 4 feet, but takes a great many years to do so. Though slow growing, it is long lived and extremely hardy. Its common name comes from the sharp needles

Needle palm (*Rhapidophyllum hystrix*)

that develop between each leaf. They serve to ward off browsing wildlife but were widely used by Native Americans and early settlers as needles.

I love the look of needle palm in the landscape, but it works best when used in an expansive setting where it can be placed away from trails. The dark green, deeply dissected fronds, silvery below, are attractive, and the dark stout base adds to its aesthetic value. Flowering occurs in late spring or early summer and clusters of brownish red, rounded fruit ripen several months later. The fruit are covered in tan hairs and are not especially valuable to wildlife. Needle palm is widely propagated by commercial nurseries. Because they grow slowly, the price you pay is a reflection of the many years the nurseryperson has invested in getting it to this size.

Azaleas (*Rhododendron* spp.)

Nearly every magazine devoted to southern gardening has used a cover photo of blooming azaleas to entice readers to purchase it. Over the years, we have come to accept azaleas as a necessary component of every attractive landscape and a great many of us have added them. While azaleas are a southern phenomenon, the species we most commonly use are from China and Japan. Most of us have ignored the many beautiful species native to Florida for no

Native azaleas, *Rhododendron canescens*, have a simple elegance and highly fragrant flowers. Though they bloom for only a few weeks each spring, their impact on a landscape can be significant.

good reason. Native azaleas rarely have the same compact growth form seen in their oriental cousins, most are deciduous, and most have smaller tubular flowers, but they compensate by being wonderfully fragrant and useful to pollinators (including hummingbirds), and by their simple elegance. Alexa and I have some non-native azaleas in a small portion of our yard and we admire our neighbors' plants when they bloom, but we *treasure* the many native specimens we have added and we have run out of space to add more or we would.

All azaleas perform best in acidic soils that are moist and fertile. Do not plant most of them in soils that stay soggy for long periods of time, or their roots may rot. They also need sunlight to bloom well. Azaleas, planted in deep shade beneath an evergreen tree, will slowly weaken and die. Used at the edge of the canopy where they receive early or late sun works much better, but the best locations are those beneath deciduous trees. The energy they receive from winter and early spring sunlight is extremely important in generating good blooms. For the rest of the year, filtered sun can suffice. Azaleas also take time to establish after planting. Like other members of this family, their fine root systems do not quickly emerge from the root ball formed inside the pot they were grown in. Water them deeply during planting and make sure the soil beneath their roots stays moist during the first year after planting in order for them to become well established. All five native species make good landscape additions to a shade garden, and they can be pushed well outside their natural ranges into central Florida, if care is given to meet their growing requirements. In former times, azaleas and rhododendrons were separated taxonomically by whether they were deciduous or evergreen. That distinction is no longer used, and all our native species are included in the genus *Rhododendron*. Native azaleas can be pruned to maintain a more compact shape, but do so after they have bloomed in late spring. All are propagated by commercial sources and are not difficult to find for home landscape purposes. Mature specimens all reach about 15 feet in height, though they grow fairly slowly.

Alabama azalea (*R. alabamensis*)

Alabama azalea is a rare plant in Florida, occurring only in a small portion of Leon and Jefferson Counties, near Tallahassee. It is also the most demanding of our five native azaleas in terms of growing conditions. Alabama azalea requires sandy soils that are frequently watered. During periods of drought, it will need some supplemental irrigation to stay healthy. Give it a good top

Alabama azalea (*Rhododendron alabamensis*)

Florida flame azalea (*Rhododendron austrinum*)

dressing of leaf mulch, too, as it prefers more fertility than most. If you can give it your attention, Alabama azalea is a beautiful plant. It will reach 10 feet at maturity and form a wide crown. Flowers are produced in abundance in the spring. They are white, with a lemon yellow spot at the base of the floral tube.

Florida flame azalea (*R. austrinum*)

If I had to choose, I would pick Florida flame azalea as my favorite of the lot, but I have always been partial to brilliant oranges and yellows and the blooms of this species are definitely brilliant. Florida flame azalea is native to the central and western panhandle, along woodland slopes and often above streams. In these areas, it can occur in mass, setting the entire woodland ablaze in color. Flower color is variable and ranges from nearly brick orange to canary yellow, but most are bright orange. Though confined naturally to extreme north Florida, the specimens in our landscape have done exceptionally well over the last decade. Blooming is best, however, following a cold winter and a moist summer and fall.

Pink azalea (*R. canescens*)

Pink (or Pinxter) azalea is one of the most widely distributed native azaleas in Florida and the one most widely planted in home landscapes. Native to north and north-central Florida in moist to seasonally wet woodlands, this species adapts well to most landscape settings and can tolerate more water at its roots than most. As its common name implies, the spring flowers are normally pink, but this can range from deep cherry-blossom pink to nearly white. It is not uncommon to find this azalea growing near Florida flame azalea in the wild. In such woodlands, pink azalea is often found a bit lower on the slope, closer to water, and it blooms about a week earlier.

Pink azalea (*Rhododendron canescens*)

Chapman's rhododendron (*Rhododendron minus* var. *chapmanii*)

Chapman's rhododendron (*R. minus* var. *chapmanii*)

Chapman's rhododendron is endemic to Florida and listed as a state and federal endangered species. Native to the edges of acidic woodlands, it is found in semiopen areas that frequently stay moist. Despite this, it adapts well to typical landscape conditions and is surprisingly hardy once established. As its common name implies, Chapman's rhododendron is an evergreen shrub. The leaves are more rounded and leathery than our other native species with rusty hairs on the lower surface, and the stems tend to be lanky with the leaves mostly clustered near the ends. Blooming occurs in spring but a bit later than pink azalea in our landscape. The flowers are more open and less tubular than our other native species and somewhat resemble the oriental azaleas. The pink blossoms are flecked with darker pink spots.

Swamp azalea (*R. viscosum*)

Though swamp azalea is the most widely distributed native azalea in Florida, it is the least used in home landscapes. Naturally occurring as far south as Glades and DeSoto Counties, near Lake Okeechobee, it prefers the seasonally wet conditions found in open pine flatwoods and other wet woodlands. In

Swamp azalea (*Rhododendron viscosum*). Photo by Christina Evans, with permission.

many ways, this native azalea is an exception to the group. It does not adapt well to most home landscape conditions unless given extra moisture during the summer. The flowers do not open until summer, well after the leaves have formed. These flowers are white and somewhat hidden by the foliage. They make their presence known by their sweet fragrance. Swamp azalea should not be used in any location that does not stay moist during the summer. It can tolerate relatively high light levels if kept moist and performs poorly if not given sufficient light during the year. This is an ideal azalea for use near a wetland feature in the landscape at the edge of a canopy or in a light gap.

Rouge plant (*Rivina humilis*)

Rouge plant can look outstanding in the right landscape conditions and exceptionally weedy in others. Over the years, I have used it in a variety of shady landscape settings, and it has performed at both extremes. When it has failed, it has been in areas where it receives too much or too little shade. Finding a balance point is not easily predictable. When grown well, rouge plant is a mostly herbaceous shrub that forms a thin, woody stem and reaches a mature height of 4–5 feet. It is an irregular plant, often with a wide crown and thin lance-shaped leaves that are deciduous in winter. The small white flowers, tinged in pink, can occur year round on spikes produced at the ends of the stems. These eventually form tiny cardinal red berries that are relished by songbirds. As rouge plant can flower and fruit for months at a time, it is an

Rouge plant (*Rivina humilis*)

extremely useful plant for the shade garden, where pollinators and wildlife are important. In too much shade or sun, however, it eventually stresses and dies. Plant it in light gaps in the understory where it will receive at least a few hours of direct sunlight daily or at the edge of a canopy where it will get morning or afternoon sun. This is also a species that looks best if periodically pruned to keep it full. Rouge plant will spread by seed if grown well. Let it fill in and form a dense ground cover. It can be used statewide and is grown by several commercial native plant nurseries.

Dwarf palm/Blue palmetto (*Sabal minor*)

Dwarf palm is a trunkless relative of the ubiquitous cabbage palm, Florida's state tree. Found throughout north and central Florida, it adds a "tropical" look to the understory of a shade garden if used correctly. I like it best when scattered in an expansive setting. In small areas, it can look crowded and out of place, and I think it loses some of its potential landscape impact when used alone as an accent. Dwarf palm has wide-spreading fronds that look bluish gray from a distance, hence its other common name. This adds a great deal of interest within a landscape. It is a long-lived, but slow-growing species; eventually it can reach six feet tall and be about as wide. Flowering occurs from spring to early fall. The flower stalks arise from the center of the stem and stand upright. The tiny white flowers are fragrant and attract a diversity

Dwarf palm
(*Sabal minor*)

of pollinating insects. Small purple fruit form on the stalk and are an excellent food source for songbirds.

Dwarf palm is highly adaptable to most landscape conditions and can tolerate low light levels better than most shrubs for north and central Florida. It is widely grown by commercial nurseries in Florida. Though I often espouse purchasing smaller plants because they establish more quickly, this is one species where paying more for a larger specimen is often worth the investment. Make sure you water it well during establishment and it will prosper for decades without further attention, except an occasional light pruning to remove dead fronds.

Saw palmetto (*Serenoa repens*)

Saw palmetto is ubiquitous in Florida and occurs nearly everywhere from exceedingly dry, sunny habitats to shady, wet woodlands. In most locations, its trunk rambles across the soil surface with the fronds appearing at the end of the stem and curving upward. In the wettest sites, it forms an upright trunk and can reach 15 feet or more. Research has found that saw palmetto rarely grows more than one inch per year, making some specimens many hundreds to a thousand or more years old. This is an exceptionally adaptable, tough plant. If you add it to your landscape, be prepared to keep it for your lifetime.

Saw palmetto (*Serenoa repens*)

Saw palmetto differs from the various *Sabal* species palms in several key ways. Most significantly, it produces sharp "teeth" along its leaf stems (i.e., petioles); hence its common name. These teeth are the bane of every landscape maintenance worker required to prune them; if you use saw palmetto, you will need to prune them. Saw palmetto is capable of forming a new top if the original is lost or pruned off. This kills all the *Sabal* palms and most other species, but it merely reduces the height and girth of a saw palmetto. This can be useful in a landscape setting if your saw palmettos become too large.

When left unchecked, saw palmetto can form multiple leads, each 6–10 feet tall, forming clumps more than 10 feet across. Blooming occurs on stout stalks in late spring. The white flowers are very fragrant and excellent nectar sources for bees and butterflies. Saw palmetto honey is one of Florida's best and one I try to keep in my kitchen year round. The fruit ripens in fall. The large black fruit are too large for birds, and are eaten mostly by raccoons, opossums, and other medium to large mammals. An extract from the fruit is currently much sought after as an ingredient in medicine to treat prostate problems. Saw palmetto is widely propagated commercially. Do not use this plant in small landscape settings or near walkways, trails, or sitting areas. Otherwise, it is a pest-free useful palm. A silver-colored form, native to Florida's east coast, makes an interesting accent to the more widely occurring green form.

Silver buckthorn
(*Sideroxylon
alachuense*)

Silver buckthorn (*Sideroxylon alachuense*)

Silver buckthorn is a rare near-endemic shrub found in only a few north-central Florida counties and a few coastal counties in Georgia. In these locations, it often occurs in the understory, but it can also tolerate full sun. A spiny, crooked, tardily deciduous shrub, silver buckthorn produces a wide crown and a mature height of about 8 feet. In addition to its distinctive shape, its dark green elliptical leaves are densely covered by silvery "hairs" on the underside. With a slight breeze blowing across its crown, the effect is spectacular. Like other buckthorns in this genus, it produces small white fragrant flowers in the spring and deep purple fruit that ripen by fall. The flowers are magnets for pollinating insects, and the fruit are eagerly consumed by songbirds.

Silver buckthorn is difficult to find from commercial nurseries but can usually be found with some determined hunting. They are connoisseur plants; you either love them or fail to appreciate their landscape value, but in the right location this species is outstanding. Use it as an accent, away from paths but near enough to enjoy the fragrance of its blooms and silvery foliage. Do not give it too much shade, or it will become leggy and fail to bloom. Silver buckthorn tolerates limey soils, but does not require them. Once established, it is a slow growing, undemanding plant.

American snowbell (*Styrax americanus*)

American snowbell occurs in seasonally wet woodlands throughout north and central Florida. It most often grows like a shrub but sometimes as a small

American snowbell (*Styrax americanus*)

tree, reaching a height of 25 feet. It has a wide crown and many stiff side branches. American snowbell is deciduous. The leaves are ovate in shape, light green, and several inches long, often with teeth along the leaf margins. Overall, it is rather inconspicuous within its native habitat. This situation changes in spring when the entire plant is covered by white bell-shaped flowers that dangle from every branch. During the several weeks that this shrub is in bloom, it cannot fail to be noticed. The flowers also attract pollinators, but the hard seed capsules that ripen in summer have little wildlife value.

American snowbell will adapt to average landscape soils once established but needs to be watered well for at least the first year. Do not use it in dry sites or in evergreen or deep shade. It requires some direct sun daily to prosper throughout the year, and it flowers best when used under a deciduous canopy. I like this species best when used as an accent in a mixed woodland understory. Place it near enough to a pathway or sitting area to admire it when in bloom, but allow it to "disappear" into the woodland at other times. Given enough moisture, it can also be effectively used in small locations to create a canopy for smaller woodland plants, or use it near a water feature.

Highbush blueberry (*Vaccinium corymbosum*)

Many native blueberries can be grown in semishade, but few produce good berry crops and lush foliage in a true shade garden. Deerberry (*V. stamineum*) has done well for me at the edge of my dry woods, but I don't recommend it

Highbush blueberry (*Vaccinium corymbosum*)

for the typical areas described in this book. In my experience, the best selection for a shade garden is highbush blueberry. Though this species occurs naturally in nearly every conceivable habitat throughout most of Florida, it often occurs in shady woodlands. It is a variable species; some taxonomists recognize two distinct species based on clearly recognizable physical characteristics. For the purposes of this book, I will treat Elliott's blueberry (*V. elliottii*) as equivalent to highbush blueberry and beg forgiveness from my plant taxonomy friends who view it otherwise.

Highbush blueberry is a many-branched deciduous shrub that can eventually reach 12 feet tall. It is narrow crowned with narrow elliptical leaves that are glossy green in color. They turn reddish in the fall and produce a good fall color display. In spring, many white bell-shaped flowers are produced in clusters at the ends of the branches. The flowers attract pollinators, but the sweet deep-purple fruit that ripen in summer attract nearly everything. Highbush blueberry is the foundation of Florida's commercial blueberry industry, and all our commercial varieties have it in their genetic background. If you want to attempt beating the birds to the fruit, the effort is worthwhile.

Blueberries perform best in acidic soils, and they adapt slowly after being planted. Water them well, and make sure you provide supplemental water for at least one year after planting if rains are not regular and deep. Highbush blueberry performs well under a wide variety of conditions, but do not plant it in deep or evergreen shade if you want it to do its best. I like this plant in small clusters in a mixed understory. Keep it close enough to pathways and sitting areas so you can pick some fruit and admire its blooms, but don't count on it as an accent as it is not that showy for most of the year. This native shrub is widely grown by commercial nurseries specializing in native plants.

Viburnums (*Viburnum* spp.)

Viburnums, native or otherwise, are important landscape shrubs that possess attributes that make their status deserving of the attention they get. Relatively pest free and easy to maintain, with attractive foliage and flowers, and quick growing, they add a variety of elements to a landscape not often equaled by other genera. They also provide excellent wildlife value. All of Florida's five native viburnum species make wonderful additions to a shade garden.

Mapleleaf viburnum (*V. acerifolium*)

Of our five native viburnum species, mapleleaf viburnum has the most restricted natural range and is the least used in home landscapes. I find this regrettable, as it is one of the most beautiful. Found in scattered locations throughout the panhandle, mapleleaf viburnum most often is associated with limestone outcroppings in upland deciduous forests. Here, it attains a mature height of 6 feet, on straight wooly stems. As its common name implies, the leaves are reminiscent of sugar maple; usually three-lobed and wide across the middle. This is a deciduous species with wonderful fall color in shades of red, purple, and orange. Flowering occurs in spring before the leaves are well formed. Wide

Mapleleaf viburnum
(*Viburnum acerifolium*)

clusters of small white flowers are formed at the ends of the stems. By fall, the deep purple fruit have ripened and are consumed by songbirds.

Mapleleaf viburnum is only occasionally available from commercial native nurseries in Florida and may take some time to locate. Over the years, I have experimented with all our native species in our Pinellas County landscape and believe it can be successfully used in much of north and central Florida. Though often associated with limey soils, I have not found it to require them, and it seems adaptable to most typical landscape conditions. I like it best as an accent in a mixed woodland understory. Its beautiful fall color, interesting foliage, spring flowers, and wildlife value provide it with enough reason to be more commonly added to the home landscape. Once established, it requires little additional care.

Southern arrowwood (*V. dentatum*)

Southern arrowwood occurs throughout most of north and north-central Florida as an understory shrub in a wide variety of conditions. I have found it near wetlands in near-saturated acidic soils and within well-drained upland forests with exposed limestone. As such, it is an extremely adaptable viburnum and capable of thriving in most home landscape conditions. As its common

Southern arrowwood
(*Viburnum dentatum*)

name implies, southern arrowwood produces numerous straight stiff stems; often it forms small colonies around the original trunk. At maturity, these stems can be 9 feet tall. The foliage is distinctive and attractive. The leaves are formed opposite each other along the stems, are ovate in shape, and have coarse teeth along the margins, hence the Latin name. Though the leaves are somewhat similar to those of mapleleaf viburnum, southern arrowwood leaves are not generally lobed, and they turn a brilliant red to red-orange in fall. Broad clusters of small white flowers are produced in late spring, usually after the foliage has returned, and large clusters of blue-purple fruit ripen in late fall.

Southern arrowwood is commonly propagated and available commercially. Use it in expansive settings as an accent shrub and allow it to form a colony around the parent plant, or use it as a screen, understanding that it is deciduous during the winter. Do not plant southern arrowwood in small gardens as it will eventually usurp most of the space by its suckering tendencies.

Possumhaw viburnum (*V. nudum*)

Possumhaw viburnum occurs in wetland forests throughout north and central Florida. As such, it is best used in moist soil areas and not attempted in droughty conditions. This species often occurs in dense colonies as it tends to sucker outward from the parent plant. Eventually these stems reach a height

Possumhaw viburnum
(*Viburnum nudum*)

of 15 feet. Possumhaw viburnum has glossy green, elliptical leaves that can be several inches long. In the fall, they turn brilliant red in color. Flowering occurs in spring, usually after the leaves have formed. Broad umbels of small white flowers are produced at the end of each stem, which give rise to clusters of round berries that start off pink and ripen to blue. These clusters of fruit are visually attractive and eagerly consumed by songbirds and other wildlife.

Possumhaw viburnum can adapt to many home landscape conditions but will not tolerate soils that are not reasonably moist during the summer. It has a great many wonderful attributes, but its propensity to sucker requires that it be planted in a setting where this can be controlled or where it doesn't matter. I like it best used at the edge of a shady wetland where it can receive some sun. For upland settings or in smaller landscapes, there are better viburnums to be used. This species is routinely propagated and sold by commercial native plant nurseries.

Walter's viburnum (*V. obovatum*)

The most widely propagated native viburnum in Florida is Walter's viburnum. Found nearly statewide, it is exceptionally adaptable and can be used in nearly any landscape setting. Normally, Walter's viburnum occurs at the edges of wetland forests, but it is sometimes found in uplands as well. The first

Walter's viburnum (*Viburnum obovatum*)

one I ever planted was near the foundation of my rental home in Largo. The spot I chose turned out to be gumbo clay, and I literally had to use a pickax to create the hole I planted it in. I watered it once and walked away. The plant took off and never needed another minute of my attention.

Walter's viburnum is nearly evergreen. Its tiny elliptical leaves are held well into the following spring and are lost for just a brief period as the plant flowers. It is often multistemmed, sometimes with a main trunk, with short stout branches. All of these are strong and stiff. Flowering occurs in early spring, well before other viburnums. The clusters of small white flowers are smaller in width than other viburnums, but each plant produces large numbers and the plants are quite showy. Small, cylindrical purple fruit ripen by late summer. They are eaten by wildlife, but not quite as quickly as those of other viburnum species.

Walter's viburnum is extremely adaptable but becomes lanky in deep shade and flowers poorly. Use it in light gaps within a woodland understory, beneath deciduous trees, or at the edge of an evergreen canopy where it will get early or late direct sun. This viburnum is very widely propagated and many forms are available to suit different landscape tastes. A compact form tends to grow more slowly than the standard one and stay denser. Dwarf, weeping, and columnar forms also are available. Walter's viburnum suckers and will form multiple stems that pop up dozens of feet away from the parent. Use it in a space where the suckers can be easily controlled or it may become a nuisance. In the right place, it is a beautiful addition to the landscape.

Rusty viburnum (*V. rufidulum*)

Rusty viburnum is another viburnum that deserves far more attention than it has received to date. Native to upland forest understories in north and north-central Florida, it is adaptable to most landscape conditions into central portions of the state. Rusty viburnum is an irregular shrub with dark blocky bark, somewhat similar to that found on flowering dogwood. Normally no taller than 15 feet, its distinctive foliage sets it apart from others in this group and makes it an interesting accent plant. The oval leaves are deep green and shiny; so shiny that they seem to be oiled. As the sun filters down across the crown of this plant, it literally glistens. By fall, the leaves have turned bright red in color. Broad flower clusters are produced at the ends of each branch in late spring, after the foliage has emerged. These small white blooms eventually form deep purple egg-shaped fruit that are eagerly consumed by songbirds.

I especially like this viburnum and believe it's best used as an accent in a

Rusty viburnum (*Viburnum rufidulum*)

mixed woodland understory, especially one where birds are a consideration. Do not put it under dense shade or it will not perform. Plant it beneath deciduous trees, in a light gap, or at the edge of an evergreen canopy where it will get some sun during early morning or late afternoon. Rusty viburnum does not sucker to the extent many others in this genus do. A few commercial native nursery sources propagate this plant. It may take some searching to find it, but its addition to your landscape will be worth the effort.

Coontie (*Zamia pumila*)

Coontie is our only native cycad, an ancient group of plants, related to pines and other conifers, that was a staple of the flora dominant during the age of dinosaurs. Found statewide in a variety of upland settings, it performs exceptionally well in deep shade as well as full sun. In the shade garden, it can be used nearly everywhere to add texture and a sense of the tropical. Coontie is evergreen. The palmlike feathery leaves emerge off a very stout, short trunk that is mostly underground. Native Americans and early settlers pounded and soaked the starch granules from these trunks to make arrowroot starch that was then used for breads and other dishes. Such widespread use of this plant caused its significant decline in the wild, and it was listed by the state of Florida and given extra protection. Coontie has made a major return to native Florida (though it is still given legal protection) and is widely propagated and planted in developed landscapes everywhere.

Coontie grows quite slowly, especially during the first few years. Mature specimens stand two feet tall with multiple tops, but this can take a decade or more to achieve. The plants are dioecious, and both sexes produce elongated cones. Female cones that have been pollinated ripen in about a year and produce dozens of seeds covered by a bright orange oily aril. These have little wildlife value, though a beautiful butterfly, the atala hairstreak, feeds on the foliage in extreme south Florida. In our Pinellas County landscape, we have used coontie in a variety of settings. Specimens planted in spots that almost never receive a direct ray of sunlight have prospered beautifully, as have those given more filtered light and those that get a few hours each day of direct sun. Coontie are sometimes subject to sooty mold as a result of scale insect infestations. I have not found this to be a long-term problem, and it has resolved itself in my landscape without the use of insecticides. Should the problem be more severe in your landscape, it is usually treatable with insecticidal soaps or neem oil. Coontie often adds a new flush of growth in spring. When it does this, the older leaves began to sag and bend down toward the stem, making the plant look wilted and causing needless concern about its health. Do not plant coontie in extremely wet sites; use it in small groupings near paths and sitting areas to create borders and aesthetic interest.

Coontie
(*Zamia pumila*)

South Florida

The shrubs I have included in this section are adapted to the semitropical conditions of extreme south Florida, but many can also be used farther north. Some are naturally confined to south Florida hammocks and are components of similar woodlands in Bermuda, the Bahamas, or other parts of the Caribbean. South Florida flora is relatively young in geological time as this region was the last part of the state to emerge from the water approximately 10,000 years ago. Some south Florida plants have been moving north since that time and are distributed up the Atlantic coast to Brevard and Volusia Counties. Many are largely absent up the western Gulf Coast. A few others have not yet made the journey on either coast, but exhibit more cold tolerance than might be expected from their restricted natural range. In the plant descriptions below, I have indicated which of these plants can be effectively used north of semitropical south Florida.

Torchwood (*Amyris elemifera*)

Torchwood is an evergreen shrub that attains a mature height of 15 feet. It is present from the Florida Keys north to Cape Canaveral on the east coast but

Torchwood
(*Amyris elemifera*)

is not naturally present on the west coast. It can be used anywhere winter temperatures do not dip below the mid-20s°F. Torchwood is a member of the same family that includes citrus (*Citrus* spp.) and prickly ashes (*Zanthoxylum* spp.). As such, it has leathery leaves rich in aromatic oils. These leaves are composed of three leaflets, each elliptical in shape, and with a drooping aspect. The foliage is shiny and attractive. It also feeds the caterpillars of the giant swallowtail, and the much rarer Bahamian and Schaus swallowtails. Blooming can occur in any month but peaks in the summer and fall. The fragrant white flowers are produced in clusters at the tips of the branches. Several months later, they develop into round purple fruit that are eagerly consumed by songbirds.

Torchwood occurs in moist soil habitats, often near the coast but is not especially salt tolerant. It can be used in typical home landscape settings once established but is slow growing. Do not plant torchwood in deep shade but in a location near the edge of the planting or in a gap in the canopy where it will get a few hours of sunlight. Despite its use as a wildlife plant and its simple beauty, torchwood is infrequently grown by commercial native plant nurseries and may take some effort to locate.

Marlberry (*Ardisia escallonioides*)

Marlberry naturally occurs across south Florida and up each coast to the central portion of the state. It is an evergreen shrub that produces several upright stems from the base of the plant. Though a slow grower, marlberry can reach nearly 20 feet tall. The narrow trunks and short branches are covered by simple lance-shaped leaves. Each is deep green, leathery, and shiny in appearance, making it an attractive foliage plant. Its real beauty, however, is apparent when it flowers. Large clusters of very fragrant white flowers are produced at any time, but most often in the fall. Most specimens in my landscape bloom twice a year. Clusters of deep purple fruit follow several months after. The common name is actually a corruption of "marbleberry," as these fruit resemble marbles. A wide variety of songbirds relish these fruit.

Marlberry has some sensitivity to cold and will suffer damage when temperatures dip below 25°F. In locations that meet this temperature need, marlberry is one of the best native shrubs for home landscapes. Its narrow crown allows it to be used in small settings, its attractive foliage and fragrant flowers are aesthetically pleasing, and its value to wildlife is significant. Marlberry does quite well in deep shade but also tolerates some sun. Full sun causes its

Marlberry (*Ardisia escallonioides*)

foliage to become yellowish and sickly looking. I like marlberry best when used in small groupings in the interior of a shade garden, though it makes a good accent plant in small gardens. Plant it close enough to a pathway or bench for its fragrance to be fully appreciated. This species is widely grown commercially and should be relatively easy to locate.

Snowberry (*Chiococca alba*)

Snowberry often grows more like a woody vine than a shrub, but older specimens eventually form a woody trunk that makes them at least shrub-like. It is evergreen, with lance-shaped leathery leaves about one inch long and opposite each other on the stems. It climbs up and over adjacent vegetation to a height of 6–9 feet, forming many side branches that arch downward. Small yellowish white flowers appear on the ends of the stems throughout the year. They are attractive, slightly fragrant, and a good nectar source for heliconius butterflies, like the zebra longwing. The flowers give rise to snow-white berries that provide its common name. These are of moderate use by songbirds and other wildlife.

Snowberry can provide interest to a naturalized landscape. It is difficult

Snowberry
(*Chiococca alba*)

to maintain, however, in landscapes where order is desired. Snowberry is adaptable to most home landscape settings, tolerates a high amount of shade, and is regularly propagated by commercial native plant nurseries. It tolerates more cold than most south Florida natives and can be used anywhere winter temperatures stay above 20°F.

Fiddlewood (*Citharexylum spinosum*)

Fiddlewood is related to the ubiquitous beautyberry, but they differ in many characteristics important to their use in a landscape. For one, fiddlewood is cold sensitive and will freeze to the ground at temperatures just several degrees below freezing. Temperatures below 25°F will kill it. In locations where it is not regularly "pruned" by cold, fiddlewood becomes a narrow shrub that reaches 20 feet tall. The stems tend to droop under the weight of the foliage, which is evergreen, shiny, and elliptical in shape. Well-grown specimens make very attractive foliage plants. It is dioecious, unlike beautyberry. Both sexes produce large numbers of racemes of small, highly fragrant pure-white flowers throughout the year. The flowers attract a variety of pollinators, including heliconius butterflies. The fruit, formed on the female plants, are rounded and fleshy; they turn from orange to black as they ripen. Birds relish the fruit.

Fiddlewood has less salt tolerance than many south Florida natives but can be used in most other landscape conditions. Its narrow crown allows it to be used as an accent in relatively small landscapes, but I think it looks best when

Fiddlewood
(*Citharexylum spinosum*)

planted in a small group of 3 to 5 individuals. Make sure you maximize the number of females if you are interested in providing wildlife habitat in your landscape. Fiddlewood also does not perform well under too much shade. Use it at the edge of your shade garden as a screen or in a light gap so that it can get several hours of direct sunlight. It is sometimes attacked by insect pests. Moth caterpillars can cause temporary defoliation. Scale insects and sooty mold can sometimes cause more persistent damage. If this becomes severe, use insecticidal soaps or neem oil. Fiddlewood is a widely propagated native that is easy to locate for landscape use.

Firebush (*Hamelia patens*)

Firebush is a south Florida native that has been reported from nearly every county north to Marion and Volusia in north-central Florida. There is even a record of it naturally occurring near Tallahassee in Leon County, but these more-northern records constitute localized populations in protected sites. Firebush is extremely cold sensitive and freezes to the ground as soon as the temperature reaches 32°F. As long as the cold is not especially protracted or severe, firebush recovers quickly and assumes its original stature within months. For this reason, it is now used in many north Florida landscapes where such "cold pruning" is tolerated. Where it doesn't typically freeze, fire-

Firebush (*Hamelia patens*)

bush reaches heights of 15 feet. It produces many stems (and can sucker as well) and has a rounded aspect. When given some direct light, or high filtered light, firebush is also dense. The leaves are thin and elliptical; the edges and the petioles (i.e., leaf stems) are often orange-red. Firebush blooms continuously in warm temperatures. Clusters of orange-red tubular flowers give rise to deep purple succulent fruit. The flowers attract a wide variety of pollinators, including hummingbirds and sulfur butterflies, while the fruit is a favorite of many songbirds. Firebush may well be Florida's best wildlife food plant and one of its most attractive shrubs.

Firebush is one of the most widely propagated native plants in Florida. A number of selections are sold that capitalize on foliage and flower attributes. Several non-native firebushes are currently also being sold. I highly discourage their use as they seem quite capable of becoming our next invasive plant problem given their attractiveness to birds. Firebush is best used in partial sun or in places where it will receive high levels of filtered light. It performs poorly in too much shade and does not adapt well to extremely droughty soils. In full sun, it often becomes stressed and the foliage looks burnt. Give it some space, a bit of sunlight, and reasonably fertile/moist soils, and it will be one of your favorite landscape plants.

Myrsine (*Myrsine cubensis*)

Myrsine is a close relative of marlberry and shares some of the same growth form characteristics. Native to nearly all of peninsular Florida, it has more

Myrsine
(*Myrsine cubensis*)

cold tolerance than marlberry. It is an upright shrub with a narrow crown and short side branches. Mature specimens reach 15 feet tall. The foliage is nearly identical to marlberry: elliptical, leathery, and shiny, but in myrsine the leaves are commonly folded under and located only at the tips of the branches. Unlike marlberry, myrsine produces rather inconspicuous greenish white flowers along the side branches. They are not fragrant, and the species is dioecious. Small purple fruit ripen along the stems on female specimens. Though the fruit are small and not nearly as succulent as marlberry, myrsine is a wonderful wildlife food plant.

Myrsine often occurs in open pinelands where it is exposed to full sun conditions, but it is equally content in shade. Use it under filtered sun or in a light gap to ensure it performs at its best, but it will adapt well to deeper shade and not get too leggy or fail to flower. I like to mix myrsine with marlberry to form a dense, lush midstory in shaded locations. They are just similar enough to mix well and different enough to keep their individual identities. Myrsine seems to grow a bit more quickly than marlberry. It is widely propagated and should not be difficult to locate. Just be sure to maximize the ratio of females to males so that you maximize the number of specimens that will produce fruit.

Bitterbush (*Picramnia pentandra*)

Bitterbush is quite rare in Florida, found only in a few hammock areas within Miami-Dade County. It is listed as a state endangered species. Despite its rarity here, it is propagated by several commercial native plant nurseries, and specimens can be purchased for home landscape use. A wide-crowned ever-green shrub, it reaches a mature height of about 15 feet. The numerous thin branches "weep" under the weight of the foliage and fruit. It has compound leaves. Each is up to 12 inches long and composed of five to nine leaflets. Flowers are produced mostly in the early summer on long racemes. They are tiny, greenish yellow in color, and not fragrant. As bitterbush is dioecious, only the females produce fruit; round, maroon-red berries that turn black when fully ripe. The fruit are an excellent wildlife food source.

Though bitterbush has a very small natural range in Florida, it has good cold tolerance and withstands temperatures to at least 25°F without damage. It is adaptable also to most typical landscape conditions. Bitterbush tolerates deep shade, but it will produce denser foliage if given higher filtered light or

Bitterbush
(*Picramnia pentandra*)

a few hours of direct sunlight daily. Because of its distinctive foliage, it makes a wonderful accent in a mixed understory, but needs to be planted in small clusters to ensure maximum fruit production.

Coffees (*Psychotria* spp.)

The native coffees are relatives of true coffees (*Coffea arabica* and others) but do not contain the caffeine in their berries that makes true coffees such sought after agricultural plants. They are extremely adaptable, attractive evergreen shrubs that are also highly useful to wildlife. Their numerous small white flowers, produced mostly in spring and summer in small clusters, are excellent nectar sources for pollinators, including heliconius butterflies. Several months later, the red berries that cover the crowns of each plant provide food for birds and other wildlife. The fruit also adds color to the landscape at a time when most everything else is simply green. Native coffees do exceptionally well in shade and are one of the few shrubs that remain full and continue to flower profusely in evergreen shade with little to no direct sunlight. We use them beneath the live oaks in our landscape where very few other shrubs have performed well. They prefer moist soils but adapt to much droughtier conditions once established, and they have some salt tolerance. Native coffees are best used in mass to form a ground cover or a midcanopy, depending on the species. They are widely propagated and easy to locate. Just make sure to get the species and variety that best suits your location. Most species can be used throughout central Florida, but they will incur some damage when temperatures dip below the mid-20s°F. I have included them in the south Florida section as they are a mostly south Florida genus that has migrated north over time.

Bahama coffee (*P. ligustrifolia*)

Bahama coffee naturally occurs only in Miami-Dade County and the Florida Keys, though it has performed well in several Pinellas County landscapes I have been involved with for more than two decades and has had minimal damage following extended periods of temperatures in the mid-20s°F. This is not the species I would recommend, however, in much of central Florida as the other two are more cold tolerant and have similar landscape uses. Bahama coffee has deep green leaves like wild coffee, described below, but the veins are not as deeply indented. The fruit is red, but not quite as cardinal red as wild coffee. Otherwise, the two species are difficult to distinguish. Bahama coffee reaches a mature height of 6 feet.

Bahama coffee (*Psychotria ligustrifolia*)

Wild coffee (*Psychotria nervosa*)

Wild coffee (*P. nervosa*)

Wild coffee is the most universally used of the three native coffees with good reason. It has the largest natural distribution because of its cold tolerance, and it can be used into north Florida if protected a bit from extremely cold temperatures. There are two forms that differ only by their mature height. A dwarf form, that never stands taller than about two feet, occurs in central and lower north Florida. The taller form that reaches 6–8 feet is typical of the

Florida boxwood is only occasionally available from commercial native nurseries in south Florida. It has minimal cold tolerance so its use should be confined to regions of the state that rarely drop below freezing. As it is dioecious, use it in small clusters if wildlife value is a consideration. It is not an especially interesting accent plant to be used alone. Provide it high amounts of filtered light or at least some direct sunlight to ensure its best growth.

Cassias (*Senna* spp.)

Cassias, and their close relatives, are an extremely diverse group that includes everything from annual weeds to tall canopy trees. Some non-natives are commonly used here as ornamental plants, and a few are invasive pests. All have value in a butterfly garden as they are the larval food of several beautiful sulfur butterflies. Our native species are tropical in origin and are cold sensitive. Both can be grown into central Florida, but temperatures below the mid-20s°F will kill them. From my experience, the seedlings are more tolerant and often survive. In most situations, seed in the soil below will sprout the following spring and maintain them in the landscape. If not occasionally cold- , caterpillar- , or human-pruned, the native cassias below often become leggy and a bit unruly. Their landscape value comes from their bright yellow flowers and their use in the butterfly garden. Both native species are widely propagated.

Privet cassia (*S. ligustrina*)

Privet cassia occurs well into north-central Florida in coastal counties and is the more cold tolerant of the two. It is a thin-crowned, lanky species that most often grows in hammock edges, in light gaps, and in disturbed places where it gets partial sun or full sun for at least a few hours daily. As it reaches its mature height of 6 feet, it bends over under the weight of its foliage and flowers and is almost never completely upright. This is a mostly herbaceous species that forms a woody stem with time. It is also quite thin crowned, with numerous short side branches. Its common name is the result of its foliage; the compound leaves are composed of many long, elliptical leaflets. Flowering can occur during any month at the top of its crown. Large clusters of canary yellow flowers (a lighter, lemon-yellow form is also available) attract bees, and the interest of female sulfur butterflies for egg-laying purposes. We use privet cassia extensively in our home landscape and allow it to reseed and appear wherever it wants to. Those in the "wrong" spots get weeded out and given away. The others provide color and butterfly use.

Privet cassia
(*Senna ligustrina*)

Bahama cassia (*Senna mexicana* var. *chapmanii*)

Bahama cassia (*S. mexicana* var. *chapmanii*)

Bahama cassia is found naturally only in portions of Miami-Dade County and the Florida Keys. It is the most widely propagated species in Florida and is planted throughout central and south Florida. This cassia is extremely salt tolerant and performs well in most any landscape situation from full sun to partial shade. It is not as shade tolerant as privet cassia, however, and will become quite leggy and fail to flower if not given at least a few hours of direct sun daily. Bahama cassia is a rounded semiwoody shrub that can reach 6 feet tall. The branches are a bit wider and stouter than privet cassia and the compound leaves are more rounded. It produces large numbers of canary yellow blooms throughout the year. In the landscapes where I have used both native species side by side, I have found that butterflies prefer this species over privet cassia.

UNDERSTORY HERBACEOUS PLANTS

Ferns

In nature, ferns are an integral part of shady landscapes. Though they do not add a lot of color, they add a texture that cannot be duplicated by other plants. Most ferns do not do well in extremely droughty soils, but they tolerate wide levels of light as long as they have moisture. Ferns can be added to the shady understory to fill in all of the open spaces. Like turf grass grows in sunny lawns, ferns form a sort of turf in the shade. Many die back to the ground in the fall and emerge again in the spring, but a few are evergreen. Those that die back emerge by forcing their coiled fiddleheads up through the leaf litter before uncurling. I find this to be one of nature's most refreshing events, and I look for it each spring. Some ferns spread quickly by underground rhizomes and eventually form a carpet; others spread slowly outward and remain clumped. Spreading ferns are excellent for those areas where a uniform planting is desired. Clumped ferns are best where a diversity of understory plants is wanted. If you want a little of both, be prepared occasionally to weed out your surplus specimens in order to maintain a balance. Weeding ferns is easy as they are shallow rooted. Pay attention also to their height at maturity. Use the lower-growing species near the front half of the planting bed and the taller ones to the rear.

Many of our native ferns grow statewide, but a few are best used only in north and central Florida where some chilling temperatures are likely in winter. I have separated the latter group from the former below.

North and Central Florida

Southern lady fern (*Athyrium felix-femina*)

Southern lady fern is one of my favorites. I love its texture and I appreciate its tidy growth form that allows me to use it in a landscape without fear of its

Southern lady fern
(*Athyrium felix-femina*)

crowding out its neighbors. It occurs naturally only in north Florida and is listed as a state threatened species. In this limited distribution, it is associated with wet to moist soil habitats, often in shade. Southern lady fern dies back to the ground each winter and reaches 2 feet in height by late spring. The fronds are finely dissected and delicate and light green in color.

I have had success with southern lady fern in my Pinellas County landscape in areas that remain moist during the summer. It has not performed well for me in the typical woodland conditions found in much of my yard. Although some of my experiences may be tempered by the fact that I am well south of its natural range, I suspect it should never be added to sites that remain droughty for much of the year. This fern mixes well with wildflowers and native grasses and generally stays where it is planted. Few commercial native nurseries currently offer this delicate fern for home landscapes, but it can be found using some perseverance.

Sensitive fern (*Onoclea sensibilis*)

Though sensitive fern has very attractive fronds and can make a stunning statement in the right landscape situation, it spreads quickly, which makes it a

Sensitive fern (*Onoclea sensibilis*)

nuisance in the wrong setting. Sensitive fern is sensitive to cold. Its fronds will die back to the ground at even the mention of the word frost in its presence. When it returns in the spring, it produces large lime-green arching fronds with simple, deeply dissected pinnae. Later, in summer, it also produces a fertile frond that looks a bit like a straight stalk of grapes. The spores are produced from this solitary frond.

Sensitive fern occurs throughout north and central Florida in wet woodlands. It adapts to most shade garden conditions, but it will not persist if kept dry for too long, especially during the late spring and summer growing season. This is not a clumping fern, but one that puts up evenly spaced fronds along the length of its underground rhizome. I really like the look of this fern, grown in mass beneath the canopy of a moist shade garden, but it will overwhelm diminutive wildflowers. Mix it with more robust species that can hold their own and do not attempt it too far south of its natural range.

Christmas fern (*Polystichum acrostichoides*)

As its common name implies, Christmas fern is evergreen. In early spring, the older fronds begin to droop and new ones emerge from the center, ready to take over for the year ahead. This is the perfect fern for shade gardens in north Florida where some color is desired in the dead of winter. While nearly every wildflower is beneath the soil and most trees and shrubs are leafless,

Christmas fern (*Polystichum acrostichoides*)

Christmas fern stays green and vibrant. The fronds are deep green and the leaflets are deeply dissected. They stand about 2 feet tall.

This fern occurs throughout much of north and central Florida in mesic woodlands. It tolerates most of the conditions typically found in home shade gardens, including occasional drought. It can be grown in both acidic and limey soils. Christmas fern is a clumping species that stays where it is planted and only slowly spreads outward over time. This attractive fern should be more widely propagated and used in home landscapes but is only sparingly available. Use it in small clusters, scattered throughout a deciduous woodland planting, and mix it with woodland wildflowers and native grasses. We have maintained this fern in our Pinellas County landscape for many years and have found it to be very forgiving of its habitat conditions.

Statewide

Maidenhair ferns (*Adiantum* spp.)

Though maidenhair ferns look delicate, they are actually quite tough and resilient, and they occur statewide under certain habitat conditions. They require alkaline soils and often can be found growing on top of limestone outcroppings, especially in areas where water frequently drips on them. Their common name is a reference to the shape of their fronds. They are long and

Southern maidenhair fern (*Adiantum capillus-veneris*)

trail downward when the plants grow on a cliff, an outcropping, or a steep incline. The individual pinnae (the leafy portion of the frond) attached to the black, hair-like rachis (the stem portion) are small, triangular shaped, and scalloped along the wide end. These elegant-looking fronds seem to look a bit like women's tresses. Maidenhair ferns are beautiful and have long been prized in the landscape.

Several rare non-native species have been collected in extreme south Florida, but only three species are considered native. Two have restricted ranges in Florida, are listed as state endangered species, and are unlikely ever to be offered for home landscape purposes; fragrant maidenhair (*A. melanoleucum*), and brittle maidenhair (*A. tenerum*). Southern maidenhair (*A. capillus-veneris*), however, is found in scattered locations statewide and is often available from commercial nurseries. Southern maidenhair is almost always found growing on limestone outcrops, but it does not require this in a home landscape. It is eventually a robust species that slowly grows outward into clumps that can exceed several feet wide. It is not forgiving of drought. In our landscape, it is often one of the first ferns to wilt when rain events are widely spaced, and it requires water to perk up. We solved this problem by growing it in large pots in the landscape with saucers beneath to hold water. In this setting, they require far less water than they would if planted directly in the landscape, and we can enjoy them better. Southern maidenhair has also colonized rocks adjacent to the water feature in our side yard. If you can provide a moist site in shade, either naturally or by some manipulation, this is a gorgeous fern that always attracts attention.

Spleenworts (*Asplenium* spp.)

There are 12 native spleenworts in Florida, plus 4 naturally occurring hybrids. The genus occurs statewide but is most often found in association with limestone outcrops. Most do not fare well in any other habitat condition. They are attractive ferns with rich green fronds and most with a jet black rachis, but they are only rarely propagated by commercial native nurseries. Many are quite rare and localized in their distribution. Only a few are well known and possible subjects for use in home landscapes. The extremely beautiful bird's nest fern (*A. serrulatum*) is a state-listed endangered species, mostly confined to cypress swamps in extreme south peninsular Florida. In these habitats, it is an epiphyte, often growing no more than 6 feet high on the trunks of trees and large shrubs. The only other spleenwort sometimes propagated is ebony spleenwort (*A. platyneuron*), described below.

Ebony spleenwort occurs throughout Florida in woodland understories. It is the only species of this group that is terrestrial: not growing as an epiphyte on trees or rocks. It prefers limestone soils, however, and I have never had success with it in other conditions. As the common name implies, the rachis

Ebony spleenwort (*Asplenium platyneuron*)

is chocolate brown to jet black. The fronds are narrow, numerous, and about 2 feet tall. It is a clumping fern that dies back to the ground in winter. Ebony spleenwort is well behaved in the landscape and its small compact size and rich color add a lot to a mixed woodland understory. Friends who have had success with it have incorporated large limestone rock into their landscapes and planted around it. If you are willing to do this, or have limestone near the surface already, ebony spleenwort is a wonderful choice. It tolerates low light and average moisture quite well. Regrettably, it is only rarely available from Florida nurseries. Do not be tempted to acquire it from out-of-state sources as it is unlikely to prosper in our climate.

Swamp fern (*Blechnum serrulatum*)

Swamp fern occurs statewide, most often in wet soil habitats from full sun to deep shade. In sunny locations, it rarely stands more than two feet tall and is

Swamp fern
(*Blechnum
serrulatum*)

yellowish green in color. In shade, it is a richer lime green with fronds that often are 3–4 feet tall. Despite its common name, swamp fern is quite drought tolerant once established and does well in average shady landscape settings. We have used it extensively in our home landscape and it has slowly colonized all of our shady locations despite the fact that we have no irrigation system. This is a fern that slowly creeps outward from its underground rhizome and forms colonies instead of distinct clumps. The fronds are mostly erect, with elliptical pinnae. The edges of each are serrated on close examination. Swamp fern is robust and not the best choice for small planting areas. Use it in more expansive settings where it can screen unsightly features and where it won't compete with more diminutive species. If it spreads to areas where smaller spring ephemeral wildflowers are planted, it is easy to weed out. Do not be afraid to weed it when warranted, but use it where it makes sense. This fern is widely propagated and should not be difficult to purchase.

Osmunda ferns (*Osmunda* spp.)

In the early days of home orchid culture, the most popular potting medium was osmunda fiber—the fibrous roots and rhizomes of *Osmunda* spp. ferns. Though this practice has now largely disappeared, *Osmunda* ferns are still protected statewide as "commercially exploited" species. Two species are native to Florida and both are quite attractive and widely propagated for home

Cinnamon fern (*Osmunda cinnamomea*)

Royal fern
(*Osmunda regalis*)

landscape use. *Osmunda* ferns occur in wet soil habitats, most often under the canopy of a wetland forest. They tolerate some drought, but not for extended periods. They have distinctive tall vegetative fronds and produce separate fertile fronds in summer. The fertile fronds are especially distinctive in appearance and coppery bronze when mature. *Osmunda* ferns are deciduous clumping ferns and do not spread throughout the landscape. As such, they make showy additions to moist soil areas. Plant them in small clusters and use them as accents in the middle portion of more expansive settings. They can be mixed with other tall ferns and low shrubs like wild coffees, and smaller ferns can be used in the forefront. Both species occur naturally statewide.

Cinnamon fern (*O. cinnamomea*) is the most adaptable of our two species and the one that produces the most luxuriant foliage. Once established, it can survive short-term drought quite well, but it performs far better when kept moist to wet. When well cultivated, the erect fronds stand 3–4 feet tall. Each has many toothed pinnae along the rachis, resembling several other medium-sized ferns discussed in this book. Its common name is derived from its fertile frond which is a rich coppery color and looks a bit like a cinnamon stick. These can be produced from spring through fall, but are most common from late spring to early summer. A mass of these ferns, with their coppery cinnamon stick fronds, is extremely showy.

Royal fern (*O. regalis*) has far less drought tolerance than cinnamon fern. Over the years, I have not been able to acclimate it to any part of our landscape except those areas that remain wet for most of the year. Its fronds are similar in size to cinnamon fern, but the pinnae branch off the main rachis in pairs; each pair is composed of elliptical pinnules that are largely without teeth along the margins. All this produces an elegant appearance but not as lush and dense as cinnamon fern. The fertile fronds of royal fern are also not as dense or showy; it produces more side branches than the dense cinnamon-stick appearance of its close cousin.

Sword ferns (*Nephrolepis* spp.)

Two native and two highly invasive non-native sword ferns occur in Florida. Of the two non-native sword ferns, tuberous sword fern (*N. cordifolia*) is the most widespread and the most invasive. Tuberous sword fern occurs throughout central and south Florida in a wide variety of settings and is rarely found in north Florida. It spreads rapidly by its underground rhizome and forms large patches in the understory of woodlands that all but exclude other species. It is difficult to remove, once established, because it also produces rounded tubers, covered by golden "hairy" scales, which often remain in the ground when the parent plants are pulled out. These tubers will sprout and produce new plants. Asian sword fern (*N. multiflora*) is cold sensitive and present only as far north as south-central Florida. It is a tall fern, often found in sunny disturbed locations.

Our native sword ferns, also known as "Boston" ferns, are better behaved but similar in appearance. If your landscape already has sword ferns, they are most likely one of the non-native invasive species. This is especially likely if they are forming large colonies that grow over everything else. There are good online publications that can help you in their identification. The one I frequently refer to was published by the University of Florida, Institute of Food and Agricultural Sciences (IFAS): http://edis.ifas.ufl.edu/ag120.

Giant sword fern (*N. biserrata*) is the largest relative in the sword fern genus. Often with fronds that reach 4–5 feet tall, it is frequently marketed by commercial nurseries as "macho fern." This is naturally native only to south Florida but is sold and planted extensively throughout central Florida as well.

Tuberous sword fern (*Nephrolepis cordifolia*) is often mistaken for native sword fern. Unlike its close relative, however, tuberous sword fern is highly invasive and eventually forms large uniform monocultures. One reason for its ability to spread is that it also produces numbers of golden tubers below ground that break off when the fern is weeded.

In most aspects, giant sword fern is simply a much larger version of native sword fern. Their fronds are similar as are their growth habits, but because giant sword fern is so robust, it can form dense patches that all but exclude other ground covers. This species is best used in shady locations where a ground cover screen is desired. It is overwhelming in small areas and in landscapes where more diversity is desired. Do not use this fern if you are also trying to incorporate wildflowers into the mix.

Native sword fern (*N. exaltata*) is found primarily in central and south Florida, though scattered records in north Florida occur. It is a medium-sized

Giant sword fern
(*Nephrolepis biserrata*)

Native sword fern (*Nephrolepis exaltata*)

fern that typically remains green throughout the winter. It stands about 2 feet tall and is somewhat a cross between a clumping fern and a spreading one. It forms clumps, but it spreads slowly over time in all directions. It only rarely produces large colonies, however, like tuberous sword fern, and it never produces the distinctive golden tubers of the latter. Native sword fern is adaptable to a wide variety of growing conditions, from wet to relatively dry and it adapts to all degrees of shade.

Shield fern (*Thelypteris* spp.)

There are 15 native species of shield fern (aka maiden fern) as well as two non-natives. As a genus, they are found statewide and are often extremely difficult to tell apart. They also have very similar cultural requirements, so for the purposes of this book, I am considering them together. Shield ferns are medium-sized species that stand 2–3 feet tall. In areas that do not freeze, they are evergreen, but they die back to the ground in colder areas of the state. I

Shield fern
(*Thelypteris* spp.)

find them to be somewhat aggressive in the landscape. Though not a clumping fern, they spread slowly outward with their underground rhizome, and
each new frond is close to an older one. Some hand-pulling may be necessary
to keep them in check, but I have not found this difficult to do in our home
landscape.

These are adaptable ferns that tolerate a very wide range of habitat conditions. They can be planted in moist soil but adapt well to dry shade and are
one of the few ferns that will provide a dense, lush appearance in such situations. They also are one of the few ferns in our landscape to spread reliably
by spores. We did not purposely plant shield ferns into our shaded back yard;
they just materialized from other places in our neighborhood, and as our
canopy develops each year and the amount of shade grows, we get new shield
ferns all on their own.

Despite this genus's adaptability, it is only sporadically grown commercially, and only southern shield fern (*T. kunthii*) is routinely offered. Other
good species include downy shield fern (*T. dentata*), variable shield fern *(T.
hispidula*), hottentot fern (*T. interrupta*), and ovate shield fern (*T. ovata*). Mix
any of these with other medium-sized ferns in average to moist soil, including
native sword fern, swamp fern, cinnamon fern, and chain fern (*Woodwardia*
spp.), to create a variable fern understory with aesthetic interest. Mixed with
coontie and wild coffee, these ferns can create a lush appearance in all but the
driest sites.

Chain ferns (*Woodwardia* spp.)

There are two chain ferns native to Florida and, though related, they are very
different species in a landscape situation. For that reason, I will describe each
in a bit more detail below. Both species are found statewide, primarily in
wet soil habitats. In extremely wet conditions, they do well in full sun, but in
less than shallow standing water, they require some shade to thrive. Neither
species is well adapted to droughty soils, though they can tolerate occasional
short-term drought once established when well shaded. Chain ferns are so
named by the single chain-like row of areoles that parallel both sides of the
mid-vein and the main vein of each pinna in their fronds. These structures
are on the undersides of the fronds and make identifying them from cinnamon fern and shield ferns relatively easy.

Chain ferns are aggressive when grown in moist soils. Their underground
rhizomes spread in all directions, and single fronds emerge at various inter-

Netted chain fern (*Woodwardia areolata*)

Virginia chain fern (*Woodwardia virginica*)

vals as they do. Over time, the rhizomes crisscross each other in the landscape, and the entire area becomes covered in its fronds. These are good ferns for expansive settings where a dense ground layer of ferns is desired. They are difficult to manage in other settings, especially Virginia chain fern (*W. virginica*), described below. Both species die back to the ground in winter, except in extreme south Florida.

Netted chain fern (*W. areolata*) is the more diminutive and better behaved of the two species. It produces fertile and sterile fronds. The sterile fronds rarely stand taller than 18 inches while the fertile ones reach another 6 inches in height. The fronds are wide with a wide, almost winged, central rachis. No other fern in Florida could be confused with this one. Because of its more diminutive size, netted chain fern does not overwhelm its neighbors the way Virginia chain fern can, but it will not persist in any situation that does not remain moist to wet. Plants I have kept for many months in cool weather have rapidly died during extended summer drought, and I have not found it possible to acclimate it to my typical shady landscape.

Virginia chain fern looks a bit like many of the shield ferns to me at first glance. They are about the same height, and the shape of their fronds is superficially quite similar. Virginia chain fern, however, is more aggressive in landscape situations and tends to die back to the ground in winter, even when temperatures do not reach freezing. Virginia chain fern will acclimate to typical landscape conditions once established but may need supplemental water during persistent drought. I consider it inferior as a landscape plant to other medium-sized ferns discussed above because of its tendency to spread, and adding it to your landscape should be carefully considered except in moist and saturated soils where a solid growth of ferns might be desired.

Grasses

The grasses that you can add to a shade garden are not the same grasses you can use in a lawn. You cannot create a lawn in the Florida shade. We need to set that straight right from the start. The native grasses available to us are mostly upright species that would be added for their ornamental value, not their ability to act as turf. In shade, most grasses are delicate and do not respond well to heavy foot traffic. They should not be mowed because their use is predicated on their attractive foliage and flower/seed heads. There are attractive native grasses in Florida, but few are available to the home gardener through commercial native nurseries. I have included what I believe are the best choices below. In the years ahead, perhaps a greater market for them will arise, and more nurseries will see the commercial return in growing them.

North and Central Florida

River oats (*Chasmanthium* spp.)

Five species of river oats (aka wood oats) are native to the Southeast, and all occur in Florida. Four have never been grown commercially, but inland river oats (*C. latifolium*) is the most widely propagated shade-tolerant grass in Florida. It is also the most attractive. All are upright species with rich green arching leaves that die back to the ground in winter. By late spring, they have reached their mature height of three feet. These are bunch grasses that form dense clumps where they are planted, but they also spread outward by underground rhizomes and form colonies over time. They are not aggressive, however, and are easily contained by occasional pruning if desired. The common names for these plants come from their seed heads that resemble oats. At one time, they were included in the same genus as sea oats (*Uniola latifolia*), also because of the similarities in their seed heads. The laterally compressed seed heads with spiky glumes are especially attractive. They turn golden brown when ripe and arch up and over the leaves by an additional 6–12 inches. All river oats occur in moist soil, in the shade produced by deciduous canopy trees. They are adaptable to periodic drought, but will decline if kept in deep shade year round or kept too dry for too long. Use them in filtered sun or in gaps where they will receive an hour or two of early or late sun. River oats are native to north and central Florida and are not good choices for counties farther south.

Inland river oats (*Chasmanthium latifolium*)

Twoflower melicgrass
(*Melica mutica*)

Twoflower melicgrass (*Melica mutica*)

I am including twoflower melicgrass though it has never been commercially propagated, because it should be. Native to north and north-central Florida, it is a perennial bunch grass that thrives in moist woodland conditions, near stream banks and in the lower pockets of deciduous forests. It is very shade tolerant and can be grown in low light. Just don't attempt it in droughty soils. Twoflower melicgrass has foliage and seed heads that superficially resemble the river oats. It blooms in spring and the flowering stalk reaches 2½ feet in height. These ripen by summer and turn light brown. Twoflower melicgrass can add interest to a shade garden with moist soil, especially on sites where the look of lush green grass is desired. In its natural habitat, it can sometimes form broad patches where it mixes well with various spring-blooming wildflowers, such as butterweed (*Packera* spp.). It dies back to the ground in winter, however, and should be mixed with species that remain green to provide some landscape interest for the months it is absent.

Statewide

Witch grass (*Dichanthelium* spp.)

Depending on your taxonomy, there are nearly 20 species of witch grass native to Florida. At one time, they were all included in the much larger panic grass (*Panicum* spp.) genus, but there are some noticeable differences between the two groups; the most important in terms of landscape purposes is that most witch grasses maintain a basal rosette of leaves through the winter while panic grasses die completely back to the ground. Some witch grasses are somewhat weedy, with narrow leaves and thin flower/seed heads that spread by underground rhizomes. Others have wider leaves and more conspicuous seed heads that give them enough aesthetic value to be considered for shady landscapes. Currently, however, very few witch grasses are available commercially in Florida. I like witch grasses planted in small patches near walkways and sitting areas. Their lower growth, interesting flower/seed heads, and

Witch grass
(*Dicanthelium* spp.)

tendency to maintain their foliage in winter makes them valuable additions when mixed with spring ephemeral wildflowers that disappear during those months. Many also have colorful foliage in the spring and fall that takes on shades of red and purple. I hope the best species for the shade garden will become more available in the future.

Basketgrass (*Oplismenus hirtellus*)

Basketgrass makes an extensive ground cover from spring to fall, but dies back to the ground in winter. Its tendency to spread throughout shady areas is a blessing or a curse depending on your landscape objectives, but when used properly and in a naturalistic setting, it can be quite attractive. Basketgrass occurs statewide in shady woodlands and is one of the few grasses that can thrive under almost any shade garden condition. It prefers moisture, but it will spread to nearly every corner of a shady location once established. This is a creeping grass that spreads by above-ground stolons, much like St. Augustine grass (*Stenotaphrum secundatum*). The rich green, short lance-shaped leaves hug the ground and eventually form robust plants in the understory, but it can be a nuisance for the more-diminutive ephemeral spring wildflowers. Flowering stems are produced through the summer season. They are somewhat inconspicuous but often stand a few inches above the rest of the foliage. Basketgrass is only sometimes available from commercial sources in Florida.

Basketgrass (*Oplismenus hirtellus*)

Wildflowers

Though shade gardens can provide color and aesthetic interest without them, I am an unabashed lover of wildflowers, especially those that make a brief appearance in early spring and disappear by early summer. These so-called ephemeral species herald the passing of winter and create a sense of anticipation that few other kinds of plants do as well. The burst of color they create, though brief, interrupts the simple shades of green that dominate most shady areas. Most have intricate blooms that attract pollinators, and all are beautiful when planted in clusters or masses within the leaf litter beneath a canopy of spring-flowering trees and shrubs.

Ephemeral wildflowers occur beneath deciduous trees and shrubs; therefore, most naturally occur only in north and north-central Florida woodlands. As the normal canopy changes from deciduous to evergreen species in south-central Florida, there are few places left for wildflowers that require high light levels in spring to bloom followed by shade to protect them in the heat of summer. Many spring ephemeral wildflowers can be grown ef-

Indian pink. Torreya State Park, Bristol, Florida. Photo by Pam Anderson, with permission.

fectively farther south of their natural range if their habitat needs are met. In our Pinellas County landscape, Alexa and I have done well with many north Florida wildflowers by extending our live oak woodland with trees that lose their leaves in winter. In some cases, we have also had to plant them in large landscape pots to provide them a better soil than what we naturally have. We have failed with a few that seem to need more cold than we can give them.

There is a second group of wildflowers that are not ephemeral; they persist through the year and do not necessarily bloom in spring. These are a much smaller subset of the overall plant palette available for shady areas, but they are important landscape plants for the color they provide. Most wildflowers need sunlight to flower and set seed. Very few can tolerate deep evergreen shade. The wildflowers that are not ephemeral should get high amounts of filtered sun, be used in a light gap beneath the canopy, or be planted at the edges where they will get a few hours of sun in early morning or late afternoon. I like to use these at the edges of my shade and let them find their own locations over time by allowing them to reseed or sucker. As my canopy changes and my shade moves around a bit, most of my nonephemeral wildflowers have moved with those changes to locations where their needs can be best met. This is true whether the shade is evergreen or deciduous. Canopies change over time. You can either prune them lightly from time to time to maintain them or let your plants move with the changes.

Many wildflowers can tolerate partial shade. The ones I've included are those species that thrive in the lower light common to a shade garden. Forcing sun-loving wildflowers to exist in lower-than-ideal light conditions makes no sense as they will not perform well and ultimately will perish.

North and Central Florida

Eastern bluestar (*Amsonia tabernaemontana*)

Eastern bluestar is native to woodland understories throughout north Florida. It can tolerate relatively high amounts of sunlight but is most often found in high filtered sun or in light gaps beneath the canopy where it gets a few hours of direct sunlight during the day. It dies back to the ground in winter. In spring, it forms an erect stem, 2–4 feet tall, with lance-shaped leaves. A single flower stalk is produced at the top of this stem and from March to April an open cluster of 5-petaled flowers is produced. The star-shaped blooms are pale blue to white in color and are produced in profusion.

Eastern bluestar (*Amsonia tabernaemontana*). Photo by Eleanor Dietrich, with permission.

Eastern bluestar has good drought tolerance, but prefers moist organic soils to achieve its full potential. Do not attempt it in deep shade as it will slowly expire. Flowering is greatly enhanced by higher light levels in the late winter and early spring. It is a member of the milkweed family, but there are no records of its being used as a butterfly larval plant. Use eastern bluestar in clusters of at least 3–5 plants for best affect. It has a simple beauty that mixes well with a great many other species, but its taller size makes it look best when planted behind shorter wildflowers. It is only infrequently available from commercial native nurseries in Florida but worth the time spent hunting it down.

Columbine (*Aquilegia canadensis*)

Eastern columbine occurs throughout the eastern two-thirds of North America but is exceedingly rare in Florida. Here, it is relegated to rich woodland soils with limestone near the surface in a three-county area centered on Florida Caverns State Park in Washington County. It is a short-lived perennial, but stock purchased from out-of-state sources is unlikely to survive a year. Despite its natural rarity, eastern columbine is rather widely propagated and grown throughout north and central Florida. Though it is lime tolerant, it does not seem dependent on high pH soils. Its tolerance, however, makes it a good choice for an understory near the foundation of a concrete block

Columbine (*Aquilegia canadensis*). Photo by Eleanor Dietrich, with permission.

home. This species dies back to the ground each winter and quickly emerges in spring. A basal rosette of leaves forms and flower stalks arise from the center. Columbines have delicate foliage and this adds a lot of aesthetic interest to the landscape even when the plants are not in bloom. The compound leaves look a bit like the fronds of maidenhair fern and arch delicately off the stem. Flowering occurs in early spring, but flowers can continue well into summer from the top of the 2–3 foot stalks. They are unique in their shape and have great charm. The flowers are composed of five orange-red sepals that fold backwards and form "horns" that stand above the bright yellow petals. The many flowers hang upside down when open and each of the "horns" holds large amounts of nectar that is irresistible to hummingbirds and bumblebees.

Eastern columbine is relatively easy to grow in north and central Florida landscapes, and farther south if special attention is given to its habitat needs. It performs best when grown in the understory of deciduous woodlands. Here, it receives ample sunlight as it reemerges in spring and initiates flowering. It then gets the protection it needs from summer and fall sun when the canopy closes over. Do not attempt this in deep evergreen shade, but it will do fine if planted in a light gap or at the edge of deep shade where it will get a few hours of sun in the early morning or late afternoon. When planted in a favorable location, it is likely to reseed and expand its position in the landscape. Do not mulch heavily around it as it will *only* persist if it can reseed.

Jack-in-the-pulpits (*Arisaema* spp.)

Few of us fail to recognize a jack-in-the-pulpit flower. They are one of those blooms that capture the attention of nearly everyone, and we see them featured in various art forms from childhood on. Despite this, I find few Floridians who realize they grow naturally throughout most of the state. There are three closely related members of this genus in Florida. Pester John (*A. quinatum*) is confined to just a few counties in the central panhandle and is not available commercially in Florida. The other two are more widely dispersed and often available. All species do especially well in low light conditions, but they perform best when given a bit of direct sunlight in late winter and filtered sun the rest of the year. They also require high soil moisture and organic matter. Do not attempt these species in sterile droughty soils. What sets all of them apart are their unique flowers. They are in the arum family so the actual flower is protected by a leafy spathe. The spathe forms the so-called pulpit on which the flower stalk "stands" and the hood that arches up and over it. The fingerlike flower stalk (the "jack") is covered by dozens of extremely small white flowers. They are pollinated mostly by very small flies, and the dense clusters of berries that follow in late fall are brilliant red. They have some value as food for songbirds.

Green dragon (*A. dracontium*)

Green dragon is restricted naturally to deciduous woodlands in north and central Florida. Its large compound leaves are composed of seven to nine leaflets and stand 2–3 feet tall at maturity. The solitary flower is formed after the leaves have fully developed and occurs beneath their canopy. The flower is much smaller than jack-in-the-pulpit, and the hood of the "pulpit" is decidedly beaked. I find green dragon most often in rich woodlands that are a bit more upland than those where true jack-in-the-pulpit (*A. triphyllum*) is found, and they seem to have more drought tolerance. I also find that they emerge and bloom several weeks later. These are interesting plants, but more so for their foliage than their flowers. Use them in mass for the best effect but never in clusters smaller than three. Green dragon is less widely propagated than jack-in-the-pulpit but can be found with some perseverance.

Green dragon (*Arisaema dracontium*)

Jack-in-the-pulpit
(*Arisaema triphyllum*).
Photo by Christina Evans,
with permission.

Jack-in-the-pulpit (*A. triphyllum*)

True jack-in-the-pulpit occurs nearly statewide but is not common in south-central and south Florida. It prefers moist to almost wet soil in summer and fall and will not do well if these conditions cannot be provided. In ideal conditions, it can form dense colonies within the forest understory. Jack-in-the-pulpit is deciduous and one of the earliest spring ephemerals to emerge, often in late winter. A large 3-parted leaf quickly reaches 1–2 feet tall, while the flower structure forms alongside it. Unlike green dragon, jack-in-the-pulpit's flower structure stands as tall as, or taller than, the foliage and is quite visible. This structure is also more robust. The large green leafy spathe is often striped in purple. It arches over the flower stalk but does not hide it to the extent seen in green dragon. Jack-in-the-pulpit dies back to the ground by summer if the flowers are not pollinated. When they are, the leaves turn yellow and the stalk, covered by bright red berries, is exposed for a second show of color.

Wild ginger (*Asarum arifolium*)

Wild ginger is found in scattered locations in extreme north Florida but can be grown well into central Florida when provided the proper growing conditions: a deciduous canopy, leaf litter mulch over a well-drained fertile soil, and a bit of moisture during the heat of summer. Wild ginger is drought tolerant once established but needs extra water during the first months. This is a ground cover, planted for its foliage instead of its inconspicuous jug-shaped brown flowers. The heart-shaped leaves remain green during the winter, unless temperatures get well below the mid-20s°F. Each is deep green and covered by irregularly shaped light green blotches. Over time, wild ginger creeps in all directions

Wild ginger (*Asarum arifolium*)

from where it was initially planted, forming a diminutive ground cover that never fails to evoke interest among our guests the first time they see it.

Wild ginger rarely stands taller than about 4 inches. Use it near pathways and sitting areas and intersperse spring ephemeral wildflowers, like violets (*Viola* spp.) and rue anemone (*Thalictrum thalictroides*) for color. Wild ginger has prospered in our home landscape for nearly ten years, well outside its natural range and with no special attention. It is only occasionally offered by commercial native nurseries, though, and will take effort to locate.

Green-and-gold (*Chrysogonum virginianum* var. *australe*)

The southern form of green-and-gold is uncommon in Florida and naturally confined to a few northern counties in the central panhandle region. It is often evergreen through the winter when temperatures stay above the mid-20s°F but dies back to the ground in colder temperatures. This is a beautiful wildflower for shady to partially shady locations. It does well under low light but blooms and spreads best when it gets at least high filtered sun or a few hours of direct sunlight. What I like best about this wildflower is that it always looks good, and it fills in "holes" in the landscape but does so unaggressively. Green-and-gold forms small rosettes of rounded fuzzy leaves that have deep-set veins and crinkled leaf margins. Each rosette is about 12 inches across and lies flat to the ground. This plant forms above-ground stolons, which are sent in various

Green-and-gold (*Chrysogonum virginianum*)

directions to form new plants, usually close to the parent. Over time, a well-grown colony of green-and-gold will form colonies of several dozen rosettes. Sporadic flowering can occur at other times but is largely confined to spring. Flattened flowers arise from the center of each rosette. They are composed of five canary yellow ray petals with a central disk of smaller yellow flowers. A blooming colony of green-and-gold is especially attractive. Green-and-gold is only rarely offered by commercial native nurseries in Florida.

Brown's savory (*Clinopodium brownei*)

As its common name implies, Brown's savory is a mint, and its small oval leaves and herbaceous stems are extremely fragrant. In fact, they make an excellent herbal tea if steeped properly. This perennial occurs statewide, mostly in moist-soil habitats from sunny to shady locations. It is extremely adaptable to various levels of sunlight but requires moisture during the summer and fall growing seasons to prosper. In our typically droughty landscape, it fares quite well with frequent summer rains after sufficient time to establish but does need a bit of extra water from time to time when rain events are infrequent. Brown's savory is a mat-forming, creeping perennial that produces many stems that venture off in all directions. Over time, it spreads across many square feet, never standing more than a few inches above ground. The pungent leaves are opposite each other on the stems, and each is slightly lobed with a wavy edge. Flowering occurs mostly in the spring but can occur in

Browne's savory (*Clinopodium brownei*)

nearly any month from spring through fall if growing conditions are ideal. The flowers arise in pairs at the leaf nodes. They are tubular, light lavender in color with deeper purple markings in the throat. Though attractive, they are very small and only noticeable on close inspection.

Brown's savory makes an attractive ground cover for semishaded areas in a moist to wet woodland garden. It will not prosper if grown in deep shade. Plant it in light gaps and allow it to spread to areas it prefers, or use it at the edge of the shade garden where it will eventually be limited by too much shade or too little moisture. This plant is only occasionally offered by commercial nurseries but can be found with some diligence.

Mistflower (*Conoclinium coelestinum*)

Mistflower is a highly adaptable wildflower that can be grown in full sun as well as in shady gardens. In some aspects it is weedy, but in the right location it can be quite attractive and provide color during the summer and fall. It also

Mistflower (*Conoclinium coelestinum*). Photo by Christina Evans, with permission.

is a good nectar source for butterflies, bees, and other pollinators. Mistflower is a perennial that dies back to the ground in winter. It often spreads via its fluffy, winged seeds and by forming underground rhizomes. It is this ability to spread that makes it weedy, but this can be easily controlled by annual weeding to keep it in the locations where it is desired. Mature specimens reach 3 feet in height on narrow erect stems with few branches. The foliage is arrow-shaped with toothed margins, the leaves opposite each other on the stem. Flowers are produced at the ends of the stems, and blooming is most abundant in summer and early fall, though it can occur throughout the year in south Florida. The flowers are produced in rounded clusters; they are cornflower blue in color and quite attractive. Not all forms of this wildflower are as showy as others, however, so make sure you start with plants that produce broad flower heads with rich blue flowers. This wildflower is sometimes marketed as "false ageratum," and the best specimens have blooms that do resemble this popular cultivated garden flower.

Mistflower occurs statewide and can tolerate nearly any typical landscape condition. It performs best, though, in light shade to locations where it receives some direct sunlight for a few hours. It also becomes more robust if not grown in extremely droughty soils. Good forms are available from several commercial native plant nurseries. If you choose to add it to your landscape, be prepared to weed it in order to contain its growth.

Elephant's foot (*Elephantopus* spp.)

Another wildflower that is sometimes considered "weedy" is elephant's foot, though well-grown clusters of this wildflower can be quite striking. Four species are native to Florida and are very similar. They differ by the types of habitat where they occur, small differences in their foliage, and their distribution in Florida. *E. nudatus* and *E. tomentosus* are native only to the northern counties of the state, while *E. carolinianus* and *E. elatus* are found nearly statewide. Of the four, only *E. elatus* is routinely offered by commercial sources in Florida. Elephant's foot is often found in sunny locations, but it performs well in partial sun or in landscapes where it receives at least a few hours of direct sunlight. They are perennial species that die to the ground in winter. Their common name comes from the appearance of their thick, rounded basal leaves that look remotely like the outline of an elephant's footprint. Tall flower stalks emerge from the center of these basal-leaf rosettes. They are tallest in *E. elatus* and reach 3–4 feet in semishade. The light lavender to pink flowers occur mostly

Elephant's foot (*Elephantopus elatus*). Photo by Christina Evans, with permission.

on the tips of the stems. As these species are in the aster family, they are excellent nectar sources for many pollinators. The peak of blooming is late summer.

Elephant's foot tends to spread over time in a landscape, mostly by underground rhizomes, and single plants soon become colonies of tightly packed basal rosettes. Plants also reseed. In certain landscape settings, elephant's foot can be attractive. As few understory wildflowers bloom in the Florida shade garden during late summer and early fall, they provide a welcome addition of color at this time. When not in bloom, the flat basal leaves form a ground cover of green that is tidy and attractive. I like elephant's foot in settings that are meant to be natural. These are not plants for manicured gardens.

Trout lily (*Erythronium umbilicatum*)

One of the very earliest spring ephemerals is trout lily. Its twin elliptical 3-inch leaves emerge in late winter just before the flowers. Each is deep green with cream and purple mottling. A solitary flower arises from each leaf pair. It stands several inches above the foliage on a nodding stem and is composed of six pale yellow tepals (sepals and petals that look alike) with irregular pur-

Trout lily (*Erythronium umbilicatum*)

plish spots. These are true lilies, and their bulbs produce side bulbs that form additional plants adjacent to their parents. Over time, trout lilies form expansive colonies that can occupy acres of a woodland understory. Nestled within the leaf litter of an otherwise bare forest floor, these colonies are spectacular to behold. They are the epitome of what it means to be a spring ephemeral.

Trout lilies are not adaptable to a broad range of conditions and should not be attempted outside north Florida. They require high sunlight during the winter and early spring, and protection, coming from a well-developed deciduous canopy, at other times. They largely disappear soon after blooming, so they are best mixed with other low unaggressive wildflowers, such as Walter violet (*Viola walteri*) or wild ginger. They are adaptable to most soil conditions, except extreme drought, but perform best in moist slightly alkaline conditions. Trout lily is only rarely available from commercial Florida nurseries. If you wish to try it, start with a small colony near a pathway or sitting area. If the conditions are right, it will spread, and you can transplant extra plants to other areas of the landscape with similar growing conditions.

Tampa verbena (*Glandularia tampensis*)

Tampa verbena is naturally quite rare in Florida and listed as a state endangered species, but it is widely propagated by commercial nurseries and often

Tampa verbena (*Glandularia tampensis*)

available for home landscape use. Once considered a true verbena (*Verbena* spp.) and a close relative of those widely used cultivated species, it has been put in a separate genus with another endangered relative, beach verbena (*G. maritima*) and a more common one, mock rose verbena (*G. canadensis*). As its Latin and common names indicate, this wildflower is native to the Tampa Bay region of west-central Florida. It occurs along both coasts of north and central peninsular Florida, but not in north Florida or the extreme southern counties. Tampa verbena is a short-lived perennial that most often occurs in disturbed sites within woodland habitats. I find it along trails, in areas where a canopy tree has fallen over, and in places where wildlife have rooted around and disturbed the forest soil. It can tolerate high levels of sunlight if given ample moisture, but it seems to perform best in partial sun or in places where it receives sunlight for a few hours in early morning or late afternoon. Even in ideal locations, Tampa verbena rarely lives more than a few years, but it will reseed. It has become a popular native wildflower because of its attractive evergreen foliage and superb flowers. It is a weak-stemmed species that will often fall over in high winds or heavy rains. If it remains upright, it can reach 3 feet tall with multiple stems. The foliage is shiny green and arrow shaped with deeply incised teeth. Flowers can be produced nearly year round if temperatures don't reach freezing. Multiple, rounded heads of deep lavender-pink blooms occur at the ends of each stem. They are especially showy and of great interest to pollinators.

Tampa verbena acts like an annual in most landscape settings. It may live several years and it may reseed, but I have never had great success with either in my own landscape. That has always been fine with me as its beauty is worth the annual need to purchase more plants. Use it in light gaps where it can be a focal point during its extended blooming season. I prefer it when used in small clusters.

Paleleaf woodland sunflower (*Helianthus strumosus*)

True to their name, most sunflowers require full sun to perform well. A noticeable exception is paleleaf woodland sunflower. This shade-tolerant sunflower is native to the Florida panhandle but has been widely used well into central Florida with success. The individuals we planted nearly a decade ago have persisted, spread slowly, and flower with annual regularity. They decline a bit in droughty years and spread a bit in wetter ones. Though its common name would suggest otherwise, pale woodland sunflower is actually more abundant in full sun than in a woodland understory. It tolerates partial shade but will not perform if shaded too much. Use it in a sunny edge and allow it to spread where it will. This is a deciduous wildflower that dies back to the ground in winter. After emerging in spring, it grows to 6 feet tall by early summer. The stems are thinner than some in this genus and they tend to droop under the weight of the blooms. The elliptical leaves are rough and whitish on the underside. Flowering begins in summer and can continue for several months. Each flower head is 1½ inches across and the outer ray petals

Paleleaf woodland sunflower (*Helianthus strumosus*)

are narrow and bright yellow. Like all sunflowers, the blooms are magnets for pollinating insects and the seeds have value to seed-eating birds.

Pale woodland sunflower should not be given too much shade or it will eventually weaken and die. It has good drought tolerance but performs much better in moist, well-drained soils. In the most favorable conditions, it produces large numbers of underground rhizomes and spreads quickly. These extra plants can be weeded out without difficulty, but this is not a wildflower for ordered gardens unless accompanied by enough labor to keep it contained. I like pale woodland sunflower best when it is allowed to grow in mass in an expansive opening within a more expansive woodland landscape. In bloom, it is a stunning wildflower, but it doesn't work well in a mixed planting, where its aggressive tendencies can be overwhelming to its neighbors.

Smooth oxeye (*Heliopsis helianthoides*)

In the Midwest, smooth oxeye is ubiquitous to the open tall grass prairie, but in Florida it is only native to a six-county area of the central panhandle where it prefers open semishaded woodlands. It is adaptable, however, and can be successfully grown well into central Florida if provided relatively rich woodland soils and protection from full summer sun. This is another wild-

Smooth oxeye
(*Heliopsis helianthoides*)

flower that grows with more sun than is typical of the average shade garden but adapts to shade as long as it is not too deep. It is a perennial that dies back to the ground each winter. In the spring, multiple stems emerge and reach a mature height of 2 feet. As its Latin name implies, it looks much like a sunflower. The leaves are opposite on the stem, lance shaped, and coarsely toothed along the margins. Flowering occurs over many months, beginning in late spring. The flower heads are borne singly on long stems and look like small sunflowers.

This is a colorful wildflower that should be more widely used. Its extended blooming period, unaggressive nature, and medium size make it an ideal plant to mix with other medium-tall wildflowers, ferns, and native grasses. Do not plant it in deep shade, however. Smooth oxeye is only rarely available from commercial native plant nurseries, but it can be found with some persistence.

St. Andrew's-cross (*Hypericum hypericoides*)

St. Andrew's-cross is an evergreen shrub native to the entire state. Though it most often occurs in wetland habitats, it is especially adaptable and thrives in all but the driest locations. St. Andrew's-cross also performs well in relatively high amounts of shade.

This is a lanky plant by nature. The thin coppery barked trunk reaches a mature height of 3–4 feet with many side branches. It forms an irregular

St. Andrew's-cross (*Hypericum hypericoides*). Photo by Christina Evans, with permission.

shape but lends itself quite well to regular pruning to keep it a bit fuller. The leaves are thin and linear in shape, are light green in color, and give the plant a willowy aspect. Flowering occurs nearly year-round in the southern half of the peninsula but is restricted to summer and fall farther north. Each bloom consists of four lemon-yellow petals that are arranged more like an "X" than a cross. The flowers attract a wide variety of bees.

St. Andrew's-cross performs best when given a few hours of direct sunlight daily or a minimum of half a day of filtered sun. It will survive deeper shade as a foliage plant but will only bloom sporadically. In our landscape, it reseeds itself freely, and we thin out the seedlings each spring that arise in areas where they are not wanted. It has been exceptionally easy to maintain, and we enjoy the character it provides the woodland edges where we keep it. This member of the St. John's-wort family is widely propagated by the nursery trade.

Cooley's justicia (*Justicia pringlei*)

Cooley's justicia is found in a four-county area of central Florida and has recently been determined to be a non-native originating from Mexico. I include it in this book because this determination is controversial. In its Florida range, it occurs on the shady forest floor in mesic limey soils. It is quite adaptable in cultivation and can be successfully grown throughout much of Florida in typical landscape settings. Alexa and I use Cooley's justicia throughout our shade garden. Our small cluster has grown over the years, through seeding of our original plants, and we have welcomed its bright green foliage and tiny

Cooley's justicia
(*Justicia pringlei*)

purple flowers. Cooley's justicia is a perennial that often holds its lower foliage through the winter. In extremely cold winters, it will die back to the ground. Individuals reach a mature height and width of 12 inches. The thin, triangular leaves are opposite each other on the stems and deeply veined. In deep shade, the leaves are rich green in color, but in higher light they become yellowish. Flowering can occur throughout much of the summer and fall but peaks in midsummer. Tiny purple flowers with an intricate white-striped lower lip are produced at the tips of the stems. Though showy, their small size requires one to stop and look to fully appreciate them. They are pollinated by small insects, and the pollinated flowers produce equally tiny seed capsules that forcibly split when ripe and scatter the seeds away from the parents. Over time, Cooley's justicia spreads throughout the shady understory and can form large colonies.

Cooley's justicia is only infrequently offered by commercial nurseries but is easy to propagate. Use it in locations with filtered sun, or beneath the canopy of deciduous trees where it will get direct sun only in winter and early spring. It does not prosper in direct sun during the summer and fall, and this will limit its spread in your landscape. This is one of the few wildflowers native to central Florida that reliably blooms in shady areas. Use it to fill openings in the understory that might otherwise be bare, but make sure a few are near enough to paths and sitting areas that its intricate flowers can be fully admired. Excess plants are easily controlled by annual weeding.

Partridge berry (*Mitchella repens*)

Partridge berry is a creeping herbaceous evergreen ground cover native to woodlands throughout north and central Florida. Numerous wiry stems spread outward in all directions from the parent plant and root as they come in contact with the soil. Over time, vast areas can be colonized by a single plant. This diminutive ground cover is not aggressive, however, and it mixes well with other wildflowers and understory plantings. The leaves are deep green, rounded to heart shaped, and opposite each other along the stems. The foliage makes a beautiful accent across the leaf litter of a woodland planting. Flowering occurs in spring. The paired bright white flowers occur at the leaf nodes. The petals are "fuzzy" on close inspection. Pollinated flowers eventually form small rounded crimson red fruit that greatly add to the aesthetic quality of the plants until the fruit are eaten by birds.

This is a relatively easy plant to maintain in the shade garden. Partridge berry tolerates a wide variety of shade and soil moisture conditions and can

Partridge berry (*Mitchella repens*)

be successfully added to most typical landscapes. Do not plant it in too much sun, do not keep it too wet, and do not use it in densely planted areas. I like it best when allowed to clamber across the leaf litter of a relatively open planting, mixed with other ground covers. In such a setting, it appears and disappears depending on its neighbors. Make sure you allow it to make its appearance near a walkway or sitting area so that its flowers and fruit can be admired. Partridge berry is infrequently offered by commercial native plant nurseries.

Peperomia (*Peperomia* spp.)

As a genus, peperomias are widely used as houseplants, and a great diversity can be found in various garden centers that specialize in indoor plants. They have attractive, succulent, evergreen foliage, and they thrive under the type of low light found indoors. Six species of peperomias are native to Florida; all are quite rare naturally and listed as state endangered species. Most are confined to extreme south Florida because most are cold sensitive and quickly killed by freezing temperatures. The two native species described below are sometimes offered commercially and make attractive additions to a shady understory. They tolerate deep shade quite well and often spread slowly by their succulent stems and by seed. Peperomias are related to black pepper. Tiny dark seeds form along the finger-like flower stalks if the extremely small whitish flowers are pollinated.

Smooth peperomia
(*Peperomia humilis*)

Smooth peperomia (*P. humilis*)

Smooth peperomia is widely scattered in coastal counties throughout peninsular Florida. It is an erect perennial that produces reddish succulent stems up to 8 inches tall. In some locations, it acts like an epiphyte and grows on fallen logs and the lower trunks of trees, but it more often forms mats of stems on the ground. Thick oval leaves are "fuzzy" and almost never exceed 1 inch in length. Smooth peperomia makes an interesting ground cover for moist shady areas. It is not especially drought tolerant, but it also cannot withstand too much water at the soil surface as this will cause the stems to rot. Use it in light gaps or in filtered sun in organic soil and allow it to spread into the areas where its habitat needs are met. If you have the right conditions, you will not need to start with more than a few plants, spaced 12–18 inches apart.

Florida peperomia (*P. obtusifolia*)

Florida peperomia is the showier of these two species. Its large glossy rounded leaves are nearly 2 inches long, and they are held on succulent stems that spread out across the ground. Overall, this is a low ground cover that rarely becomes upright; most often it clambers over downed logs and the lower trunks of trees as an epiphyte that roots periodically along the stems. The fingerlike flower

Florida peperomia
(*Peperomia obtusifolia*)

spikes are 2–3 inches long and quite noticeable. This species has far less cold tolerance than smooth peperomia and should be used only in frost-free areas of the state or grown in large pots in the landscape that can be protected during especially cold weather.

Wild blue phlox (*Phlox divaricata*)

Phlox are extremely popular landscape plants throughout most of North America, but only wild blue phlox is suitable for the shade garden in Florida. Other species require high amounts of sun or are not native here and perform poorly in our state. Wild blue phlox is native only to a small region of the central panhandle in the understory of deciduous woodlands, where it receives high amounts of sun in winter and early spring and dappled sun the rest of the year. Given these conditions, this wonderful wildflower can be grown successfully well into central Florida. Wild blue phlox is a perennial that dies back to the ground in winter. By early spring, it stands 8–12 inches tall with multiple erect stems. Narrow, elliptical leaves are attached opposite each other along the stems and clusters of flower buds form at the top. These blooms are light lavender to purplish pink, but not blue in the true sense of

Wild blue phlox
(*Phlox divaricata*)

the word. Like all phlox, the five petals flare around a central tube. They are of great interest to pollinating insects, especially butterflies.

Wild blue phlox is widely propagated by commercial sources and should not be difficult to find. Use Florida plants (not plants from farther north) for best success and provide high sunlight levels in early spring to ensure good flower production. This is not a species for evergreen shade. Phlox spreads slowly by producing underground stems adjacent to the parent plant. The seed capsules burst open forcefully when fully ripe and scatter the seeds up to several feet away. If you provide it with the proper growing conditions, you will eventually have wonderful patches in your landscape. Begin by planting small patches of three to five plants in light gaps and scatter the patches throughout the open understory near trails and sitting areas.

Native plumbago (*Plumbago zeylanica*)

Blue plumbago (*P. auriculata*) is a widely used landscape plant in much of Florida, but it is not native. Native plumbago is far less aesthetically interesting but can be used quite effectively in a naturalistic landscape setting. It is also an important component of a Florida butterfly garden as it serves as the

Native plumbago (*Plumbago zeylanica*)

larval plant for the Cassius blue. Native plumbago occurs in much of peninsular Florida but is most common in the southern one-third. It is adaptable
to a range of growing sites and can be found from open disturbed areas to the
understory of evergreen shade. In evergreen shade, it performs much better if
used in a light gap beneath the canopy or in high amounts of filtered sun. Do
not attempt it in deep shade where it does not receive at least some direct sunlight. Native plumbago is a weak-stemmed semiwoody shrub with vine-like
branches that extend horizontally off the main stem and rarely stand more
than 12 inches above the ground. Thin oval leaves alternate along the stems,
and flower spikes form at the ends of each. The flowers are bright white, tubular in shape, with five petals. The ripened seeds are covered with hooks that
catch in clothing and animal fur, a characteristic that helps it spread.

This is not an exceptionally well-behaved plant for a highly ordered setting and is difficult to keep adequately pruned for gardeners who like to keep
things tidy. It is a useful wildflower, however, for butterfly gardeners interested in creating a naturalistic look. Because of this, it is widely propagated
by commercial native plant nurseries. Do not plant it closer together than 3
feet apart, and use it sparingly in all but the most spacious landscapes.

Smooth Solomon's-seal (*Polygonatum biflorum*)

Smooth Solomon's-seal is widely distributed throughout much of North
America and occurs in much of north and north-central Florida. Here it is a
wildflower of deciduous woodlands where it receives protection from the full
force of the summer sun but gets ample light as it emerges in late winter and

Smooth Solomon's seal (*Polygonatum biflorum*)

blooms in early spring. Smooth Solomon's-seal is a perennial that dies back to the ground in early winter. Multiple stems emerge in early spring and arch delicately above the ground, oriented almost horizontally. Each stem reaches a length of about 4 inches, sometimes longer in ideal growing conditions. Dark green elliptical leaves occur opposite each other along the stems and give them a ladderlike appearance. As the Latin names indicate, the flowers are formed in pairs along the stem. They are greenish white, bell shaped, and dangle downward. If pollinated, purple berries ripen by midsummer.

I have grown smooth Solomon's-seal in my central Florida landscape for years, but it has never fully prospered. It seems best suited to the understory of deciduous woodlands where winter temperatures regularly dip below freezing. I love the delicate look of this wildflower more for its foliage than its flowers. It mixes well with other spring ephemeral wildflowers. Use it in patches of at least three plants in an open understory setting with showier wildflowers and ferns such as southern lady, Christmas, and/or ebony spleenwort.

Cutleaf coneflower (*Rudbeckia laciniata*)

Most black-eyed Susans (*Rudbeckia* spp.) are poor candidates for the shade garden. Cutleaf coneflower is the most significant exception because it prospers in partial sun or in highly filtered sun as long as its moisture needs are met. Resident to only a few north Florida counties, it is extremely common to our north and most often occurs along the upper edges of slow-moving streams and in wet depressions where the soil is moist to wet during the summer months.

Cutleaf coneflower (*Rudbeckia laciniata*)

Cutleaf coneflower is a perennial and keeps its attractive deeply toothed basal leaves through winter if temperatures are not extreme. These leaves reach a length of 12–18 inches. In early spring, a stalk is produced from the center of this rosette and it continues to grow until midsummer, eventually reaching 4–6 feet in height and forming multiple side stalks near the top. The leaves along these stems are somewhat diamond shaped and deeply notched along the margins.

Flowers are produced in profusion at the ends of each stem in mid- to late summer. The outer ray petals are lemon yellow and droop downward from the central disk. The rounded disk is composed of green flowers, not the dark brown ones typical of most black-eyed Susans. In bloom, cutleaf coneflower is quite showy and attracts a great many pollinating insects.

We have had great success with this wildflower in our Pinellas County landscape, well south of its natural geographic range, but find that it wilts quickly if not kept moist. It also has been susceptible to mealy bugs at times, which attack its roots. These must be controlled for the plant to survive. Given a moist to almost wet location, cutleaf coneflower can be grown in full sun to partly sunny locations. Its height makes it a good candidate to screen areas behind it or it can be used in front of even taller wildflowers such as native hibiscus. This species is being propagated by several native plant nurseries and can be found with a bit of diligence.

Wild petunia (*Ruellia caroliniensis*)

There are few native wildflowers more adaptable to site conditions than wild petunia. It occurs statewide from well-drained sunny uplands to the understory of shady woodlands and tolerates nearly every condition likely to be encountered in a home landscape. Wild petunia performs best in sun but can be effectively added to a shade garden if consideration is given to its need for at least some sunlight during the day. This is an herbaceous perennial that dies back to the ground in winter. In partly sunny sites, it eventually forms a main stem that stands 12–18 inches tall. It has oval to almost linear leaves opposite each other along the stem and flower buds are produced in succession at the top. Each bloom is light lavender to deep pink in color and funnelform in shape, looking much like a true petunia (*Petunia* spp.), though the two genera are not related. Blooms generally open in the morning and fade by midday, though plants in the shade tend to keep their blossoms well into the afternoon. Each flower lasts for one day, but individual plants produce a succession of flowers from late spring into fall. The flowers attract pollinators.

Because of its great adaptability, wild petunia is widely propagated by native nurseries and easy to locate. Plants spread by seed; the dry capsules open forcefully when ripe and expel the seeds great distances from the parents. Use this in light gaps or under high filtered light for best results. Though wild petunia can survive very low light conditions, it rarely blooms and the stems

Wild petunia (*Ruellia caroliniensis*)

become weak in these conditions. I like to use this plant in small clusters for best effect, but plants will move about the landscape over time. This works best in naturalistic landscapes, not well-ordered formal ones. Small patches of wild petunia provide color at a time when most shade-garden wildflowers have finished. Do not confuse this "wild petunia" with the non-native Mexican species (*R. simplex*; aka *R. tweediana*, *R. brittoniana*), widely sold in garden centers. Mexican wild petunia is highly invasive and has become a severe problem to natural areas in Florida.

Sages (*Salvia* spp.)

Members of this genus are mints; they produce highly aromatic foliage and colorful tubular-shaped flowers that are important nectar sources for pollinators. They are hardy and spread easily by the production of large numbers of seeds. Sages are adaptable perennial wildflowers that tolerate a wide variety of growing conditions. Most perform best in sunny conditions; the species listed below are those that perform well under degrees of shade.

Scarlet sage (*S. coccinea*)

Scarlet sage is one of the most widely propagated native wildflowers in Florida and one of the most adaptable plants for home landscapes. Sometimes called "tropical sage," it occurs most widely in the southern third of the state but has been reported nearly statewide. In frost-free areas, it acts like an evergreen and becomes quite tall and somewhat woody. In colder areas, it often freezes to the ground but persists by reseeding. Scarlet sage is best pruned periodically to maintain its shape and to encourage maximum flowering. I think it best to keep it between 3 and 5 feet tall. At this height, it is still ideal for hummingbirds, and they are especially attracted to its bright red flowers. Flowering occurs throughout the year in frost-free areas. Though red is the typical color, several other color varieties are available, including white, pink, salmon, and lavender. The latter colors are recessive and tend to disappear over time as the parent plants die and seedlings take their place. In our landscape, the pink forms have persisted in reduced numbers.

Scarlet sage needs some sunlight to keep its stems strong and for it to bloom well. Use it in sun gaps, at the edge of an evergreen canopy, or under filtered sun. It is especially drought tolerant and can be planted in nearly every soil condition except extreme moisture. I like it best when used in small clusters with other understory wildflowers, grasses, and ferns. Hummingbirds rarely venture

Scarlet sage
(*Salvia coccinea*)

deep into shade to nectar, so plants used near an opening are more apt to draw them. This is also true for butterflies, especially sulfurs and swallowtails.

Lyre-leaved sage (*S. lyrata*)

Lyre-leaved sage is most apt to occur naturally in the understory of open woodlands or in gaps beneath the canopy of deeper forests, though it fares well in open sunny locations if given sufficient moisture. It is especially adaptable and can tolerate high amounts of shade and still bloom well. It is a perennial that persists through the winter as a rosette of basal leaves. This makes it a good choice for areas where some foliage is desired at a time when most others have died back to the ground. The leaves are irregularly shaped and somewhat resemble the outline of a lyre, the ancient precursor to the violin. The leaves are thick and rough to the touch; the deep green color is often interrupted by blotches of purple. For most of the year, lyre-leaved sage remains as a cluster of basal leaves. In spring, flower stalks emerge from the center and reach a height of 18–24 inches. The light blue to lavender flowers open at the upper part of the stem in succession from the bottom up and the

Lyre-leaved sage
(*Salvia lyrata*)

plants remain in bloom for several weeks. Often a second set of flower stalks is produced in fall. These flowers are cleistogamous: the buds do not open and pollination occurs inside the buds without a pollinator. With both types of flowers, large numbers of seeds are produced and colonies of this plant form.

Lyre-leaved sage is not especially showy and the flowering period is much shorter than scarlet sage, but colonies of this wildflower can be especially attractive in the right setting. In a formal garden, remove the spent stalks after the seed has ripened. I like it best when it is allowed to spread naturally at the edge of a canopy. It is easily weeded from areas where it is not wanted. This species is widely propagated by commercial sources.

River sage (*S. misella*)

River sage is restricted to shady moist locations, though it has some drought tolerance when used in a landscape. Found only in peninsular Florida, it is a mostly tropical species that performs best in frost-free areas. It is an evergreen ground cover, creeping across the understory, rooting periodically, and eventually forming large mats that rarely stand taller than 8 inches. Small triangular

River sage (*Salvia misella*)

leaves with toothed margins are opposite each other along the stem. Flower stalks are produced mostly in the spring. They are sometimes horizontal to the ground and sometimes erect, standing several inches above the foliage. The flowers are azure blue, but tiny, and can go largely unnoticed when planted distant to a trail or sitting area. In the southern third of Florida, river sage makes an effective ground cover for shady locations that are not droughty. If used near a path or sitting area, its bright azure flowers add to its aesthetics. This is not a good choice for areas where more diminutive species are also desired as river sage is rather aggressive, but it mixes well with robust ground covers that can stand above it. River sage is not widely grown by commercial sources.

Bloodroot (*Sanguinaria canadensis*)

Bloodroot is a northern spring ephemeral that barely makes its appearance in the Florida panhandle. Here it occurs in rich deciduous woodlands. It is a perennial that dies to the ground each winter. In very early spring, palmate leaves arise from the leaf litter. They are deep green on the upper surface, silvery white below, and deeply lobed. The leaves stand upright on red stems, held perpendicular to the ground, and patches of these leaves are especially distinctive. By late February, the snow-white flowers appear. Each is more than 1 inch across, with up to 16 petals surrounding the canary yellow anthers. Pollinated flowers form an elliptical capsule.

Bloodroot (*Sanguinaria canadensis*)

Like trout lily, bloodroot signals the end of winter and the emergence of spring. Use them in deciduous shade in organic soil with moderate drainage, and plant them in mass. This is a wildflower that loses its effect if used in small numbers. Plant at least seven in a cluster, no closer than 6 inches apart. They will spread by their underground rhizomes. Bloodroot is only infrequently offered by Florida sources. Do not attempt it using out-of-state stock or anywhere except the northern tier of counties.

Skullcaps (*Scutellaria* spp.)

Skullcaps are herbaceous perennial mints that die back to the ground each winter. They have highly aromatic foliage and distinctive hooded tubular flowers in shades of blue to lavender. Their common name comes from the curious shape of the seed capsules that persist well after the flowers have been pollinated, held perpendicular to the flower stalk. Skullcaps spread aggressively in a landscape by underground rhizomes. For this reason, they can become a nuisance in small spaces or in very formal settings. In a shade garden, however, this tendency is somewhat curtailed, and suckers can be easily pulled if they venture beyond their assigned planting space. Most species, like the common skullcap (*S. integrifolia*), can tolerate some shade but are best grown in sunny locations. Several, however, are good candidates for shadier locations. I describe these below.

Hoary skullcap
(*Scutellaria incana*)

Hoary skullcap (*S. incana*)

Hoary skullcap is often found in open habitats but also occurs in open woodlands where it receives only a few hours of direct sunlight each day. It is a robust species that forms stiff upright stems that stand 2–3 feet tall. The arrowshaped leaves are opposite each other on the stem and have deeply toothed margins. Flowering occurs from spring to fall. Numerous flower stalks are produced at the top of each stem. They attract bumblebees, rarely butterflies, and other pollinators. This distinctive skullcap has many aesthetic qualities but is only very rarely offered in Florida by commercial sources. If you can locate specimens, use them in a mixed understory with other medium-sized wildflowers that can hold their own. Plant them in small clusters in the middle portion of the shade garden where they will get at least a few hours of sunlight. In this setting, expect the clumps to spread outward over time.

Heartleaf skullcap (*S. ovata*)

Heartleaf skullcap is widespread in eastern North America but has a very disjunct distribution in Florida. It occurs in Escambia County, adjacent to Alabama, in the far western panhandle and in Hernando County in lime rock soils beneath the canopy of deciduous woodlands. As its common name indi-

Heartleaf skullcap
(*Scutellaria ovata*)

cates, the leaves are heart-shaped, rather broad and distinctive for this genus. Specimens stand 18–24 inches tall. The flower stalks are formed at the end of the stems, and the flowers open in summer. They are light lavender in color, larger than most other species but produced in smaller numbers. Heartleaf skullcap is not currently offered commercially in Florida, and I have not had success with stock originating from other states. Because of its excellent tolerance of shade, beautiful foliage, and distinctive flowers, I hope it will find its way into commercial production someday soon.

Catchflies (*Silene* spp.)

There are several beautiful catchflies with very limited distributions in Florida that can be used in deciduous woodland settings in extreme north Florida. The best of these are Carolina catchfly (*S. caroliniana*), fringed campion (*Silene catesbaei*), and royal catchfly (*S. regia*). Each requires fairly similar growing requirements: a deciduous canopy and organic soils that are moist but well drained. Of the three species above, royal catchfly prefers slightly higher light levels to perform at its best. All are perennials that die back to the ground each winter, and each has spectacular blooms unmatched by other genera.

Carolina catchfly is a low-growing species that spends much of the year

Carolina catchfly (*Silene caroliniana*)

Fringed campion (*Silene catesbaei*)

as a basal rosette of leaves no taller than several inches. Flowering occurs in early spring on short stalks emerging from the center of each basal clump. The blooms are deep pink in color. Over time, Carolina catchfly spreads outward by underground stems.

Fringed campion is one of my favorite native wildflowers. Like Carolina catchfly, it forms basal rosettes of leaves that remain close to the ground, and these spread outward over time by above-ground stems to form colonies. Flowering occurs in early spring, on nodding stems that keep the blooms close to the ground. They are large for the genus (1 inch across) and composed

Royal catchfly
(*Silene regia*)

of five fringed petals that are soft pink in color. Colonies of this species in full bloom are extremely showy.

Royal catchfly emerges in spring and forms an upright rosette of deep green leaves. Flower stalks emerge in late spring and into the summer. They stand several feet tall and on each are dozens of scarlet blooms. Few flowers in nature are this brilliant red, and they attract hummingbirds, butterflies, and an assortment of other pollinators.

Though rare in Florida, commercial native plant nurseries have recently begun to propagate all three of these species. Alexa and I have grown them quite successfully in our landscape by keeping them in large pots where we can better control soil and moisture conditions. If planted in the ground, use them only in north Florida in filtered sun or beneath the canopy of deciduous trees where they will receive only a few hours of direct sunlight during the harsh summer and fall. Carolina catchfly and fringed campion will form colonies over time. They should be allowed to spread and should be kept near paths and sitting areas so their blooms can be fully admired. Royal catchfly will form multiple stems over time, but will not form colonies like the other two. Plant this species in clusters of at least five plants, set back a bit from the front of the planting bed.

Bear's-foot (*Smallanthus uvedalia*)

Bear's-foot is a woodland understory wildflower that occurs throughout north and central Florida. It adapts to a variety of growing conditions but performs best when grown in partial sun or in light gaps where it receives limited direct sunlight per day. This perennial dies back to the ground each fall and quickly forms a set of basal leaves in spring. The large coarse leaves are up to 6 inches long and nearly as broad. Though they are said to resemble a bear's foot in shape, I do not see it. To my eye, they look somewhat like a maple leaf. It is a large robust herbaceous semishrub by late spring, standing 4–6 feet tall. The stems are hollow, however, and tend to break if subjected to severe weather. Flowering occurs from summer to fall, and the yellow sunflower-like blooms are produced at the ends of all the stems. Each is nearly 1 inch across and attracts a wide variety of pollinators.

Bear's-foot becomes a dominant member of the understory and should be used with low shrubs like wild coffee and rouge plant or other large wildflowers like frostweed to be effective. Over time, it spreads by seed. Because it flowers over many months during the summer when few other woodland wildflowers bloom, it can be an interesting accent to a mixed understory. If it spreads into unwanted areas it can be easily pulled, and it tolerates pruning if it becomes too robust. Do not use this plant in small settings, however. Bear's-foot is only rarely offered commercially and may take some time to locate. Once established, it is very adaptable and easy to keep.

Bear's foot
(*Smallanthus uvedalia*)

Indian pink (*Spigelia marilandica*)

Indian pink is one of Florida's showiest woodland wildflowers. It occurs naturally only in central and western panhandle counties but can be propagated into central Florida if provided the growing conditions it needs. It occurs in well-drained soils in open deciduous woods where it receives some protection from the heat of the summer sun and full sun in spring to produce its flowers. Indian pink is a perennial that dies back to the ground in winter. Multiple stems emerge in early spring and eventually stand 2 feet tall or more. The broadly ovate leaves are opposite each other on the stems and a rich green in color. Each stem is somewhat lanky overall, however, and not especially interesting. What sets this plant apart are its flowers. They are produced on short stalks at the end of each stem from late spring to early summer and are spectacular. The buds are crimson red. Each bursts open at the tip to form a five-pointed star that is bright yellow in color. The contrasting red and yellow is truly unique among Florida's native wildflowers and can be seen for long distances.

Indian pink spreads slowly by underground rhizomes to form colonies over time. It also reseeds. Use it in a mixed woodland setting, and mix it with other woodland wildflowers, such as wild blue phlox, that tolerate well-drained soils. It is best used in a landscape where it can form substantial colonies. Do not allow it to remain wet for too long or it will rot. Indian pink is only occasionally propagated by commercial nurseries in Florida but can

Indian pink (*Spigelia marilandica*)

be found with some diligence. If you can provide it the right conditions, there are few other wildflowers that can match it. As a member of the strychnine family, however, it should not be ingested.

Wavy leaf meadowrue (*Thalictrum revolutum*)

Wavy leaf meadowrue is a perennial that dies back to the ground each winter. It emerges again in early spring and reaches a mature height of 2–3 feet before blooming in late spring. Like other members of this genus, it has delicate compound leaves that look similar to columbine. The flowers are rather small and open in late spring. Unlike its close relative, rue anemone (*T. thalictroides*), described below, wavy leaf meadowrue is dioecious, and the two sexes are very different in floral structure. Male plants have flowers with no petals, but short white sepals and numerous stamens that dangle downward. Female flowers also lack petals, but are green and lack much aesthetic interest. This species occurs in only three counties of north Florida in well-drained deciduous woodland understories but can be grown well into central Florida if

Wavy leaf meadowrue
(*Thalictrum revolutum*)

provided the right soil, moisture, and light conditions. Protect it from summer sun but give it ample light in spring, mulch it with leaf litter, and give it moisture but good drainage. This species mixes well with other woodland wildflowers, ferns, and grasses and is best used for its beautiful foliage as an accent. Because it is dioecious, plant it in small clumps, and do your best to get at least one of each sex. As the male flowers are more interesting, this is one time that having more males than females makes the most landscape sense. Wavy leaf meadowrue is only rarely offered by commercial nurseries specializing in native plants.

Rue anemone (*T. thalictroides*)

Rue anemone is the best-known member of this genus as a landscape plant. In regions like the Northeast, it is widely planted in mixed wildflower beds, but in Florida it occurs naturally only in a three-county region of the central panhandle and has virtually been ignored in landscapes. That is especially regrettable as rue anemone is resilient and can be grown well outside its limited natural range. It is a perennial that dies back to the ground each winter. In early spring, it forms a basal clump of delicate compound leaves and stands only 6–9 inches tall. Across the top of each plant forms open clusters of bright white flowers; the many petal-like sepals are sometimes flushed with pink and up to 1 inch in diameter.

Rue anemone is an early spring ephemeral and requires organic woodland soils with good drainage, but some moisture, to thrive. Like other spring

Rue anemone (*Thalictrum thalictroides*)

ephemerals, it also needs high light in late winter and early spring but a well-formed canopy during the rest of the year. Though a state endangered species, it is sometimes offered by commercial sources. Use it in large masses near walkways and sitting areas for best effect and mix it with other low-growing wildflowers such as Walter violet (*Viola walteri*) and wild ginger.

Spiderwort (*Tradescantia ohiensis*)

To some, spiderwort is a weed. It occurs nearly everywhere in north and central Florida (as well as much of eastern North America) and often spreads aggressively by seed, but this tenacity also makes it an exceedingly hardy plant and useful in a shade garden where formality is unimportant. Spiderwort dies back to the ground in all but the warmest winters. Thick, grass-like leaves emerge in spring and form a rosette that stands about 12 inches tall. In shade, it may stand several inches taller. Upright flower stalks arise from the center of these leaf masses and reach another 6 inches above the foliage. From the top, a succession of flower buds is formed. Each flower lasts only one morning before wilting, but several may be open on any given day, and plants bloom from late spring through summer. The petals are typically deep blue in color, with bright yellow contrasting anthers and spidery projections from the deep blue filaments below. Many other color forms have been developed, and it is possible to find pink, white, and light blue forms.

Spiderwort can be grown in full sun to nearly full shade and in virtually

Spiderwort (*Tradescantia ohiensis*)

every soil type typically encountered in a home landscape. In shade, it tends to grow lankier and bloom a bit less, so it is best used in light gaps, the edge of evergreen shade, or under high filtered sun. Clumps grow outward each year and plants also reseed, so it will increase over time. This is not a species easily used in formal plantings, but it works well in more natural ones if care is taken to control its spread. This is a difficult species to hand pull once fully established so it should be weeded when young. Spiderwort is widely grown and sold by commercial nurseries.

Trilliums (*Trillium* spp.)

In much of North America, trilliums are the symbol of a natural landscape woodland wildflower. Many have broad lush foliage and showy blooms, they form beautiful clumps within the shade garden that remain attractive for the entire growing season, and they add a sense of elegance few other wildflowers can. Florida trilliums, however, are a bit understated compared to many, and they have not achieved the level of landscape use seen in many other parts of the country. We have four species that differ by small differences in foliage and flower shape. All are native to north Florida woodlands with deciduous canopies. Trilliums require high light in the late winter and early spring to leaf out and flower, but they quickly wither if given too much sun later in the year. Many seem to do best in alkaline soils, with a well-developed organic leaf litter,

Spotted wakerobin (*Trillium maculatum*)

good drainage, and not too droughty. Of our four species, spotted wakerobin (*T. maculatum*) has the widest natural distribution and occurs as far south as the Gainesville area. Long-bract wakerobin (*T. underwoodii*) occurs through-out a wide region of the central and eastern panhandle, while Chattahoochie and lanceleaf wakerobin (*T. decipiens* and *T. lancifolium*, respectively) have extremely limited natural ranges in the central panhandle. Our native trilli-ums produce three-parted leaves beneath the solitary flower. They rarely stand taller than 8 inches, and the leaves are variable in color. Most are a deep green with some spotting of silver, cream, and/or purple. Over time, plants spread slowly by their underground rhizome. First year plants have a solitary, undi-vided leaf; the three-parted leaf is formed in later years. Flowering occurs in early spring. The sepals of most species are deep maroon in color, though they are greenish in spotted wakerobin. The petals of all four species are maroon, and they vary in shape and length. Yellow-petal forms of spotted wakerobin are not uncommon. Trilliums form complex relationships with ants, which collect and disperse the seeds once the capsules ripen in summer.

Use native trilliums in mixed collections of other spring ephemerals, such as bloodroot and trout lily. They are drought tolerant once established but require cold winter temperatures to persist and the correct light and soil con-ditions to prosper. Of the four native trilliums, spotted wakerobin is the most commonly propagated. Plant them in mass, never less than five per clump, for maximum effect.

Frostweed/Winged stem (*Verbesina virginica*)

There are several yellow-flowered species in this genus that are potential candidates for the shade garden, but their very limited distribution in the Florida panhandle greatly limits their landscape use, and they are not cur-rently offered for sale by commercial native plant nurseries in Florida. Only the white-flowered frostweed is both widely distributed and available to the home gardener. Frostweed occurs nearly statewide in a variety of settings but is common in light gaps and edges of shady areas. It is a perennial that dies back to the ground in winter, even in south Florida, and becomes quite robust by fall. Mature specimens reach heights of 6–7 feet. The stems are semiwoody and keeled, which gives rise to its other common name, winged stem. Both the stems and leaves are rough to the touch. The lower leaves are deeply lobed, alternate along the stem, and often more than 6 inches long. They are smaller near the top of the stem and sometimes unlobed. The com-

Frostweed (*Verbesina virginica*)

mon name, frostweed, is a reference to its late fall blooming season. This is one of the last wildflowers to produce blooms and, for this reason, they attract the attention of a great many butterflies and other pollinators. Large numbers of pure white flowers are produced in heads at the tips of each stem, and this mass of blooms is quite showy.

Frostweed is a rather weedy looking wildflower for much of the year, but it makes amends in the late fall with its floral display. Use this wildflower at the back of the planting bed in a location where it will receive strong filtered sun or a few hours of direct sun to promote strong stems and good flowering. This is not a plant for a small planting area; it will reseed heavily and spread over time if not routinely weeded. I like it best when mixed with evergreen shrubs such as marlberry, myrsine, and wild coffee. In such a setting, its somewhat weedy growth form is hidden for much of the year, and its presence is revealed in late fall when it blooms.

Giant ironweed (*Vernonia gigantea*)

Ironweeds are found throughout North America, and most occur in open sunny habitats. As such, they are poor candidates for the shade garden. The one exception in Florida is giant ironweed. Giant ironweed occurs throughout north and central Florida in a wide variety of settings but is tolerant of partial shade. It is not a good candidate for deep shade and requires at least

Giant ironweed (*Vernonia gigantea*). Photo by Christina Evans, with permission.

some direct sunlight daily to thrive. Giant ironweed is a perennial that dies to the ground each winter. Large, wide, finely toothed leaves (up to 12 inches long and 3 inches wide) emerge in spring and form a rosette at the soil surface. Shortly after, a main stem arises from the center and quickly grows upward. As the common name suggests, this stem reaches great heights, sometimes 9 feet, before flowering commences. Like other members of this genus, broad clusters of deep lavender flowers are produced at the top of each stem. The blooming season is prolonged, often lasting several months, from summer to early fall. Pruning the spent flower stalks encourages the production of side stems that will also bloom. Ironweed flowers attract a great many pollinators.

Giant ironweed performs best at the edge of a shade garden, and its large size makes its best use at the back of the planting where it will get some direct sunlight, act as a screen, and draw butterflies and other pollinators during its time in the sun. All ironweeds spread by underground rhizomes. Allow it to form masses for best effect, but limit its spread, if necessary, by routine weeding of the new suckers. This is not a good candidate for a small space unless used alone as an accent. Giant ironweed is commonly propagated by commercial sources in Florida and should be relatively easy to locate.

Violets (*Viola* spp.)

My mother, Louise, was not a gardener, but she took great delight each spring in the appearance of her garden flowers. One that she never failed to mention was her violets. Since my earliest childhood, I have delighted in violets and measured the arrival of spring by their flowering. Violets in Florida sometimes keep their lower leaves through winter if temperatures remain above freezing, but they always bloom in early spring. Their heart-shaped foliage and colorful flowers add much to a shady landscape, and their ability to spread by seed eventually distributes them to all corners of the planting bed. Masses of violets seem a natural occurrence in shade to my eye and I use them in my own landscape. They mix well with other species and fill in the holes whenever one occurs. For some reason, violets are not an especially common landscape plant in Florida. That is not for want of species to use. Florida is home to eight species of native violets. A few are limited to extreme north Florida, but others occur nearly statewide and can be used well into south Florida landscapes. None of our native species, however, are widely propagated at this time but can be found with some searching. It is my hope that this situation will change in the future and that a demand for them will generate a better market.

Violets are best used in expansive settings where they can spread and form masses. They perform best beneath deciduous shade where they can receive high sunlight as they emerge in spring and begin generating flower buds. In evergreen shade, they need high filtered sun or a few hours of direct sun in a canopy gap. Plant no less than five plants 4–6 inches apart in clusters. Over time, they will spread throughout the understory and be limited only by encountering too much sun or soils that are too droughty. Most violets (and all the species discussed below) are drought tolerant, once established, but they will eventually perish if kept too dry for extended periods. The species discussed below are the most widespread violets in Florida and the best candidates for home landscapes.

Early blue violet (*V. palmata*)

Early blue violet is not necessarily the first violet to bloom each spring, but its deep blue flowers can be seen from late February through early summer. I often encounter this violet in open pinelands where it receives high amounts of filtered sun, but it also occurs beneath woodland canopies. Early blue vio-

Early blue violet
(*Viola palmata*)

White violet (*Viola primulifolia*). Photo by Eleanor Dietrich, with permission.

let has been given a great many Latin names over the last century and it is somewhat variable, but its distinctive characteristic is its foliage. Unlike most species, the leaves are deeply lobed near the base. This gives the leaves an appearance somewhat resembling a hand with fingers, hence its Latin name.

White violet (*V. primulifolia*)

White violet is actually one of two white-flowered species. Bog violet (*V. lan-ceolata*) occurs statewide but requires wet soils to prosper and is not discussed further in this book. White violet, however, is extremely adaptable to typical home landscape settings and occurs naturally throughout Florida, except the most southern tier of counties. I use this species extensively in our home landscape. The heart-shaped leaves persist in all but the coldest periods, and the bright white flowers are produced for several months in spring. The lower lip of each bloom is streaked with purple lines.

Blue violet (*V. sororia*)

Blue violet is an extremely variable species that some taxonomists split into several species. In many ways, it is similar to white violet and is difficult to distinguish from it when not in bloom. Its flowers are the typical violet blue in color, though the depth of this color is quite variable and white forms are common. The lower lip is often striped with dark lines. I like to mix this species with white violet for the contrasting colors of the flowers.

Walter's violet (*V. walteri*)

Walter's violet is the most distinctive of the violet species described in this book. It occurs sporadically in central north Florida and in Hernando County, most commonly on limestone soils beneath the canopy of decidu-

Blue violet (*Viola sororia*)   Walter's violet (*Viola walteri*)

ous woodlands. It is adaptable to other soils but does not seem to perform as well on soils that are acidic. Walter's violet creeps across the ground, rotting periodically at places where the stems make good contact with the soil. Its small, heart-shaped leaves are light green, accented by dark green veins. On some specimens, the leaves are mottled. Small light lavender flowers stand several inches upright above the leaves in early spring. The petals are streaked in purple. I truly enjoy this diminutive violet, but have not had good success with it when grown directly in my central Florida landscape. It has persisted for years, however, in a large pot I keep in my landscape and it has reseeded to nearby pots. Use Walter's violet as a low ground cover near pathways or sitting areas or it will get "lost" in the understory and you won't be able to fully admire its wonderful blooms.

Wet Places

Not all of us are blessed with naturally wet places in which to garden, but all of us are capable of creating such places if we desire it. Most plants that require wet soil adapt well to high sunlight. Even most ferns will tolerate sun if kept wet, but only a small subset of wetland wildflowers perform well in the shade. The species described below are shade tolerant, but none thrive in deep shade. Most require at least a few hours of direct sunlight or they become lanky and fail to flower. To maximize the opportunity to use wildflowers in a created wetland in your landscape, position the wetland at the edge of the canopy so that it receives early morning or late afternoon sun. If you have a naturally wet spot, use selective pruning of the canopy to open a light gap. Otherwise, you will mostly be limited to ferns.

Golden canna (*Canna flaccida*)

Golden canna occurs statewide in seasonally flooded habitats. It can tolerate less moisture for short periods, but will not persist if not kept extremely wet during the summer and fall when temperatures are at their highest. It is a perennial that dies to the ground each winter. The large, pleated leaves arise in spring, standing erect to a height of several feet. The flower stalks emerge from the center of the leaf cluster in late spring and stand up to a foot above the foliage. The bright lemon yellow flowers are then produced in succession over several months. Each bloom lasts only a morning, but each plant often has several open at any given time. They are composed of three sepals and three petals, all broadly ovate in shape with a frilly margin. A mass of golden canna can

Golden canna (*Canna flaccida*). Photo by Christina Evans, with permission.

be spectacular in bloom at the height of the season. It is the larval food of the Brazilian skipper as well. Evidence of the caterpillars is noticeable by slits along the leaf margins with the leaves folded over and held that way by silken threads.

Golden canna spreads rapidly in wet soils by its woody underground rhizomes. It is difficult to maintain in a small setting and is best used along a pond margin or other expansive planting bed where it can form masses. It is widely propagated by commercial sources and should be easy to locate.

Swamp/String lily (*Crinum americanum*)

Swamp lily is not a lily, but an amaryllis, and though a great many non-native members of this genus are used extensively in Florida landscapes (especially Asian swamp lily, *C. asiaticum*), only one species is native to Florida. Swamp lily occurs statewide in areas that are seasonally flooded, though it is somewhat adaptable and relatively drought tolerant compared to most species in this section. Do not use it in droughty soils, but it will persist for short periods in typical landscape conditions once established. It is a perennial that

Swamp lily (*Crinum americanum*). Photo by Christina Evans, with permission.

maintains its basal leaves in south Florida but dies back to its bulb in colder locations. Long (2–3 feet) strap-like leaves arch and produce a whorl in the spring. They are deep green and succulent. The 2–3-foot-tall flower stalks arise from the center of each whorl in summer and produce four to six buds each. The flowers open at the same time and persist for a week or more. Each is composed of six porcelain white narrow tepals with contrasting orange to pinkish stamens. The blooms are exquisitely fragrant and quite showy.

Swamp lily spreads slowly over time by divisions of its underground bulb, so eventually it forms small clumps. In small masses it is attractive for its foliage and showy when in bloom. In extreme south Florida, the blooming season can occur all year, but it is confined to summer and early fall further north. This plant mixes well with other wetland wildflowers, but is at its best when used in expansive landscapes where it can mass in large numbers or as an accent in smaller landscapes where it is used solely for impact. Swamp lily is widely grown by commercial sources.

Spider lilies (*Hymenocallis* spp.)

There are 13 species of spider lilies native to Florida. Many are narrowly endemic to small regions of the state, but all are very similar in appearance

Spider lily
(*Hymenocallis palmeri*).
Photo by Christina
Evans, with permission.

and have similar uses in the home landscape. Spider lilies, of one species or another, can be grown statewide. Many typically occur in moist pinelands as well the edges of wetlands, and they exhibit good drought tolerance as long as they are kept moist during the summer and fall. Spider lilies are closely related to swamp lilies; both are members of the amaryllis family, have underground onion-like bulbs, and produce fleshy strap-like leaves, which are evergreen in south Florida but deciduous further north. In spider lilies the leaves do not form a distinct whorl around the bulb, but are more upright and have a fanlike aspect. The flower stalks emerge from the center of this fan and stand 2–4 feet tall. Depending on the species, 2–10 or more flower buds are produced on top of each stalk. The flowers open successively (often several at a time) and last for up to a week. The spidery thin crystalline white tepals surround a funnelform central disc; the shape is similar to a daffodil. Spider lilies have a definite blooming season, regardless of the species or its geographic location. Most blooming occurs in summer, and the flowers are fragrant.

Spider lilies can be effectively mixed with swamp lilies, but each should be clumped in small masses to maximize their unique differences. Spider lilies will spread by bulblets formed off the main bulb. Do not plant them in standing water but in areas that might be inundated for short periods during the summer rainy season. This is a species best used at the higher elevation of a wet area. Of the many species possibly offered for sale commercially in Florida, beach spider lily (*H. latifolia*) is the most widely grown. As its name implies, it is salt tolerant. Not all species are.

Irises (*Iris* spp.)

Worldwide, irises are widely grown as garden flowers, and as many as 300 species exist that form the foundation of a major horticultural industry. All produce woody underground rhizomes that spread slowly through the landscape, sending erect narrow strap-like leaves above ground and taller flower stalks that produce unique blooms consisting of three large drooping sepals and three erect smaller petals.

Florida has six native irises, but only two are widely distributed. The others have very limited ranges in extreme north Florida. Nearly all are restricted to wetland habitats, where they are frequently inundated by six inches of water throughout the rainy season. They have limited drought tolerance and do not thrive if grown in droughty conditions for any length of time. All have deep

Dixie iris (*Iris hexagona*). Photo by Christina Evans, with permission.

blue flowers, except copper iris (*I. fulva*), a coppery flowered species found only in Santa Rosa County in the far western panhandle. Of our six native species, the best choices for most landscape settings are Dixie iris (*I. hexagona*) and blue-flag iris (*I. virginica*). These very similar species differ mostly by small differences in the way their flowers attach to the stem. Dixie iris is more widely distributed than blue-flag iris and is the better choice for south Florida.

Use any of our native irises in shallow pond edges, or the edge of similar large water features. They are not good choices for small areas as they spread aggressively and are not easily confined. They mix well, however, with other aggressive wetland wildflowers such as golden canna, and masses of these species can be extremely attractive. Irises tolerate low light levels, but will not bloom well if not given several hours of direct sunlight.

Cardinal flower (*Lobelia cardinalis*)

In Florida, cardinal flower is most apt to occur along the edges of springs and rivers, in the floodplain where it is inundated by several inches of water during the rainy season. It has tolerance to some drought, but unlike specimens farther north, does not perform well if not provided wet conditions

Cardinal flower (*Lobelia cardinalis*). Photo by Christina Evans, with permission.

during the summer and fall. In fact, my best successes with this plant have come from planting it directly in shallow water. I have not had it persist for long in other types of landscape settings. Cardinal flower is a perennial that dies back to the ground each winter. In warmer winters, its rosette of basal leaves may persist. In early spring, this set of leaves increases in diameter, but they continue to hug the ground. Often, additional clumps of leaves form as "pups" adjacent to the main cluster, and beginning in late spring, each sends a fleshy flower stalk upward that reaches a mature height of up to 6 feet by summer. The flowers open from the bottom of the stalk and proceed upward over a span of several weeks. Few flowers in nature match the brilliant crimson red of cardinal flower. Patches of this wildflower, in full bloom, are one of the most spectacular sights in the floral world. Their broad, deeply notched lower lip and narrow, doubly notched upper lip surround a floral tube that is especially attractive to a wide assortment of pollinators, including hummingbirds. Eventually, these pollinated flowers form seed capsules along the stem that allow it to reseed near the parent plant. It is also possible to propagate this plant by bending the spent flower stalk so that it is in contact with water. Each node, where a flower bud was formed, is capable of forming a new plant over time and can be separated from the stalk once roots have formed.

Cardinal flower should be planted in clumps of no less than three to be most dramatic. Larger masses will form over time and, in my opinion, you can never have too many. As this wildflower gets quite tall before blooming, it is best planted behind more diminutive species or spring-blooming species, like golden ragwort (*Packera* spp.), described below. Because of its great beauty, cardinal flower is widely propagated in Florida. Do not purchase plants originating from more northern populations as they will not survive long in our climate.

Golden ragwort/Perennial butterweed (*Packera aurea*)

The butterweeds are a genus composed of five very similar species. Small's ragwort (*P. anonyma*) is most common in open sunny habitats, while the others are resident to shade and partly shady locations. The extremely common butterweed (*P. glabella*) is an annual and difficult to maintain in a landscape setting, while two other excellent perennial candidates for the shady wetland garden (roundleaf ragwort, *P. obovata*, and balsam groundsel, *P. paupercula*) are of limited distribution in the Florida panhandle and not currently offered by commercial native plant nurseries. Only the perennial butterweed is

Golden ragwort (*Packera aurea*). Photo by Eleanor Dietrich, with permission.

sometimes grown commercially. Golden ragwort emerges in early spring and quickly forms a clump of heart-shaped basal leaves with sharply toothed margins that stand several inches tall. This species produces a stout underground rhizome and spreads slowly in all directions. Over time, it forms a mass and works extremely well as a ground cover. For much of the year, these masses of basal-leaf clusters are quite attractive. Flower stalks are produced from the center of each in early spring. Each stands 2–3 feet high, and a great many flower buds are produced at the top in a rounded head. As the common name indicates, the flowers are golden yellow in color. Patches of these golden-daisy flower heads are outstanding.

Golden ragwort is a bit weedy by nature, however. Besides spreading slowly outward by its underground stems, it also reseeds if allowed to. Prevent this by removing the spent flower stalks once flowering has finished. Although this species is naturally limited to a few north Florida counties, we have had great success with it in our own central Florida landscape, and I suspect it would prosper in much of the state. It prefers moist soil but does not require it to be saturated. Do not use it in droughty locations, and give it high filtered sun or a few hours of direct sun to encourage flowering.

Spoonflowers (*Peltandra* spp.)

Spoonflowers are only very rarely sold by commercial native plant nurseries in Florida but make an attractive addition to a wetland shade garden. Their large,

Green spoonflower (*Peltandra virginica*)

glossy leaves make them an especially attractive foliage plant from spring through fall while their jack-in-the-pulpit type flowers are interesting accents. These spikes of tiny flowers, partly surrounded by a broad spathe, can be produced in most months, except winter. Pollinated flowers produce a round berry that is eaten by birds. Two species occur in Florida. White spoonflower (*P. sagittifolia*) is showier. Its spathe is white in color and its leaves are shaped like arrowheads. The ripened berries are bright red. White spoonflower naturally occurs from north Florida into the central peninsula. Green spoonflower (*P. virginica*) occurs statewide. Its spathe is identical in color to the deep green foliage and often hides the flower spike. The berries are greenish brown and the foliage is arrow-shaped but much narrower than white spoonflower.

Both species perform best in shallow water, no deeper than six inches for extended periods of time. As such, it works well with golden canna, iris, and cardinal flower. Do not use it in soils that are not inundated during the summer. Spoonflowers are best used as accent plants in a mixed pond edge. Cluster them in small groups for best effect. Both species perform well in deep shade but will do better if given at least high filtered sun.

Lizard's tail (*Saururus cernuus*)

Lizard's tail is an adaptable species for wet sites and can be used statewide. Though it occurs in open sunny locations, along the edges of ponds and

Lizard's tail (*Saururus cernuus*). Photo by Bill Bilodeau, with permission.

streams, it also does well in shadier wetland sites. It is an herbaceous perennial that dies back to the ground each winter, except in extreme south Florida. The glossy heart-shaped leaves emerge early on upright stems that stand up to 3 feet tall. Lizard's tail produces stout rhizomes and spreads rapidly in the wetland landscape, producing dense colonies. Flower spikes are produced in early summer. Tiny white fragrant flowers are produced along the curved length of the spike, and each remains in bloom for several weeks. Pollinated flowers produce tiny brown seeds that have little wildlife value.

Lizard's tail is widely propagated and easy to locate for home landscaping purposes. I believe it is best used in expansive settings, such as pond edges, where it can spread and form large colonies. It is a difficult plant to confine in smaller settings. It does not mix well with less-robust species, so it often becomes a monotypic mass. Such masses are attractive, however. Though lizard's tail can survive moist soils, it will perform best in settings where it is inundated by several inches of water during the summer rainy season.

Vines

By nature, vines adapt to shade by climbing out of it and into the tree canopy where they reach the light they need. Most vines are aggressive. They produce large numbers of seed, and they often also spread by producing additional stems from their extensive root systems. Vines can be herbaceous or woody, and they can climb using coiled tendrils and hooks or by simply twining around and through branches and trunks. The vast majority of vines can be used in a shade garden, but they aren't really shade tolerant if their sole goal is to escape into the canopy and the sun. A few, however, can actually perform well in shade and have aesthetic and/or ecological features that make their inclusion in a shade garden a consideration. I have included these in the descriptions below.

Cross-vine (*Bignonia capreolata*)

Cross-vine is one of the most aggressive native vines available to the home gardener. It freely suckers once established and can quickly escape any attempt to keep it confined. Its stout woody stems quickly climb into the canopy using tendrils that arise at each leaf axil. The paired evergreen leaflets are opposite each other along the stems. Cross-vine's redeeming value in the landscape comes from its flowers. They are produced in spring, are large and trumpet shaped, and deep orange to red with a yellowish throat. These flowers are visited by hummingbirds.

Cross-vine (*Bignonia capreolata*)

Cross-vine is especially difficult to control and should be used with caution. It can be a useful addition to a naturalistic landscape designed for hummingbirds, but even then, the blooms are most often produced in the canopy where viewing these magnificent birds is difficult. Once added to a landscape, cross-vine is nearly impossible to eradicate should you change your mind. It is widely propagated by commercial sources because of its attractive blooms and value to hummingbirds. It is native to north and central Florida and can be used in most typical landscape settings.

Trumpet creeper (*Campsis radicans*)

Trumpet creeper may be even more aggressive than cross-vine and tolerates a wide range of growing conditions. In the Iowa farm house where I once lived, it grew up the walls of the home, worked its way through the side boards and overtook the clothes I had hanging in my closet. Its stout woody stems produce aerial rootlets that anchor themselves on any substrate as they climb to the canopy. Trumpet creeper is evergreen; the leaflets are opposite each other

Trumpet creeper (*Campsis radicans*). Photo by Gil Nelson, with permission.

on the stems and compound. Each leaflet is oval in shape with rounded teeth along its margins. Like cross-vine, its landscape value comes from its flowers, which are produced in late spring and summer. They occur in small clusters along the stems, are bright orange in color, and are tubular. They are eagerly visited by hummingbirds.

Like cross-vine, trumpet creeper should be added to a landscape only after careful consideration. It is impossible to contain once established and suckers freely. Its best use is in naturalistic landscapes where hummingbirds are a major consideration. Trumpet creeper can be grown in all but the most southerly Florida counties. It is exceedingly adaptable and is propagated by many commercial nurseries.

Climbing hydrangea (*Decumaria barbara*)

Climbing hydrangea is a member of the hydrangea family and shares the family trait of producing showy blooms. It is one of the few vines naturally confined to shady locations, and though it climbs up the trunks of trees by means of small aerial roots that anchor it to the bark, it generally remains in the shade instead of climbing all the way to the canopy. A deciduous woody vine, it is native to moist soil habitats, such as forested wetlands and moist hammocks throughout north and central Florida. It has some drought tolerance but should not be attempted in droughty soils. Dark green, heart-shaped

Climbing hydrangea (*Decumaria barbara*)

leaves occur opposite each other along the woody stems. The flower buds are produced at the tips of the new growth in spring, and showy clusters of fragrant white flowers open in late spring through early summer.

Climbing hydrangea is infrequently offered by commercial nurseries for home landscapes. It can be used in most shade situations but should be watered well during the first year to ensure it is well established. Because the flowers are often produced well below the canopy, their fragrance and color can be appreciated.

Carolina yellow jessamine (*Gelsemium sempervirens*)

Carolina yellow jessamine occurs in sunny and partly sunny locations throughout north and central Florida. It is exceedingly adaptable and tolerates most typical landscape conditions except excessive moisture. It is a thin-stemmed vine that twines its way up to the canopy. Its glossy leaves are willowlike. Flowering occurs from December to March; I often think of it as the Valentine's Day flower. Bright canary yellow tubular flowers occur along the stems at the leaf axils. They are exceedingly fragrant, and their perfume carries a great distance from the plant itself. The flowers attract hummingbirds as well as bees and butterflies.

Carolina yellow jessamine is widely propagated. Its glossy evergreen foliage and brilliant blooms make it one of the best native vines for home land-

Carolina yellow jessamine (*Gelsemium sempervirens*)

scapes, but it suckers and can sometimes be difficult to control. In a shade garden, it may sucker beneath the mulch and find its way around and up all your shade trees over time. This can be a problem in well-ordered gardens, but less so in naturalistic settings. Consider this trait before adding it to your landscape, and do not put it in deep evergreen shade. In deciduous shade, it will bloom well before the canopy closes.

Passionvine (*Passiflora* spp.)

Early Spanish priests saw the passion (i.e., crucifixion) of Christ in the intricate flower structure of passionvines. The five petals and five sepals are the ten disciples less Judas and Peter. The corona filaments are the crown of thorns. The five stamens with anthers match the five sacred wounds and the three stigmas the nails. All passionvines have these complex flowers, but the species that perform best in shady habitats tend to have small drab blooms that require close inspection to notice them. Passionvines are largely a tropical family and only a few occur north of central Florida. In the warmer portions of Florida, passionvines are evergreen, but they tend to die back to the ground in colder winters. All passionvines sucker from underground rhizomes and spread in the garden. Unwanted suckers can be easily hand-pulled, but this is an adaptation to herbivory and allows them to survive being eaten to the ground by butterfly caterpillars. Not all passionvines serve as larval host plants, but our native species do; they are relished by zebra and Julia heliconias as well as gulf fritillaries. The former two butterflies are most apt to consume those grown in a shade garden, but the Julia is a butterfly common only to extreme south Florida.

Yellow passionvine (*P. lutea*)

Yellow passionvine is a northern species whose Florida range includes most of north Florida and a few counties in the north-central region of the peninsula. It is a perennial that dies back to the ground each winter, producing multiple vines from the base each spring that can extend 1–15 feet in all directions. In nature, yellow passionvine typically occurs in moist woods where it receives partial sun to mostly shade. As such, it is a good candidate for the shade garden as long as it is not planted in areas that remain droughty. In my experience, it does not adapt well to prolonged drought even after a significant establishment period. This is an excellent choice for butterfly gardeners, but the foliage and flowers are not aesthetically significant. Small, shallowly lobed leaves are produced at intervals along the stems. Each is about 1 inch

Yellow passionvine
(*Passiflora lutea*)

across. Small yellowish green flowers are produced for several months in late spring through summer, and the pollinated blooms ripen to purplish black fruit several months later. These are eaten by birds.

Yellow passionvine is only rarely available from Florida native plant nurseries. If you have average to moist soils, use it along a fence or trellis in partial to nearly full shade. It can also be allowed to ramble in a woodland understory where it will climb shrubs and small trees. In this situation, it rarely becomes too aggressive as butterfly caterpillars normally eat it as fast as it can grow.

Corky-stem passionvine (*P. suberosa*)

Corky-stem passionvine occurs throughout peninsular Florida and is the best choice for landscapes south of the upper two tiers of counties. Like yellow passionvine, it is rather drab in terms of aesthetic qualities, but it is excellent at providing food for zebra longwing and Julia heliconias. Corky-stem passionvine is extremely adaptable and can be grown in nearly any situation found in the home landscape. Though it can prosper under high amounts of sunlight, it does best in partial shade and under filtered sun in relatively deep shade. In the southern half of Florida, it is an evergreen perennial, but often dies back to the ground where it experiences winter temperatures below the mid-20s°F. Its common name refers to the "wings" that form along the

Corky-stem
passionvine
(*Passiflora suberosa*)

main stems that give them a corky appearance. The leaves of this species are extremely variable in shape; some are lobed (but never as shallowly lobed as yellow passionvine), but others are elliptical with no lobes. The flowers are tiny and greenish in color. This passionvine is an excellent butterfly and bird plant.

Corky stem passionvine is frequently cultivated by commercial nurseries. Use it on a fence or trellis beneath a woodland canopy, or allow it to ramble up and through the woodland understory. Birds frequently spread its seeds throughout the landscape, but it is easy to control if it appears in areas where it is unwanted. From my experience, butterfly caterpillars never allow it to spread too far before eating it back to the main stem.

10

Epilogue

Living in Florida means longing for shade. Very few of us wish to spend all our day in the sun. In the heat of summer, the respite we create in our landscapes through shade allows us the time outdoors most of us treasure.

The spaces we create are our own. Whether we enlist the assistance of a landscape architect or venture off alone, our shade gardens must reflect our own desires. They need to be aesthetically attractive so that the time we spend inside them refreshes our senses and cools our nerves as well as our bodies. No landscape design should result in a space that does not invite us inside. I am a firm believer in aesthetic beauty.

Native plants, adapted to shade, can be used to make ecologically significant landscapes that are also aesthetically attractive.

I also believe that the time has come to venture deeper into those spaces, below the surface, to a place that is also alive. We cannot do that solely by creating beautiful gardens if those gardens are as two-dimensional as a painting. We can admire paintings, but we cannot explore them. We explore spaces that are multidimensional, spaces that are more than color and more than comfortable.

I believe that landscapes should have an ecological purpose as well as an aesthetic one. They should do more than paint a picture; they should be alive, they should change with the seasons, and they should create expectation. A multidimensional landscape invites exploration. It creates opportunities to catch the ruby sheen of a hummingbird's throat as it turns to visit a flower, the darting flash of a migratory warbler as it hawks an insect come to pollinate a springtime burst of woodland flowers, the hovering grace of a heliconia butterfly nectaring in the understory or laying eggs within a light gap. Landscapes should be music, not paintings; alive, not static.

Adding life to a landscape is best done by using the plants that add that life naturally: native plants. Though there are exceptions, it seems unrealistic to expect plants from other continents to nurture the life that has adapted to Florida living. Plants are more than aesthetic objects; they create life opportunities, and Florida plants have evolved to create these opportunities in Florida.

I hope this book has awakened this concept and demonstrated that our native plants are worthy of forming the foundation of your shady garden. We have so many wonderful species to consider without the crutch of purchasing the foundation from other places. A living shade garden, built on native Florida plants, designed with a multidimensional purpose, will be far more satisfying than one that is not. We own our landscapes so the outcome is solely ours to direct. Consider your goals, don't hesitate to pursue them, and explore your final product with the anticipation you once had as a child. In a living landscape, you never know what you may find. The element of surprise is never old.

Additional Resources

Books

About Shade Gardening

Brandies, M. 2003. *Shade Gardening for Florida*. St. Petersburg: Great Outdoor Publishing Co. 144 pp.

Chatto, B. 2002. *Beth Chatto's Shade Garden*. London: Cassell Illustrated. 224 pp.

Darke, R. 2002. *The American Woodland Garden: Capturing the Spirit of the Deciduous Forest*. Portland, Ore.: Timber Press. 377 pp.

Druse, K. 1992. *The Natural Shade Garden*. New York: Clarkson Potter Publishers. 280 pp.

Ellis, B. W. 2003. *Shady Retreats: 20 Plans for Colorful, Private Spaces in Your Backyard*. North Adams, Mass.: 182 pp.

Hodgson, L. 2005. *Making the Most of Shade: How to Plan, Plant, and Grow a Fabulous Garden That Lightens Up the Shadows*. Emmaus, Pa.: Rodale. 408 pp.

Rice, G. 2011. *Planting the Dry Shade Garden: The Best Plants for the Toughest Spot in Your Garden*. Portland, Ore.: Timber Press. 192 pp.

Schenk, G. 1984. *The Complete Shade Gardener*. Reprint 2002, Portland, Ore.: Timber Press. 377 pp.

Tannenbaum, F., ed. 1994. *Taylor's Guide to Shade Gardening*. Boston: Houghton Mifflin. 501 pp.

Wiley, K. 2007. *Shade: Ideas and Inspiration for Shady Gardens*. Portland, Ore.: Timber Press. 176 pp.

About Native Plant Landscaping—Florida

Haele, R. G., and J. Brookwell. 1999. *Native Florida Plants: Low Maintenance Landscaping and Gardening*. Houston: Gulf Publishing Company. 360 pp.

Huegel, C. N. 2012. *Native Wildflowers and Other Ground Covers for Florida Landscapes*. Gainesville: University Press of Florida. 328 pp.

————. 2010. *Native Plant Landscaping for Florida Wildlife.* Gainesville: University Press of Florida. 284 pp.

————. 1995. *Florida Plants for Wildlife: A Selection Guide to Native Trees and Shrubs.* Orlando: Florida Native Plant Society. 118 pp.

Jameson, M., and R. Moyroud, eds. 1991. *Xeric Landscaping with Florida Native Plants.* San Antonio, Fla.: Association of Florida Native Nurseries. 67 pp.

Nelson, G. 2010. *Best Native Plants for Southern Gardens: A Handbook for Gardeners, Homeowners, and Professionals.* Gainesville: University Press of Florida. 284 pp.

————. 2003. *Florida's Best Native Landscape Plants: 200 Readily Available Species for Homeowners and Professionals.* Gainesville: University Press of Florida. 412 pp.

Osorio, R. 2001. *A Gardener's Guide to Florida's Native Plants.* Gainesville: University Press of Florida. 346 pp.

Walton, D., and L. Schiller. 2007. *Natural Florida Landscaping: Using Native Plants for a Beautiful, Life-Supporting, and Environmentally Sensitive Landscape.* Sarasota: Pineapple Press. 110 pp.

Workman, R. W. 1980. *Growing Native: Native Plants for Landscape Use in Coastal South Florida.* Sanibel, Fla.: Sanibel-Captiva Conservation Foundation, Inc. 137 pp.

About Native Plant Landscaping—General

Christopher, T., ed. 2011. *The New American Landscape: Leading Voices on the Future of Sustainable Gardening.* Portland, Ore.: Timber Press. 255 pp.

Darke, R. *In Harmony with Nature: Lessons from the Arts and Crafts Garden.* New York: Friedman/Fairfax Publishers. 160 pp.

————, and D. W. Tallamy. 2014. The Living Landscape: Designing for Beauty and Diversity in the Home Garden. Portland, Ore.: Timber Press. 392 pp.

Diekelmann, J., and R. Schuster. 2002. *Natural Landscaping: Designing with Native Plant Communities.* 2nd ed. Madison: University of Wisconsin Press. 301 pp.

Loewer, P. 1988. *American Gardens: A Tour of the Nation's Finest Private Gardens.* New York: Simon and Shuster. 193 pp.

Robinson, W., and R. Darke. 2009. *The Wild Garden: Expanded Edition.* Portland, Ore.: Timber Press. 355 pp.

Summers, C. 2010. *Designing Gardens with the Flora of the American East.* New Brunswick, N.J.: Rutgers University Press. 222 pp.

Wasowski, S., and A. Wasowski. 1994. *Gardening with Native Plants of the South.* Dallas: Taylor Publishing. 196 pp.

————. 1988. *Native Texas Plants: Landscaping Region by Region.* Austin: Texas Monthly Press. 406 pp.

Other Resources

Florida Association of Native Nurseries
c/o JCM
PO Box 972
Melbourne, FL 32902-0972
321-917-1960
http://www.afnn.org
http://plantrealflorida.org (homeowner resources)

Florida Native Plant Society
PO Box 278
Melbourne, FL 32666-0434
321-271-6702
http://www.fnps.org

Florida Wildflower Foundation
Executive Director
PO Box 941066
Maitland, FL 32794-1066
407-353-6164
http://floridawildflowerfoundation.org

Hawthorn Hill Wildflowers
http://hawthornhillwildflowers.blogspot.com

Institute for Regional Conservation
22601 SW 152 Ave.
Miami, Florida 33170
305-247-6547
http://www.regionalconservation.org

Institute for Systematic Botany
Department of Cell Biology, Microbiology, and Molecular Biology
University of South Florida
4202 East Fowler Avenue, BSF 218
Tampa, FL 33620-5150
813-974-6238
http://www.florida.plantatlas.usf.edu

PanFlora
http://www.gilnelson.com/PanFlora

USDA Plants
http://plants.usda.gov

Index

Bolded page numbers indicate photographs.

Craig N. Huegel is the owner and operator of Hawthorn Hill Native Wildflowers. He is the author of two UPF books: *Native Plant Landscaping for Florida Wildlife* and *Native Wildflowers and Other Ground Covers for Florida Landscapes*.